Changing Hospital Architecture

Changing Hospital Architecture

Edited by
Sunand Prasad

RIBA ⫴ **Publishing** corus

Frontispiece: Evelina Children's Hospital
pviii: Community Hospital of the Monterey Peninsula

© RIBA Enterprises Ltd., 2008
Published by RIBA Publishing, 15 Bonhill Street, London EC2P 2EA

ISBN 978 1 85946 167 9

Stock Code 55094

British Library Cataloguing in Publications Data
A catalogue record for this book is available from the British Library.

Publisher: Steven Cross
Commissioning Editor: Matthew Thompson
Project Editor: Anna Walters
Copy-editor: NHS Estates, with Wendy Toole
Designed by Alex Lazarou, Surbiton, UK
Typeset by Alex Lazarou, Surbiton, UK
Printed and bound by Cambridge University Press, Cambridge

While every effort has been made to check the accuracy of the information given in this book, readers should always make their own checks. Neither the Authors nor the Publisher accept any responsibility for misstatements made in it or misunderstandings arising from it.

RIBA Publishing is part of RIBA Enterprises Ltd
www.ribaenterprises.com

Contents

Contributors

SUNAND PRASAD MA, AA DIP, PHD, RIBA, FRSA

Sunand Prasad is co-founder and senior partner of Penoyre & Prasad LLP, an architectural practice known for its award-winning designs, many in the health sector. President of the Royal Institute of British Architects (RIBA) 2007–2009, he previously guided the institute's policy and strategy including action on climate change. As a founding commissioner of the Commission for Architecture and the Built Environment (CABE) he launched its enabling programme and chaired its skills programme. He played a key part in the development of the Construction Industry Council's (CIC) Design Quality Indicator. Sunand's extensive written work ranges from architectural culture, urban form and the work of Le Corbusier to *Transformations: the architecture of Penoyre & Prasad*.

DEREK STOW OBE, FRIBA

After eight years as an Associate with Powell & Moya, in 1962 Derek established Derek Stow & Partners. The Practice's principle field of endeavor, in both the UK and overseas, has been healthcare architecture. This has embraced Research & Development, Strategic and Development Control Planning, Landscape and Interior Design, together with the design of Components and whole Building Systems. The work of the Practice has been widely published and recognized by eight major awards. Derek Stow has been closely associated with Architectural Education, firstly as a tutor at the AA School, and subsequently as a lecturer and external examiner to MARU.

JOHN WORTHINGTON

Since co-founding DEGW in 1973, John has been concerned with supporting both the public and private sectors in making the most effective use of resources, by matching available space to organisational demands. He has applied the lessons learnt in workplace design to the fields of healthcare, education and urban design with an emphasis on linking the processes of briefing and evaluation to design.

John has held a number of academic posts and currently holds the Graham Willis professorship in Architecture at the University of Sheffield, is a Professorial fellow at the University of Melbourne and a visiting scholar at Pembroke College Cambridge. He is a board member of the London Thames Gateway Development Corporation, past chair of CABE/RIBA Building Futures and a past president and current trustee of the Urban Design Group.

He lectures internationally and his recent books include *Managing the Brief for Better Design* (Spon 2001), co-authored with Alistair Blyth, and *Reinventing the Workplace* (Architectural Press second edition 2006).

MICHAEL DAVIS

Mike became a founding director of the Catalyst Healthcare consortium in 1994 and is currently the asset management director of Catalyst Lend Lease Ltd. He is responsible for providing management services to a portfolio of eighteen PFI project companies in the healthcare, education and government accommodation sectors, with £2.5 billion of funds invested, about half of which is in eight hospital PFIs.

PAUL HYETT

Paul Hyett is Chairman of RyderHKS International and a Principal of HKS Inc – the largest firm of healthcare architects in the US. A past president of the RIBA, he currently chairs the Carbon Trust's £8 million research programme on ecologically responsible design. He is a Director of the Building Centre and has written extensively on architecture, urban design and ecologically responsible building.

JOHN JENNER DipAA, RIBA

John Jenner is a founding director of Greenhill Jenner Architects and leads on the design and delivery of healthcare buildings in the practice. He has lectured widely on healthcare design in both the UK and the USA. He is currently involved in advising NHS Trusts on major PFI proposals in his capacity as a senior member of the NHS Design Review Panel.

SUSAN FRANCIS

Susan Francis is Special Advisor for Health to CABE and works closely with the Department of Health for whom she chairs their NHS Design Review Panels. She is developing initiatives to encourage the making of well-designed buildings for modern care in healthy neighbourhoods for a sustainable future.

Trained as an architect, Susan has worked as a practitioner, researcher and lecturer. She has published and presented extensively in the UK and abroad.

DOUGLAS L. OLSON AIA, RIBA

Doug was founding director of Chong Partners London and co-founder of FB|CP LLP. Doug is currently Healthcare Practice Leader for the San Francisco Office of NBBJ. With 26 years of architectural experience, Doug has been responsible for all aspects of planning and design of medical facilities ranging up to £300 million.

LAWRENCE NIELD LFRAIA, ANZIA, RIBA

Lawrence Nield is a founding prinicipal of Bligh Voller Nield Architects in Australia. Bligh Voller Nield has been designing major hospitals, healthcare and research buildings in Australia and New Zealand since 1978. These have gained national and international awards. He was previously the Professor of Architector at the University of Sydney and he is now a Visiting Professor at the University of Sydney and the University of New South Wales. He is a graduate of the University of Sydney and Cambridge.

Typology diagrams

The project descriptions in Chapters 4 to 7 are accompanied with thumbnail diagrams of their typology for easy, if somewhat simplistic, comparison. Hospital typologies can be differentiated through specific elements of the hospital programme; for example showing how the four basic components, treatment areas (including theatres), wards (nursing units), outpatients (including diagnostics) and servicing are arranged, together with the associated service and circulation cores. Rather than such a strictly programmatic description of typology, we have adopted a more form-oriented approach as used in general architectural typology – one that shows the overall massing, composition and relations between outdoor and indoor space. The diagrams do not describe all the parts of the hospital, and are not to scale. In practice hospitals may be a hybrid of two or more typologies, so in some case the diagrams indicate the typology to which the overall arrangement best approximates.

1. Linked pavilion or finger plan

The oldest typology and still in common use. The pavilions would often have clinical spaces on lower levels with wards above.

Examples
Woolwich Hospital and St Thomas's Hospital, London;
Hotel Dieu, Paris; many others worldwide

2. Low-rise multi-courtyard or checkerboard

This typology can offer a human scale in contrast to the institutional character that tends to overwhelm most hospital design. However it will tend to apply to the larger, non-urban sites or smaller hospitals.

Examples
Wexham Park Hospital; Venice Hospital (unrealized design by Le Corbusier); Homerton Hospital, London

3. Monoblock

The classic compact and circulation efficient type. The small atria/lightwells can take many forms and the lower floors may have fewer, with deep planning for non-patient areas or operating theatres. There is a need for artificial ventilation and the opportunity to incorporate Interstitial Service Floors.

Examples
Greenwich Hospital, London (demolished); Boston City Hospital; McMaster University Hospital, Ontario

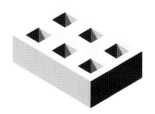

4a. Podium and slab/tower
(also 'Bundled' or 'Stacked' in US)

The wards are generally in the tower with the clinical and technical areas in the slab. This typology can be effective on urban sites with small footprints but the upper floors can be problematic in terms of travelling distance.

Examples
Bridgeport Hospital, Connecticut; Prince of Wales Hospital, Sydney; Royal Free Hospital, London; UCL Hospital (PFI), London

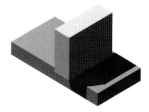

4b. Podium with two or more towers/ blocks over

This typology avoids some of the potential travel distance and scale problems of no. 4a above but will require a larger site.

Examples
Birmingham Hospitals (PFI)

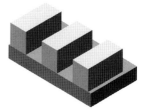

5. Street

The attraction of this type has lain in its flexibility and extendibility as well as the legibility that the street itself offers to patients.

Examples
Wythenshawe Hospital, Manchester; Northwick Park Hospital, London; Westmead Hospital, Sydney, Rikshospitalet, Oslo

6. Atrium/galleria

Atria have become extremely common in open plan office buildings where daylight can penetrate working floors from both sides. The cellular character of hospital buildings make atrtri a less obvious solution but there are a number of successful uses of this typology

Examples
New Children's Hospital, Sydney; Chelsea and Westminster Hospital, London; Hospital for Sick Children, Toronto; University of Maryland Homer Gudelsky Building

7. Unbundled

Unbundled is a pattern of segregation of the diagnostic and treatment functions on the one hand, and on the other the nursing functions along a shared circulation/support spine. 'Unbundled' is a North American term and the typology is dominant in current design there; but it is also used worldwide.

Examples
Norfolk and Norwich Hospital; many US examples

8. Campus

Individual buildings disposed around the site with or without enclosed circulation network.

Examples
Hospital sites that have been built up over the years with successive additions.

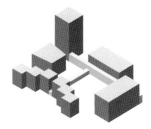

SPONSOR – CORUS

Corus is Europe's second largest steel producer with revenues of £9.7 billion and crude steel production of 18.3 million tonnes in 2006, primarily in the UK and the Netherlands. Corus' three principal divisions comprising Strip Products, Long Products and Distribution & Building Systems provide innovative solutions to the most demanding markets around the world such as construction, automotive, aerospace, packaging, rail and general engineering worldwide. Corus is a subsidiary of Tata Steel, the world's sixth largest steel producer. With a combined presence in nearly 50 countries, Tata Steel including Corus has 84,000 employees across five continents and a pro forma crude steel production of 27 million tonnes in 2007.

SUPPORTER – THE NUFFIELD TRUST

The Nuffield Trust is one of the leading independent health policy charitable trusts in the UK. Its mission is to promote independent analysis and informed debate on UK healthcare policy. Its purpose is to communicate evidence and encourage an exchange around developed or developing knowledge in order to illuminate recognised and emerging issues. This book was inspired by Achieving Quality in Hospital Design – Broadening the Vision, a conference hosted by The Nuffield Trust and co-sponsored by the Royal Institute of British Architects, the Commission for the Built Environment and the Medical Architecture Research Unit on 6 February 2003.

Introduction

SUNAND PRASAD

Hospitals have a very long architectural history. Given the high state of development of the arts of medicine in ancient Mesopotamian, Chinese, Indian and Egyptian civilisations, it is possible that these cultures had proto hospitals. But it is from ancient Greece and Rome that we know for certain that the architectural genealogy of hospitals starts in the ancient world. The temples of Askelpios in Epidaurus and Kos (ca 500 BC), where the sick came to be diagnosed and healed, placed faith in the power of sacred settings and ritual. Ancient Roman hospitals on the other hand were developed for military purposes with plans based on barracks. These two traditions – the military and the religious – are consistent threads in the development of hospitals right up to the twentieth century. They continue to be paralleled today in the sometimes competing and sometimes complementary ideas of a hospital as an efficient mechanism for delivering treatment and a hospital as a place for healing.

Despite this long history the hospital as a building type features only occasionally in architectural histories. Brunelleschi's Foundling Hospital in Florence is generally agreed to be the first building of Renaissance architecture (Figure 1). The Tuberculosis Sanatorium that Alvar Aalto designed in Paimio is a seminal work of the Modern Movement (Figure 2). There are a few other celebrated hospitals but generally hospitals have been 'background' buildings that have not excited passions in mainstream architectural and design culture. Today they feature infrequently in architectural and design magazines and even more rarely among projects set in schools of architecture. Few win architecture awards.

Public perceptions of hospitals as places to be in, as distinct from their immediate functional purpose, are equally ambivalent. On the one hand people associate hospital environments with soulless mazes of corridors, harsh lighting, an anxiety-inducing smell and waiting areas that create the wrong kind of anonymity. Recently hospital stays have come to be seen as positively dangerous because of scares about hospital-acquired infections. On the other hand, especially in the United Kingdom, the local hospital has a powerful place in the construction of community identity. It inspires strong loyalty, expressed through local charitable activities, volunteer work and fund-raising and also through campaigns when one is threatened with closure or relocation. A hospital is part of the security bedrock of a stable society. A celebrated demonstration in the UK of the emotional and social place of the hospital was the election to Parliament of Dr Richard Taylor in 2001 solely on the platform of retaining services at Kidderminster Hospital. While much of the debate centred on ease of access to hospital services, the campaign would not have had the power it had without the emotionally charged idea of 'our hospital'.

1
Filippo Brunelleschi's Foundling Hospital, Florence (1419–45)

Typically hospitals are as big as a village. Some are as big as small towns. They are part of the civic realm in a locality. Modern society will not function without them. They employ huge numbers of people. They cost a lot of money to build and run. So why is hospital design apparently considered to be a backwater by so many of the most lauded architects? Why do the public tolerate the poor environments that would have them filling in complaint forms in a hotel – a word derived after all from the Latin *hospitale*?

Perhaps at root this is because no one really wants to be in a hospital. But there are more immediate reasons.

Process vs place

Since the middle of the twentieth century hospital design has almost everywhere been dominated by the functionalist strand of the Modern Movement in architecture. Medical and surgical processes have been considered to be virtually deterministic as regards the layout, even though they change rapidly in response to technological and clinical developments. Perhaps because the smooth flow of these processes can literally be a matter of life or death, medical

2
Alvar Aalto's Paimio Sanatorium

architecture has escaped the critique of functionalism that began in the 1950s and by the end of the 1960s had shattered the consensus around the International Style. Understandably hospitals have not been a prime setting for the experiments of the avant garde. However, as a result, the efficient accommodation of *processes* rather than the making of *places* has continued to dominate the design of hospitals.

Although, as Derek Stow demonstrates in Chapter 1, the most interesting innovations have been in the pursuit of generic models with high adaptability, hospital designers rightly stress the need to respond to the specifics of particular clinical models and operational policies. This emphasis too often leads to the belief that hospitals are so extraordinarily complex to organise in plan and section that the creative freedom that exists in other building typologies must inevitably be diminished in this specialised field. So the creation of good architecture must always be pushed into the background by the implacable demands of optimising clinical adjacency.

This miserable 'either/or' doctrine has gained such currency that architects not engaged with hospital design have also come to believe it and to regard this as a highly specialised field where architectural ambitions will come a poor second, and which is too difficult to include in a design curriculum. So hospital architecture has become isolated as a specialist field, lagging behind the most inventive and progressive developments in the art and science of architecture, and indeed losing the commitment and skill required in the making of places that mean something to people. The reconnection of hospital design with the wider architectural and design culture and the involvement of more committed and skilful architects and designers currently outside the field are crucial to improving the quality of hospital environments.

Customer focus

Fortunately, a small number of outstanding hospitals, as well as buildings of other complex building types such as airports, demonstrate that excellent architecture can go hand in hand with excellent functional design. Indeed truly functional design – satisfying immediate operational needs, catering for the emotional needs of patients and staff, making good connections with the locality, anticipating future change – must be the basis of excellent architecture. Chapter 4 to 7 of this book illustrate hospital designs from the UK, a number of other European countries, the US and Australia that aim to fulfil such architectural ambitions.

Equally happily, there is now greater recognition of the importance of the human beings that are the centre of the health services and the complexity of their needs and responses. Terms like 'a patient-centred approach' began to be used in the 1970s[1] and its natural corollary, 'patient-focused design', appeared in the 1980s. NHS Estates' publication *Better by Design*[2] (1994) was the first piece of official guidance in the UK, and possibly the world, to recognise the importance of the design quality of healthcare environments as distinct from the logical accommodation of healthcare processes. Since then evidence has been accumulating to show that patients are likely to recover more quickly, need less drug therapy, and feel more trust in the delivery of healthcare if the hospital environment is more convivial. An area of design that has been dominated by the consideration of *process* is waking up to the need to consider the making of *places*.

Patient focus is the health variant of customer focus that many corporations have adopted for business reasons in our increasingly consumer-oriented culture. Indeed currently in the NHS of the early twenty-first century there has been a particular recognition of 'consumerism' – the need to identify and provide things that patients and their relatives want from the service. In addition to more staff contact, less waiting, better standards of cleanliness and good food, the environment comes high on the list. More recently there has been a growing realisation that close attention to the needs of the staff – including nurses and auxiliary staff – is essential for delivering patient-focused care; for it is the behaviour of staff that makes the greatest difference to patients' well-being and *sense* of well-being. Working conditions for staff are therefore of crucial importance. Experience of and studies in the design of modern offices suggests that the quality of the working environment has a key influence on corporate performance.[3] This realisation is filtering though to health services. In Chapter 2, John Worthington draws on his extensive experience of radical improvements in office design to set out an effective approach to the all important task of formulating the brief.

A consequence of increasing consumer orientation in the health service has been the realisation that the better informed the consumers of healthcare are, the healthier will be the population. This leads to the concept of the 'expert patient' able to play a leading part in managing his or her own health. By increasing the likelihood of prevention over cure, such a patient will reduce expenditure in the health system. The costs of creating the expert patient must be far less than the cost of treatment of preventable diseases.

Another aspect of the growing realisation that design must put people at its centre is the increase in consultation with 'stakeholders' to the point of institutionalisation. A stakeholder is whoever will in some way be affected by the creation of the new facility – whether as a member of a 'user group' (doctor, nurse, surgeon, midwife, administrator, ambulance driver); or as a patient; or a local amenity society; or a statutory body. In major hospital projects there may be a hundred user groups alone. Stakeholder consultation should mean true participation of key people in the briefing and design but can be reduced to opportunistic lip service to the idea.

The people who will be relying on the building to deliver their services possess precious knowledge and unique insight that will immensely benefit the quality of the design. But the process needs leadership, expert management and highly skilled and imaginative designers. Without the presence of all these it runs the twin risks of failed expectations on the one hand, and on the other a design driven by mere expediency and compromised by conflicting and unresolved pulls. Such a design tends to have a short shelf life, becoming redundant with the inevitable changes in the operational policies to which it was over-specifically tailored. The Design Review panel of the UK's Commission for Architecture and the Built Environment has found a number of hospital designs that suffer from an over-rigid interpretation of clinical adjacencies.[4] The ability to listen to, understand and draw out the underlying substance in stakeholders' views, to grasp the deeper organisational structure that will satisfy but also transcend the demands of current processes and logistics to produce generic, adaptable and versatile design solutions: that is the basis of excellent hospital design today.

The healing environment

If, as noted at the beginning, the religious and the military conceptions of hospitals are a constant thread in their history, we have recently been undergoing something of a religious revival. In the last half of the twentieth century – and the first half-century of the UK National Health Service – functionalism and process dominated hospital design. While they are still the largest influence, there is a growing recognition that the medical approach that underpinned this preference failed to see the patient as a whole person whose emotions and intellect as well as body had needs; and indeed that all these aspects were inextricably, intricately and variably linked. At an obvious level it is widely known that stress inhibits healing. It is also generally recognised that most modern hospital environments and patients' experiences of these environments is often very stressful. The stress factors include the anxiety-inducing uncertainty of waiting, the poor acoustics produced by easy-clean low-maintenance surfaces, the smells, the harsh lighting, the difficulty of finding your way around a maze of impersonal corridors and the plethora of signs and scrappy notices. It is ironical that the very places where people could most do without stress seem to be calculated in their operational and sensory aspects to most induce it.

The rediscovery of the power of the patients' environment to help rather than hinder the healing process has been gradual, starting with an increased attention to the inclusion of art and of plants in hospitals. In the 1970s Peter Senior pioneered the concept of 'Arts for Health' and demonstrated its value at Wythenshawe Hospital in Manchester. In the meanwhile Claire Cooper Marcus working at the Department of Landscape Architecture at Berkeley was conducting research into the psychology of the relationship between people and their homes and into public space and the built environment generally. Marcus's work eventually led her to focus on the therapeutic effects of gardens and to show these effects in the book *Healing Gardens*.[5] These two pioneers are not solely responsible for the growing acceptance of the contribution art and landscape can make but they represent a movement towards the idea of the healing environment, which is now accepted widely. A number of studies have shown correlations between patient outcomes and the presence of nature and art. A celebrated study by Dr Roger Ulrich in 1993[6] found that heart patients with a view of the natural environment were likely to recover more quickly. Work at Chelsea and Westminster Hospital, which has an extensive arts programme, has shown that art, and in particular the performing arts, increase people's sense of well-being. Dr Ulrich has recently gone on to demonstrate that plants and flowers increase workplace productivity. People who have been taking flowers to their hospitalised relatives for as long as anyone can remember seem to have worked out something similar.

The idea of the healing environment of which art and landscape are vital components is now part of mainstream thinking in hospital design. However, it tends to be an add-on rather than integral to the design concept. Some of the examples in this book, in particular Scandinavian ones, show how a functional hospital can also be a healing environment.

The economic value of design

By the beginning of the current decade it was clear that in the UK, in an atmosphere that demanded public accountability and where all public spending decisions were required to demonstrate 'value for money', it was no longer enough to argue for good design on the basis of a 'higher good' or cultural value. The same applied to other countries with a significant public sector. In the US the yardstick is the profitability of insurance companies and health maintenance organisations (HMOs) and the only argument for better design is through the cost–benefit equation: either directly through operational efficiency or indirectly through competitive advantage, brand enhancement and market share. In other words the contemporary context for the design of hospitals requires better design to be argued on the basis of economic value.

Even taken separately the influence of well-designed environments, on patients on the one hand and on staff on the other, offers a strong argument that good design produces economic value. Taken together, with evidence coming from more than one sector of public life and the economy, the argument is even stronger. So it is that a number of agencies have been arguing with some success that better design – defined holistically – is essential to the better delivery of the health services. These include in the UK the Department of Health's Estates and Facilities Directorate (formerly NHS Estates) and the Commission for Architecture and the Built Environment (CABE) and in the US the Center for Health Design. The winning of this argument and real implementation of its implications is perhaps the best hope today of creating contemporary hospitals of excellent design.

Crucial to the discussion is the distinction between first cost and life-cycle cost. It is clearly possible to build more hospitals more cheaply if their long-term performance is of no consequence. However, if long-term performance is taken into account some illuminating statistics appear. Breakdowns of costs, amortised over 25 years, for the total operation of a modern downtown office show that if one unit represents the capital cost of constructing the accommodation then maintaining and running the building will cost 1.5 units and the operational costs of the service delivered will be typically 65 units.[7] For a UK district general hospital an analysis of annual accounts of a trust will indicate that operational costs are around ten times greater than premises costs.[8] As design costs of hospitals are typically a tenth of construction cost, these figures at least open the possibility that relatively small initial expenditure will pay for itself in the long run, perhaps many times over. Although a number of factors, examined below, are currently conspiring against turning this theory into practice, intellectually the argument has gained wide acceptance, including within HM Treasury, UK.

Sustainability

A long-term view of design, construction and operation is by definition what sustainability means, with the added ingredient of an awareness of the impact of these activities on the wider environment, local to global. Although the pioneers of environmentally conscious design have been at work for over 30 years, it is only in the last ten that the complex interdependencies of such design have been gathered under the mantle of sustainability. In that time the aspirational and evangelical, strong on intent but vague about solutions, have given way to greater precision assisted by ever improving science. A key driver for the increasing interest in sustainable design is the realisation that the construction and operation of buildings accounts for 50% of the CO_2 emissions that are now all but proved to be causing climate change with its anticipated catastrophic consequences. As the health services are among the largest sectors of the economy in the west, hospitals and health buildings must be making a significant contribution to environmental degradation. However, healthcare design has been notably lagging in addressing sustainability.[9] This will have to change, partially through legislation but also through an increasing emphasis on long-term value. Aside from reducing net energy consumption, a key tenet of sustainability is the ability of the design to accommodate change and reuse. This means a keener search for the essential, generic and versatile rather than the specific and tightly fitted to immediate need: the slogan of 'long life, loose fit, low energy'[10] overlaid with technologically sophisticated and high-performing building structure and fabric. If a greater attention to people means a shift from process to place then an attention to sustainability is a shift to the quality of the building as a high-performance tool.

The hospital and the town

Not only has much post-war hospital design neglected the patient experience and lagged in sustainable design, it has quite literally turned its back on the urban public realm. For most of the last 50 years there has been a preference for siting hospitals on greenfield sites where

3
Square of St Bartholomew's
Hospital, London, c. 1908

4
St Olave's Hospital, Trondheim, masterplan by
Neils Torp based on city blocks

possible, often away from town centres, giving freedom for layout design. It was assumed, until the oil crisis of the 1970s, that universal car use was desirable and inevitable. The relatively high costs of urban land contributed to this trend. Where urban sites were used or reused the design of modern hospitals, almost without exception, has been as hermetic entities, often confusing for a patient to enter. Making an architectural contribution to the civic realm has clearly not been on the agenda. And yet hospitals, as noted above, are in themselves as large as many settlements and even small towns. Their design, in terms of legibility of layout, the hierarchy of the parts and the capacity for growth and change, can learn a great deal from good town planning principles. Furthermore, as well-considered extensions to the urban realm they have great potential as agents of regeneration, helping to increase economic activity in the neighbourhood.

There is no shortage of clues in architectural history as to how there might be better integration of the hospital and the city. Nineteenth-century English hospitals like St Bartholomew's Hospital, Guy's Hospital and Leeds General Infirmary have powerful civic presences and display an elegant and functional continuity with the urban public realm. They do so not only through a self-confident architectural language but also through the creation of urban space useable by citizens not necessarily on hospital business. This is a two-way transaction: the public space of the city benefits from the hospital, and the patients, visitors and staff have a hugely richer set of options on hand. As recently as the 1990s recovering patients were even wheeled out to relax in the square of St Bartholomew's which was a public through route for pedestrians (Figure 3). Le Corbusier's unbuilt Venice Hospital project of 1963 was a radical humanist essay in designing the hospital as a continuation of the urban fabric, a series of linked squares with routes connecting to the city streets. Two entries in the competition for the design of the new University Hospital in Trondheim in 1995, the winning entry by Neils Torp (Figure 4) and runners-up Edward Cullinan Architects, showed how a hospital can fully be part of a city.

What is design quality?

All attempts to improve design quality in any sector have come up against the problem that there has been no shared language for describing, and therefore discussing and assessing, design quality. An architect's notion of design quality may be very different from that of a hospital estates manager, which in turn is different from that of a clinician or the patient, or the builder or a local artist making work for the hospital. The contemporary emphasis on consultation and the presence of many voices lend an added urgency to the need for a shared language.

Until the 1980s there was no challenge to the assumption that the expert architects and designers knew best, and the best among them did make a point of understanding and addressing the needs of the people most affected by their designs. The mediocre tended to repeat previous models or, worse, produce poor solutions of their own. In an increasingly critical consumer culture such autonomy for designers is no longer possible. Consultation with 'users' – usually those who will provide the services, rather than the patients – is a requirement. This does not necessarily result in better design. If simply asked for their views users tend to describe what they have previously seen to work or not to work and sometimes to express apparently contradictory views. A good designer is able to interrogate and extrapolate from this and reflect back potential a priori solutions through understandable language and visualisation. In less design-aware hands consultation can lead merely to more convoluted solutions, as apparently irreconcilable demands are clumsily negotiated or previous practice is implemented unquestioned.

As early as 1997 Susan Francis, the author of Chapter 5, was working at the Medical Architectural Research Unit (MARU) in London to devise measures of design quality applicable in particular to health buildings. This was later taken up by NHS Estates. In the meantime the Construction Industry Council,[11] through a well-resourced and partially government-funded project, devised the Design Quality Indicator (DQI) which drew on a wide pool of contributions but distilled it into a simple and robust framework. The intellectual framework of the DQI was combined with the healthcare-specific considerations assembled by NHS Estates to produce a coherent design evaluation tool, the AEDET.[12] The AEDET, which is seen as a sector-specific version of the industry standard DQI, has become widely adopted in the UK and has begun to establish a shared set of terms and concepts through which all involved in the process can map the quality of design. There is interest from outside the UK in the DQI methodology and for the first time there is a likelihood of a shared language to discuss and negotiate design quality, ranging from mathematically measurable attributes like thermal comfort through less precise but high-value-adding attributes like adaptability, and all the way to intangibles like the capacity of the design to raise the spirits. Hospitals costing half a billion pounds and more, procured through the Private Finance Initiative (PFI), with over 50 separate contracts to be in place at financial close, are being interrogated for their ability to raise the visitors' spirits. They may be found wanting but at least it is on the record.

Procurement and cost

At the time of writing the UK National Health Service is nearing the end of its largest hospital building programme ever. Unlike previous construction projects, these hospitals are being built via the PFI. This leads to a form of building procurement whereby a private sector entity finances the designing, construction and facility management of the building under a 25-year contract (typically) and recovers its costs and makes a profit through a periodic 'unitary charge' paid by the hospital trust. PFI remains controversial in many quarters for the principal reason that it is seen as a means to shift wealth away from the public sector to the private sector. Critics argue that since governments can obtain the best borrowing terms it is strange to pay the relatively higher cost of private sector debt and reward the banks, in effect paying for an asset several times over through the 25–30-year lease period. While the point about lower costs of public borrowing is valid, any lease entails an overall payment over the lease period. On the whole in the recent past the public sector has been inefficient in building and maintaining its estate – serious cost and time overruns in contracts have been the norm rather than the exception; the buildings have been expensive to maintain and have too often been of indifferent design quality. If this had not been true PFI might well not have succeeded in being embraced within UK government policy in spite of its appeal to some of the baser instincts of politicians and money men.

The reasons PFI was adopted may well have included some wrong ones, such as successive governments' wish to remove the capital costs of investment in public infrastructure from the Public Sector Borrowing Requirement, the growth of a risk-averse culture seeking to shift all the risk away from the client side, and an ideological belief in the private sector's efficiency and effectiveness. However, the simple idea at the core of PFI is sound – if a single organisation is responsible for the delivery of the entirety of a service, from infrastructure to client contact, it will be incentivised to perfect the quality of the component parts of that service so that they work most effectively with each other. Thus it would be in the interest of the service provider to ensure that the design of a hospital gets the best out of the doctors and nurses, decreases patient recovery times and reduces running costs. There would be an attention to true whole life costing and therefore sustainability. It would not matter if this meant a greater first cost because the savings in revenue costs would more than pay for it. Making the state such a single provider has not worked, so the theory of PFI envisaged only private sector providers. However, very little PFI in the UK has followed this pure model. This is because in a political economy like the UK's the delivery of the service itself is firmly embedded in the public sector, and likely to remain so for good reasons, not least the ideals of public service that are at the core of the longevity of the National Health Service. Even the drive to make NHS organisations commissioning bodies rather than suppliers of services is unlikely to change this in the near future. So we have a 'hybrid' PFI model – the private sector providing the accommodation, but the public sector remaining responsible for delivering the service to the clients/patients.

The continuity of the 'incentive chain' is therefore broken. While it is in the interest of the private sector consortium delivering the building to ensure that its long-term maintenance and technical performance are taken into account at the outset, better working conditions for the staff or outcomes for the patients are of no direct concern. At the same time, given the competitive context, the providers will try to drive down capital cost, which accounts for around 70% of the unitary charge. The cost of service delivery of course falls outside the unitary charge in such a hybrid arrangement.

Despite these imperfections PFI, or PPP (Public Private Partnership), continues to be increasingly adopted round the world. It is often seen as the only way of making capital investment in public services, direct exchequer funding having been deemed to be impossible because of its implication for taxation and dominant notions of fiscal prudence. Mike Davis, the author of Chapter 3, believes that, if operated in the right way, public private partnerships are capable of promoting very high design quality and harnessing its value in new ways.

In the UK, by June 2007 over 40 new or substantially new hospitals had been completed or were in construction under the PFI and a further 30 or so were under way and at various stages. The design quality of the early results of the PFI were widely criticised as being disappointing, both in the press and by organisations such as CABE, the King's Fund and Unison, the trade union. Some later examples, as illustrated, for instance, in Chapter 4, have shown clear improvements. At the same time almost all of these contracts have been completed generally to time and budget and are providing the accommodation asked for by the client hospital trust. Also, there is no evidence that these designs as a whole are any worse than the majority of what went before. The mood generally among those championing design quality has therefore been to accept that PFI/PPP is here to stay but to improve the development processes within them to deliver higher quality.

The purpose of this book

In the UK the balance of power and money in the health service is undergoing its most radical transformation in 50 years. The post-war health service had the hospitals at its apex – now 75% of National Health Service money will be channelled through the primary care sector, the so-called shift from the acute to the 'primary care led NHS'. Among other things this change is a simple acknowledgment of the fact that less than 10% of the 'health events' passing through the NHS are handled by the acute sector. This leads to a more integrated view of the health service as whole. Why then a book just about hospitals?

We decided to concentrate on hospitals for better precision and focus. In spite of the reconfigurations and the rapid changes in technology and society, hospitals will remain recognisable and coherent entities for the foreseeable future. Because of their scale it is in hospitals where the effect of getting things wrong in terms of design is the most serious. The hospital remains a highly distinct typology in the healthcare spectrum, showing considerable consistency of component parts and key issues around the world. That being said, the hospital clearly exists within a wider healthcare context and the interrelationships of the two are significant.

Like the idealised hospital described above, this book is intended to be a tool. Its aim is to help improve the quality of design by pointing to potential exemplars, presenting key issues and occasionally signalling caution. This book is not intended to be a world survey. The countries selected for inclusion all have developed industrial economies and healthcare practices of direct relevance to the UK. The funding of healthcare in these countries differs in its balance of private insurance, national insurance and general taxation. These funding regimes exert influences on the nature of the hospital and are touched on by the authors in their chapters. We could have cited excellent hospital designs from Japan, Switzerland, Austria and other countries. The selection of the projects for inclusion is not any reflection on the quality of a number of individual hospitals in many other countries.

A word that recurs in the chapter titles is 'change'. If this book is a tool it is intended for the hands of change agents. To that end the authors have concentrated on real evidence that design quality in its fullest sense can be achieved in hospital design, and shown how.

The book divides into two main sections. Three chapters set the scene – Derek Stow on the post-war history of the British hospital; John Worthington on the crucial and undervalued early stages of the creation of a hospital; and Mike Davies on the changing context of the financing and construction of hospitals. There follow four 'regional' chapters on the UK (Paul Hyett and John Jenner), Europe (Susan Francis), USA (Doug Olson) and Australia (Lawrence Nield). The book closes with a speculation by Lawrence Nield on the architectural form of the future hospital.

The future hospital

A fascinating aspect of the current situation is that no one has anything like a complete possible answer to tomorrow's healthcare needs. It has been pointed out that there are 50 million hospital beds in the UK, but they are in people's homes. If we can find the technology to convert this lateral thought into reality we will no longer need hospital design.

The book *Building a 2020 Vision: Future Health Care Environments*[13] anticipated a pattern of future healthcare based on four settings for the delivery of healthcare in the future:

the home, integrated health and social care centres, community care centres (dealing principally with mental health), and finally in the scale of increasing acuity, specialist care centres. Only care that needs a high-technology environment with specialist equipment and skills will remain in these specialist care centres. Developments in technology have caused a huge increase in ambulatory care and the consequent drop in the requirements for in-patient beds is far greater than the increases due to the ageing population and greater scope for medical intervention. So hospitals as we understand them today will have a far smaller place in the spectrum of health services. On the other hand, the UK Government's pledge to reduce hospital waiting lists, combined with the popular resistance to reducing hospital bed numbers (as exemplified by the campaign about Kidderminster Hospital), means that thousands of new hospital beds will become available in the next ten years. Will a large proportion of these be redundant by 2020? The hospitals being designed today will not be open to patients until around 2010 so we are nearer 2020 than one might initially think. What will happen to these hospital buildings? Can we design hospitals that could accommodate quite other uses in the future? If factories, churches and indeed hospitals can be converted into desirable flats, as is happening nowadays, it must be perfectly possible with foresight to design hospitals adaptable to other uses. Arguably this is the great lesson of the life and growth of settlements – that certain qualities of connectedness, image, environmental performance and structural stability enable buildings and the spaces between them to transcend matters of functional arrangement. Learning this lesson is a key challenge for hospital design.

Notes and references

1. Howard Goodman of the UK Ministry of Health chaired a seminar in January 1971 with this title (see Derek Stow, Chapter 1).
2. NHS Estates, *Better by Design* (1994).
3. Sebastian Macmillan (ed.), *Designing Better Buildings* (London and New York: Spon, 2004).
4. CABE, *Design Reviewed – 2* (London, 2005).
5. Clare Cooper Marcus and Marni Barnes, *Healing Gardens: Therapeutic Benefits and Design Recommendations* (New Jersey: John Wiley and Sons, 1999).
6. R. S. Ulrich, O. Lundén and J. L. Eltinge, 'Effects of exposure to nature and abstract pictures on patients recovering from heart surgery' (Paper presented at the 33rd Meetings of the Society for Psychophysiological Research, Rottach-Egern, Germany, 1993). Abstract published in *Psychophysiology* 30 (Supplement 1, 1993): 7.
7. There are a number of sources for such analyses: Royal Academy of Engineering/CABE *Creating Excellent Buildings/Building Magazine*.
8. This is based on conversations with senior figures in the NHS.
9. Great Western Hospital, Swindon (PFI Consortium led by Carillion Health; architects BDP), remains the only hospital project to pay special attention to sustainability. This is in contrast to what has been happening in other sectors in the UK.
10. Coined by Alex Gordon, President of the Royal Institute of British Architects ('Architects and Resource Conservation', *RIBA Journal* 81(1), 1974).
11. The CIC is an association of professional bodies in the construction industry.
12. The 'Achieving Excellence Design Evaluation Tool' has now been further developed by Professor Bryan Lawson and Professor Michael Phirie of the University of Sheffield.
13. Susan Francis and Rosemary Glanville, *Building a 2020 Vision: Future Health Care Environments*, Nuffield Trust and RIBA Future Studies (London: The Stationery Office, 2001).

CHAPTER ONE

Transformation in healthcare architecture: from the hospital to a healthcare organism

DEREK STOW

Derek Stow describes, from the point of view of someone who was in the thick of it for most of the period, the evolution of hospital design in the UK in parallel with the evolution of the National Health Service founded in 1948. The NHS remains a cherished institution and its central aim of providing healthcare to all who need it, free at the point of delivery, is a true milestone of civilisation. However, a striking aspect of the story is the lack of continuity of purpose, as governments came and went, initiating this and abolishing that. This frustrated not only the development of a rational and long-term view of how a comprehensive health service could be built but also the efforts of health planners and architects like Stow. Nevertheless, in the first 30 years of the NHS, design and construction professionals – in private practice and, especially, in the UK government's variously incarnated health departments – built an internationally respected knowledge base of the design and operation of health facilities. Much of this knowledge was explicitly evidence-based and continually improved, albeit through a highly centralised body. Stow shows how the whole of the supporting apparatus was steadily dismantled from the end of the 1970s. When the next big hospital building programme came along at the end of 1990s the UK hospital sector had to turn to the US and other countries for the latest advances in design. In 2008, as this book is being written, with over 60 hospitals designed, built or being built, in the last ten years there has accrued again a very considerable knowledge base but it is dispersed and difficult to access, except by the large firms who dominate the sector. At the same moment, the body to which the centralised functions were devolved is itself about to be abolished. The chapter describes two 30-year cycles between the poles of big vs small, centralised vs devolved and comprehensive vs specialised. Showing that we are at another threshold, it prompts the question: will the emerging organisation of healthcare support the green shoots of high-quality design that are struggling to emerge?

1948 – The inheritance: a tripartite system

Though superficially they may display the trappings of the stylistic fashions of their day, buildings in the field of healthcare – their location, content and built form – are determined by the wealth, culture and ethics of the society responding to the needs of the population, as perceived at the time of their construction.

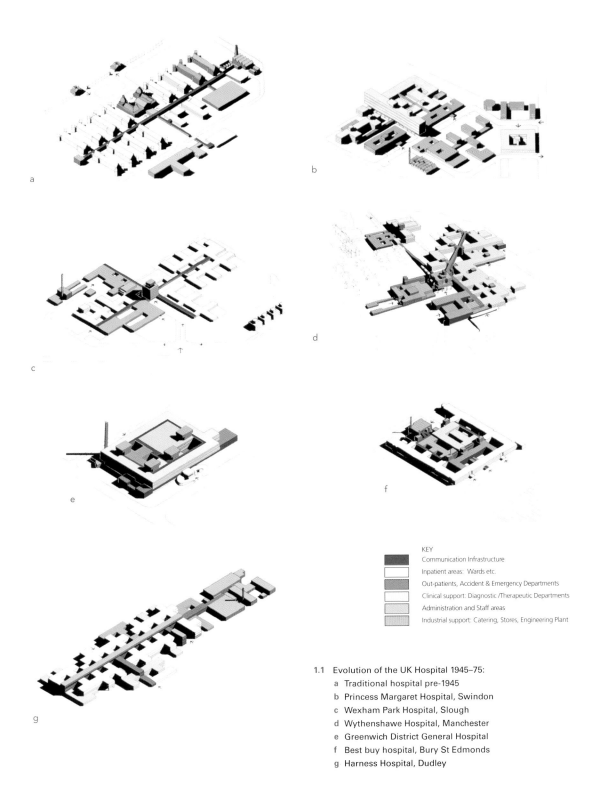

KEY

Communication Infrastructure

Inpatient areas: Wards etc.

Out-patients, Accident & Emergency Departments

Clinical support: Diagnostic /Therapeutic Departments

Administration and Staff areas

Industrial support: Catering, Stores, Engineering Plant

1.1 Evolution of the UK Hospital 1945–75:
   a Traditional hospital pre-1945
   b Princess Margaret Hospital, Swindon
   c Wexham Park Hospital, Slough
   d Wythenshawe Hospital, Manchester
   e Greenwich District General Hospital
   f Best buy hospital, Bury St Edmonds
   g Harness Hospital, Dudley

The healthcare estate inherited by the NHS when it came into being in 1948 was dispersed, varied and inconsistent in the way it was administered. It had grown as an ad hoc response to the needs of the local population and the epidemics and diseases of an earlier era, as well as the demands placed upon it during two world wars. Hence the country's 2,000-plus hospitals were made up of large university teaching hospitals with their own in-house architects, county and municipal hospitals, specialist hospitals, charitable trust hospitals and war memorial hospitals, down to local cottage hospitals of 50 or so beds. The outbreaks of water-borne disease in the nineteenth century had resulted in a programme of isolation hospitals, while the prevalence of tuberculosis in the early twentieth century gave rise to the building of sanatoria and open-air hospitals. There were also many prefabricated war emergency hospitals, such as Harefield, which had a built form so configured that it could be recognised from the air as the ANZAC Forces' cap badge.

In the absence of present-day technology, with its diagnostic and therapeutic capability, a patient's best chance of recovery lay in the quality of the nursing care and the avoidance of cross infection. Thus in pre-war hospitals the nursing or bedded areas predominate, while orientation to maximise sunlight, fresh air and good cross ventilation were the prime design criteria. The traditional British hospital comprised a series of pavilions linked by a single-storey street at ground level. A hospital's campus was often extensive, with landscaped grounds in which patients could convalesce. It was usual for hospitals to have their own industrial support departments, laundry, bulk stores, engineering workshops, etc. and some even grew their own garden produce (Figure 1.1a).

Nowhere was the concept of the self-sufficient hospital more in evidence than in the large mental health institutions that had been built on the peripheries of the country's major cities. Predominantly these were to care for those suffering from the 'general paralysis of the insane' – syphilis. None was more remarkable than the Epsom Cluster, a group of five mental hospitals, with its own farms and linked to the national rail network by its own narrow gauge railway. In 1944, the Cluster had sufficient spare capacity to accept all the British casualties following the D-Day landings in Normandy.

Within the community, environmental and welfare health services, maternity and child welfare clinics, etc. were provided by local authorities, and personal healthcare by the family doctor service, that is GPs mostly working as sole practitioners. Across the country there was no consistent standard of provision. For example, in Liverpool, as a result of the cultural diversity of its population, the number of hospital beds was three times the national average because Roman Catholics had their own hospitals.

There had been a national health insurance scheme since 1912 that, subject to means testing, entitled low-wage earners to free treatment by GPs. However, the majority of the population did not qualify. The poor could either seek public assistance or resort to the casualty department of the local hospital.

From the outset, when it came into being in 1948, the mission of the National Health Service has been to provide healthcare to the whole population free at the point of access, approximately 90% of the cost being raised by taxation and the remainder by compulsory National Insurance contributions.[1] Over the years, this principle has been watered down by contingency measures, such as the introduction of prescription charges, in order to relieve the financial burden on the Exchequer. Nevertheless, we are assured that the overall objective remains the same today.

The new NHS's first act was to formally endorse the status quo by adopting the tripartite system it had inherited:

- Secondary and tertiary care would be the responsibility of the Ministry of Health and administered through 15 regional hospital boards.
- Community, welfare and public health services would be the responsibility of local government and administered by the local authorities.
- Personal health services would be provided by GPs acting as independent contractors to the National Health Service.

1950s – The first wave: NHS hospitals

In an era of austerity, post-war governments had declared the national priorities to be firstly housing, secondly education and thirdly healthcare. Thus it was hoped to create a healthy, well-informed population that would place the minimum demand on the new NHS, albeit that advances in technology and improved diagnostic capability were uncovering an ever increasing demand for healthcare from within the population. The consequence was a hiatus of seven years, and it was not until 1955 that buildings produced under the new NHS began to appear.

However, the intervening time was not lost for it was in 1955 that the Nuffield Provincial Trust published *Studies in the Functions and Design of Hospitals.*[2] It was to have a profound influence on the design of hospitals in general and of wards in particular. The Nuffield ward, its break with the traditional open Nightingale ward and the methodology behind its inception, followed by its demonstration at Musgrove Park, Belfast, and at Larkfield, Greenock, promoted the concept of the exemplar project.[3] Architects of the first wave of post-war hospitals had little else by way of precedent to guide them.

The famous icons were projects from another era:

1932 Alvar Aalto's Piamio TB Sanatorium
1935 Sir Owen William's Pioneer Peckham Health Centre
1938 Tecton's Finsbury Healthcentre

The tower on a podium hospital

It was a time of fierce competition. Appointments were made not as a result of fee tendering but on an architect's proven ability to analyse the client's requirements, formulate the brief, find the most efficient solution and produce the highest build quality within the lowest budget feasible. Functionality and economy were everything. It is remarkable, therefore, that architects of that time, having no previous experience in the field of healthcare but only in those of housing and education, should have evolved a built form that not only satisfied the client and became a model for new hospitals worldwide, but can still be found in projects conceived in this century. The concept was to stack the repetitive private elements – that is, the wards – over a two- or three-storey podium containing on either side of an entrance concourse the public elements: the deep-planned ambulatory care and diagnostic/therapeutic departments, which were space-expansive and subject to growth and change. Specialist units such as maternity and paediatrics could be added to the periphery. Such an arrangement, though dependent on the capability of its lift installation, was obviously highly efficient and cost-effective.

Commissioned in 1953, Powell and Moya with Llewelyn-Davies Weeks as consultants, at Princess Margaret Hospital, Swindon, produced the first hospital embodying this philosophy.

1.2
Princess Margaret Hospital, Swindon.
Architects: Powell and Moya

Over a three-storey podium containing the public element, which cascaded down the sloping site and was entered at the highest level, the private elements, that is the beds, were stacked in a four-storey linear block. On each side of a central lift hall was a Nuffield duplex ward of 40 beds, with a generous terrace, or solarium, at its extremity (Figures 1.1b and 1.2).

This built form was designated by Paul James and William Tatton-Brown, in their book *Hospital Design and Development*, as the 'simple tower on podium hospital'.[4] Its merits won international recognition. In the following decade examples appeared in Scandinavia, Europe and North America. With a five-storey tower on a two-storey podium, it was adopted as the standard 'turnkey hospital' by the Ministry of Health in the Kingdom of Saudi Arabia. Variants on the theme, named the 'complex tower on a podium hospital', continued to be in favour into the 1970s. Notable examples are:

- The Lister Hospital in Stevenage with its 543 beds in a seven-storey, four-wing nursing tower. Architects: Northwest Thames Regional Health Authority.
- The Royal Free Hospital London with its 843 beds in a nine-storey tower over a five-storey podium (Figure 1.3). Architects: Watkins Gray Woodgate International.

1.3
Royal Free Hospital.
Architects: Watkins
Gray International

The 'radial tower on a podium', based on Jeremy Bentham's 'Panoptican', where the beds in wards radiate from, and can be supervised from, a single central nursing station, never found favour in the UK, though there are notable examples built in Switzerland, Germany and the US.

The new street hospital

The 1951 Festival of Britain ('a tonic for the nation') launched a decade of national recovery, optimism, idealism and confidence in the welfare state, which found expression in Powell and Moya's Wexham Park Hospital in Slough. The original scheme was based on a built form similar to their Princess Margaret Hospital at Swindon. At the last minute this proposal was withdrawn and the hospital was built with all the clinical and patient accommodation at ground level. It was inspired by the traditional British 'street and pavilion hospital'. A cruciform circulation infrastructure of hospital streets linked the support zone of kitchens, stores, etc. to the ambulatory care and cinical departments, which were planned around courtyards, and to the inpatient zone where the wards were configured to form sheltered gardens.

The 32-bed wards were L-shaped, comprising a Nuffield duplex with two 16-bed nursing units at right angles to each other. The main entrance, at the intersection of the hospital streets, was beneath a suspended five-storey tower containing administration and on-call staff accommodation. Naturally lit and ventilated throughout, waiting areas became lungs, and the roof a potential window, with the whole hospital opened up to the landscape in which it was set. It was the ultimate expression of the quest for the therapeutic environment – the original patient-focused hospital (Figures 1.1c and 1.4).[5]

1.4

Wexham Park Hospital, Slough. Architects: Powell and Moya

1960s – Technology leads: the auto-dominant society

The 1960s began with man in space orbiting the earth, and ended with Concorde coming into service. Taking office in 1963, the Wilson government promised to harness 'the white heat of new technology', and set up a Ministry of Technology. In order to boost the flagging housing programme, in 1966 Richard Crossman transformed the construction industry, introduced new methods of procurement and changed the landscape of urban Britain by granting blanket approval to any mass housing project provided that the contract was sealed before the coming election and that it employed a proven industrial building system.

The Greater London Council's new town at Thamesmead became the largest building project in Europe and the Aylesbury Estate in Southwark saw the development of Europe's longest block of flats.

In 1962 Enoch Powell, the then Minister of Health, published *Hospital Plan for England and Wales*,[6] thereby endorsing the findings of the 1960 Bonham Carter Committee and declaring that the 'General District Hospital serving a population of 300,000 approx. [is] to be the cornerstone of the National Health Service'. It was to have around 900 beds, that is to say three beds per 1,000 of the population served. This was in order to provide sufficient clinical mass to support the appointment of two consultants to each specialty.

An ambitious road-building programme combined with a rapid growth in private car ownership was perceived to increase the mobility of the population to the extent that the new district general hospitals (DGHs) could be planned on open expansive sites at the periphery, rather than at the centre, of the urban developments they served.

However, in the interim, following the Suez debacle, there had been a profound change within the country: optimism and confidence in the future had evaporated. A phenomenon occurred, known at the time as 'the flight from the patient'. Large numbers of medical and nursing staff left the UK and migrated to the US and the Antipodes. For the first time staff, always the NHS's most valuable resource, were in desperately short supply.

Racetrack wards, multi-level streets and interstitial space

The critical factor in the design of the next wave of NHS hospitals became the need to maximise their operational efficiency and to minimise the demands on the staff delivering the service. Three examples of the architectural profession's differing approach in responding to the new situation were:

- At High Wycombe, a 'simple tower on a podium hospital', Powell and Moya abandoned the 40-bed Nuffield duplex wards in favour of two 20-bed units in a racetrack configuration – the first use of the racetrack ward in the UK (Figure 1.5).
- At Wythenshawe, by the same architects, the basic elements of an enlarged Wexham Park were stacked over three storeys to a much more compact footprint and thereby created the first 'multi-level street hospital' (Figure 1.1d).
- At Greenwich District Hospital, the Department of Health's architects deployed the most advanced technology available in order to create a hospital of unique built form, with the objective of maximising the effectiveness of the staff engaged in the care of the patient (Figure 1.1e).

The design of Greenwich was inspired by Gordon Friesen's concept of an 'automated hospital'.[7] Over a semi-basement containing a food-preparation area, the boiler house and car park, the accommodation is arranged in a compact rectangular block with a footprint that covers the available site. The diagnostic/therapeutic departments form a three-storey core around which is disposed ambulatory care at ground floor, with the 800 beds in continuous bands around the perimeter of the upper two floors. The block is pierced by three full-height courtyards and four shafts containing lifts and engineering services. The principal vertical circulation is by escalator. As originally conceived, a mechanised supply and disposal system was provided.

1.5   High Wycombe District General Hospital

1.6
Greenwich District General Hospital.
Architects: DHSS Architects Department

For the UK, and the time in which it was built, Greenwich had three unique features:

- A long-span warehouse-type structure with a column grid of 19.5 m × 4.88 m.
- Accessible interstitial space 1.7 m high above each floor to carry environmental engineering.
- A sealed external envelope with the whole of the occupied space mechanically ventilated.

Theoretically, on a polluted urban site the interior would remain clean and its complex engineering installation could be maintained without disturbance to the occupied clinical areas. It was claimed that the long-span open structure would facilitate change and growth by its ability to carry an additional floor if necessary at a future date (Figure 1.6).

During the 1960s the concept of interstitial space was taken up enthusiastically by architects practising in the hospital field. However, the most famous example – the McMaster University Health Science Centre, in Hamilton, Ontario, Canada – on completion was found, in context, by its vast scale, to overpower the community that it was built to serve. Grandeur of scale is inherent in buildings that incorporate interstitial space between floors.

Comprehensive healthcare planning (CHP): an integrated service

The new Greenwich District Hospital was to replace the existing St Alphege's Hospital but before its construction could commence several active departments on the site had to be relocated. The then South East Regional Hospital Board recognised the opportunity that this gave to rationalise the support services in an area of south-east London extending from Guy's Hospital in the west to Erith in the east. In 1964 Derek Stow and Partners were appointed by the Hospital Board as architects and planners for the project, and by the GLC, on behalf of the boroughs of Greenwich and Bexley, for the community health services in the new town of Thamesmead, which fell within the boundary of the scheme.

The rationale underpinning the project was that, by bringing together all the different parties responsible for the delivery of healthcare, an integrated service could be comprehensively planned within the area in order to make the best use of the resources available, to the maximum benefit of the population served. Central to the overall strategy was the decision to concentrate all the support services on a single site and thereby assemble the critical mass necessary to take advantage of the latest industrial technology and automation, while at the same time freeing land for development at the hospitals served. The site chosen was at Hither Green Hospital, which was ideally located in relation to the road and rail network interconnecting the users of the service.

In the first instance, the industrial zone comprised a 160,000-piece laundry and a central linen and automated central sterile supply department serving seven hospital management committees with 3,500 beds in 17 hospitals, together with all the community health services within the area. Later it was expanded to include the regional transfusion and blood products service. The 85,000 gallons of water consumed daily was drawn from the hospital's own bore hole and the laundry pioneered the operation of a full heat and water recovery system. Already existing on the site was the stains and media department, which not only supplied sterile fluids to the NHS nationwide but enjoyed a profitable export market in Europe (Figure 1.7).[8]

Concurrently, in 1964 the Nuffield Foundation gave a substantial grant to Professor Butterfield of the Department of Medicine at Guy's Hospital to develop a system for planning the provision of medical care in the new community of Thamesmead that would provide the University with a base for the teaching of community medicine. Guy's General Practice Research Unit (GPRU) was set up to undertake the task. In parallel, the Joint Health Services Advisory Committee (JHSAC) was inaugurated to represent the two borough councils, two executive councils and the regional hospital board. The GPRU and the JHSAC, together with the GLC, became the client body. It was the architects' responsibility to formulate the physical brief, design the buildings and produce a development control plan that would locate them. It was a requirement that frontline services were to be operational and available when the first occupants took up residence.

1.7
Industrial Zone, Hither Green Hospital. Architects: Derek Stow and Partners

1.8
Thamesmead, Lakeside Health Centre. Architects: Derek Stow and Partners

1.9
Thamesmead, Gallions Reach Health Centre. Architects: Derek Stow and Partners

23

A four-module relocatable health centre was available to provide these frontline services when the first families arrived.[9] This was superseded in 1972, when the population had grown to 10,000, by Lakeside Health Centre, which in turn was expanded in 1980 to serve the whole population in the southern sector of the town (Figure 1.8).[10] Finally, in 1985 Gallions Reach, the main Thamesmead health centre, opened, providing specialist acute care as well as the whole range of community care services to the 45,000 who represented the remainder of the population. Twenty-one years after its inception Gallions Reach, the client's original brief for which had called for a '200-bed hospital without beds', became the base for Guy's schools of community medicine and dentistry (Figure 1.9).

'The best buy hospital'

Even before it came into commission, it was perceived that, in the light of the worsening financial climate and the looming oil crisis, Greenwich District Hospital, with its consequential high operating costs and standards of provision, could not be put forward as the exemplar DGH for the next decade.

The Department's response was to develop and promote 'the best buy hospital', that is two for the price of one! One was built at Frimley Park and the other in Bury St Edmunds.

In essence, they were to have the built form of Greenwich simplified, the footprint spread, the height reduced to two storeys, the building's mass opened up with a generous provision of large courtyards, and the whole naturally ventilated. Most significantly, the findings of the Bonham Carter Committee were to be abandoned, with a reduction of bed numbers from 800 (3.3 per 1,000) to 540 (1.8 per 1,000), together with a reduction in the supporting functional content, thus providing a reduced standard of provision. Subsequently, 540 beds was to become the accepted norm for new DGHs (Figure 1.1f).

The construction of a new DGH would invariably lead to the closure of any cottage hospitals that were functioning within its catchment area. It was expected that the community health services (primary care) would make up the shortfall in the provision of the services provided by the DGH (secondary care). Unfortunately, although an attempt was made at Frimley Park with Ministerial backing, there existed no legal framework under which the three arms of the NHS could be brought together to comprehensively plan an integrated health service, as had happened in south-east London in support of the Greenwich DGH.

As a result of an initiative launched by a group of local GPs, proposals were drawn up for a community health centre at Yateley in support of Frimley Park. The project, a true precursor to PFI, was to be financed and built by a local developer and leased to Hampshire County Council. Ahead of its time, it fell at the last fence.

With the Ministry's attention firmly focused on the hospital programme and local authorities giving priority to housing and education, very few examples where healthcare had been comprehensively planned existed. Those that did tended to be centred on large-scale urban developments, new towns and the like, where the incoming population generated a demand for new health services that required to be integrated with those already in existence. The best-known example was Harlow New Town, to be followed by Milton Keyes, Killingworth, Runcorn and Livingston in Scotland.

In response to the widespread concern at the apparent lack of coordination in the provision of healthcare, the King's Fund organised a series of conferences to which a wide spectrum of those engaged in the planning and provision of healthcare were invited. Although no precise recommendation as to the way forward emerged that could be reported back to the government, it became clear that the three separate arms of the then current tripartite service should be brought under a single administrative umbrella if progress was to be made. Only then could the delivery of an integrated healthcare service be comprehensively planned, with its buildings designed to provide the most appropriate environment for patient care.

NHS guidance systems: research and development

The burgeoning hospital building programme threatened to overwhelm the resources, in terms of skills, experience and basic information, of the multi-disciplinary professional teams charged with its implementation. To address this problem, the Hospital Division of the Ministry of Health, which was ultimately responsible for the success of the programme, recognised that in order to maintain, on a nationwide basis, common standards of provision that complied with established working practices, and to keep control of the capital investment, a body of information should be assembled consisting of design and procedural guidance that could then be disseminated to all those involved. The first Hospital Building Notes (subsequently Health Building Notes) were published in 1961:

HBN1: Buildings for the Hospital Service
HBN2: The Cost of Hospital Buildings
HBN3: The District General Hospital

Over the years the system, which has survived into the twenty-first century, was expanded to include:

- CUBITH: Coordinated Use of Industrialised Building Technology for Hospitals*
- MDB: Manufacturer's Data Base – approved building components*
- ADB: Activity Data Base – all the data required to design a space for a specific activity
- DBS: Design Briefing System*
- HTMs: Hospital Technical Memoranda – codes of practice
- Capricode: the mandatory procedural framework for managing and processing NHS Capital Building Projects*
- CIM: Capital Investment Manual.

* These tools and guides have not survived.

To be accepted in the field and remain effective, such a guidance system relies on the quality of the data upon which it is based. Equally, it is dependent on a continuous programme of research: firstly to provide the data, secondly to prove its effectiveness in use and thirdly to update the guidance that the system disseminates in order to take account of advances in technology and changes in practice. The Hospital Building Division embarked on such a programme into which private architects, engineers and surveyors working in the healthcare field were drawn, either by being commissioned to undertake specific research projects or by seconding staff to the central Department.

Independent research was carried out by the Medical Architecture Research Unit (MARU), established in 1965 by Professor Raymond Moss to undertake research as a multi-disciplinary team. MARU's first commission was to assist in the drafting of an outline brief as part of the feasibility study into the provision of a community health service for Thamesmead.

The Nuffield Provincial Hospital Trust supported the development of Professor Thomas McKeon's concept of 'the balanced teaching hospital'. The theory was that hospitals of the future should be large hospital complexes each wholly serving the hospital needs of the population depending on it. These should replace the varied separate hospitals for the acutely ill, the mentally ill and those suffering from special diseases which we have inherited from an unplanned past. One such hospital should provide all the beds and outpatient clinics and all attendant services that its population requires.[7]

Professor Llewelyn-Davies was commissioned to join the study and Nuffield demonstrated the theory by drawing up proposals for the development of the Queen Elizabeth Hospital Birmingham as part of the University campus. The scheme did not proceed, and the concept of the healthcare campus would have to await the coming of the millennium before it was taken up.

At University College London, Llewelyn-Davies and John Weeks developed their theory of indeterminate loose-fit architecture. The hospital was to be conceived as a village with its separate elements, varying in height and length, served by a central hospital street that followed the contours of the site. Their concept found concrete expression at Northwick Park Hospital which, starting at the same time as Greenwich, accepted its first patients in 1970.

1970s – The heroic decade: a total healthcare delivery system

Across the Atlantic the 'mega hospital' had already arrived, in two distinct built forms.

- **The vertical monolith.** The most extreme example of the vertical monolith, 'the cube hospital', was the Bellevue Hospital in New York. It was built up to the edge of the pavement on all four sides, and was 25 storeys high with a floor plate of 6,039 m^2 (65,000 ft^2). Only the 2,000 beds, arranged in wards around the perimeter of the building, enjoyed natural daylight. The staff providing the clinical support were condemned to work in the artificially lit and ventilated deep-planned internal space surrounding the central vertical circulation core.[11] The nearest equivalents in the UK – York, Rosenberg and Mardell's main phase block at St Thomas's Hospital (Figure 1.10), and Llewelyn-Davies Weeks's new block at St Mary's Hospital Paddington – are on a much more human scale. In both, the relationships between the main functional elements have been rationalised so that the wards sit on a podium containing the clinical departments, the two separated by an intervening service floor, which houses the environmental engineering plant.
- **The interstitial space hospital.** The most extreme example of the interstitial space hospital was the McMaster University Health Science Centre, the underlying concept of which was to continue to influence the next generation of hospitals.

The Harness Hospitals Building System

In the UK the decade opened with the launch of what was probably the most ambitious hospital building project ever contemplated. The Directorate of Works DHSS in succession to the Hospital Buildings Division, charged with responsibility for the construction of 70 new DGHs, had assembled the data and published the guidance necessary to set the standards and control the process – the 'software' was in place. Since 1969 it had been overseeing the development of the

1.10
St Thomas's Hospital, North Block.
Architects: York, Rosenberg and Mardell

1.11
Harness prototype, East Birmingham Hospital. Architects: DHSS/West Midlands RHA/William Nicholls Associates

'hardware' – the Harness Hospitals Building System, a system that sought to incorporate the lessons of the previous decade.

In a Harness hospital, the basic clinical elements were arranged either side of a central spine, the hospital street, at one extremity of which were the industrial zone, energy centre, etc., leaving the other free to extend to serve future expansion. Over the central spine a continuous engineering plant room ran from the energy centre for the full length of the hospital street – the 'harness'. The clinical elements were free to expand outwards from the street and upwards to a limit of four storeys. The whole complex was to be built up of 15 m × 15 m modules of occupied space with a 600 mm engineering/structural zone on each side and a 1.8 m interstitial ceiling/roof zone over. This provided for great flexibility for planning within a 16.2 m master grid.

In a move to overcome the acute shortage of professionals with the experience to develop such a system, at the same time to win nationwide support, the Department brought into the project the 15 regional authorities to whom, depending on their expertise, was delegated the drafting of operational policies and planning of specialist departments. Multi-disciplinary teams of building professionals experienced in the field were commissioned to design the fabric, external envelope, internal sub-division and engineering systems, and to draw up manuals giving guidance on the application of the system and procedures for its erection on site. To meet regional variations across the country, to suit local conditions and to provide an element of choice, a range of alternative cladding systems was developed.

In the best industrial tradition, and in order to test the system before the main programme got under way, two prototypes were built: one at Shortlands Hospital Worthing and the other a pathology department at East Birmingham Hospital (Figure 1.11). Harness combined the interstitial engineering space of Greenwich with the linear built form of Northwick Park to accommodate a functional content determined by the aspirations of the users. An appraisal commissioned by the Department demonstrated that, as a result of the enhanced space standards and the inclusion of interstitial floors, a Harness hospital was 30% larger in floor area, with a 60% greater enclosed cube, compared with a one-off DGH providing the same facilities.

Tragically, the Harness programme became a casualty of the economic crisis and oil crisis of 1973. Only two Harness hospitals were ever built: one the Dudley Hospital in Birmingham, the first to be planned in 1970, and the other at Stafford. At Dudley the length of the hospital street, as planned, was 423.3 m (1,389 ft) – more than a quarter of a mile – as compared with St Thomas's where the street is 274.3 m (900 ft) long.

In May 1970, the same year that the development control plan for Dudley was drawn up, the *Architectural Review* published its special 'Manplan' issue on *Health and Welfare,* as an overview of the state of the whole spectrum of architecture for the health and social services in the UK.[12] It found fault with the central Department for focusing on the acute hospital to the exclusion of the rest of the sector. It criticised Hull Royal Infirmary and Northwick Park as being overlarge and daunting, and drew attention to the unsustainably high operating costs of Greenwich. It doubted that these high-profile projects could be taken as models for the future. It called for the unification of the existing fragmented services into a single 'cradle-to-grave' health and welfare delivery service system.

At the same time, the King's Fund continued to champion the case for CHP with a new series of seminars. The first seminar, on 11 January 1971, entitled 'A patient-centred approach', was chaired by Howard Goodman. The call was for a strategically devolved delivery system based on the measurement of need, planned from the 'grass roots' up, but with the allocation of resources coordinated by the central Department. The Conservative government, under Prime Minister Edward Heath, listened and the Department of Health and Social Security (DHSS) came into being.

With all their services under one administrative umbrella, and their estate still intact, the health and welfare services in the UK reached their apotheosis. Now, for the first time, it would be possible on a national scale to plan and implement a comprehensive integrated health and social service to provide 'cradle-to-grave' care for the whole population of the country.

Plans had been drawn up and Departmental approval granted for a conference centre and residential college for the new DHSS on the banks of the River Granta at Owlstone Croft, as part of Cambridge University. Its purpose was to spread the gospel of the new culture among the diverse disciplines that would be brought together within a unified National Health and Social Service. The very first act of the new labour Secretary of State, Barbara Castle, on her first day of taking up office in 1974, was to cancel the project. She went on to declare her intention to provide 'hospitals for the people'.[13]

In 1975 her successor, Dr David Owen, declared that the hospital building programme was completely out of control and that there was an overriding need to reduce capital expenditure within the NHS.

The Nucleus hospital

Rather than cancel any of the proposed new hospitals, the Department responded to the crisis by setting a cost limit of £6 million for building the nucleus of each new DGH in the programme. At the same time the development of a new system to replace Harness was put in train. The new system was to be named Nucleus and to become adopted as the approved Standard Hospital System in the UK. It was to remain so for the next 15 years.

The standard Nucleus hospital retained the linear built form of Harness with the same central hospital street serving the clinical content planned around courtyards. However, it was reduced in scale, being generally of two storeys, without interstitial space and the continuous Harness plant room. Although conforming to the Harness 15 m x 15 m bay, each functional unit was

1.12
Nucleus hospital, Maidstone. Architects: Powell and Moya

planned within a 1,000 m cruciform template. Such a coarse-grained unit of accommodation greatly reduced the flexibility of the system: the phrase 'the tyranny of the template' became common parlance among those charged with planning a Nucleus hospital on a restrictive site. Nevertheless, it enabled the Department, with limited professional resources, to oversee the construction of more than a hundred Nucleus hospitals while keeping control of the capital expenditure. At Maidstone DGH Powell and Moya proved that the system could be deployed to produce good architecture and a humane hospital that was sympathetic to its rural context (Figure 1.12). The system aroused interest overseas and a programme of suitably modified Nucleus hospitals was built in Malaysia.

The devolution of care to the community

A watershed had been reached. Like its predecessor the best buy hospital, the Nucleus hospital, with its reduced clinical content, relied on supporting services being provided within the community. The argument put forward for this strategy was that the capital and revenue costs of providing care in the community were far lower than the costs of providing it within an acute hospital. The champions of the devolution of care had won the day – by default.

There had been precedents. The Oxford Regional Hospital Board, commencing in the mid-1960s under the Regional Architect A. L. Arschavir, had embarked on a number of community, psychiatric and district hospitals as well as various specialist units. Those at Wallingford and Milton Keynes brought together within the community primary care, hospital specialist and diagnostic support, and also social services, providing consulting facilities, day care and,

1.13
Evesham Psychiatric Day Hospital.
Architects: Derek Stow and Partners

for inpatients, 17 medical and 17 maternity beds. The region's burgeoning programme was sufficiently large to support the development of its own prefabricated building system, known as 'The Oxford Method'. This proved to be highly successful. In its developed form it was used to build large hospitals in Italy at Brescia and Cremona. Later it was adopted by Powell and Moya for the construction of the Queen Elizabeth Military Hospital at Woolwich.

In Worcestershire, in the late 1960s, a disastrous fire had led to the closure of Powick Mental Hospital and the dispersal of its patients. After a comprehensive planning study carried out under the aegis of the central Department it was decided to establish three psychiatric day hospitals in the surrounding district. The first was to be an adjunct to the new local hospital planned at Kidderminster. This hospital, which came to be much loved by the community it served, was to become a cause célèbre in the next century. When the hospital was threatened with closure its defender, Dr Richard Taylor, standing as an independent candidate, was returned to Parliament following the general election of 2001. The second day hospital, that at Malvern, was created by the conversion of a terrace of Georgian houses in the centre of the town. The third, after an exhaustive option appraisal of five alternative sites within Evesham, was built at Avonside Hospital where it was designed to form the first phase of the redevelopment of the whole campus as a new community hospital (Figure 1.13).

Under the newly unified DHSS, regional health authorities were for the first time able to comprehensively plan the delivery of services within the area under their jurisdiction and thereby redress any perceived shortcomings or imbalances in the system as it existed. Enterprising authorities focused their attention on what were seen to be the four main issues of the day:

- To relieve the overcrowded mental institutions by re-locating patients who could be better cared for in community-based facilities; for example, the South West Thames Regional Health Authority's (SWTRHA) strategy of developing a standard 18-bed unit for young mentally handicapped patients, which could be plugged into local community-based hospitals, thus enabling them to be transferred from Botley's Park Mental Hospital. Two units were built at Northfields Hospital, Aldershot (Figure 1.14), and a further four units at Greenfields Hospital, Farnham.
- To reduce the number of long-stay patients occupying beds in acute hospitals by providing local specialist day care with social service backup that would enable them to continue to live in their own homes. The same region, SWTRHA, embarked on a

1.14
Mentally Handicapped Units,
Northfields Hospital. Architects:
Derek Stow and Partners

1.15
Geriatric Day Hospital, Ellesmere
Hospital. Architects: Derek Stow and
Partners

programme of standard 50-place geriatric day hospitals. The first, Ellesmere, was
completed at Walton-on-Thames in 1979 (Figure 1.15).[14]

- To bring about an effective integration of family doctor, community health and social
  services, providing the patient with a single point of contact. On a self-contained site
  at Langthorne Hospital, Leytonstone, the North East Thames Regional Health Authority
  proposed a multi-service community health centre bringing together 14 local GPs each
  acting as a single-handed practitioner, the community health services and, on a separate
  floor, the offices and local headquarters of the Department of Social Services.
- In various parts of the country, towns and cities were forced to respond to the imposition
  of new transport infrastructures, fundamental changes to their industrial base and

patterns of employment, and the needs of their new catchment population. Nowhere was the situation perceived to be potentially more dramatic than that resulting from the closure of the London Docks and its proposed redevelopment as a major commercial centre with new rail and road links to the City.

The City and East London Area Health Authority commissioned a study to seek a new pattern for the delivery of services that would address the future healthcare needs within its area, in both the long and the short term. The outcome of the study was the decision that in order to address the uncertain dynamics of the situation, as a first phase, it would be necessary to establish in advance of the proposed development a modular clinic at South Poplar that was capable of being relocated at a future date, together with a permanent fixed modular health centre (The Barkentine Clinic), with an inbuilt expansion capability, on the Isle of Dogs.

Systems: rationalising the process and the product

Faced with an expansion of their remit to cover the delivery of a fully comprehensive health service, it became common practice for authorities to attempt to rationalise both the process and the resultant new building types for which they would now be responsible. Procedures were set for assessing the need, formulating the brief to fixed standards of provision, selecting the site, developing the design, and procuring, constructing and commissioning the completed project, in order to cope with an extended range of building types.

In 1971 the DHSS had published the working party's report proposing a development control plan sub-system.[15] Anticipating the IT revolution and the adoption of computer-aided design, this set out a task-based system that rationalised and coordinated the administrative and design team activities into a series of work stages from the inception of the project through to the completion and adoption of the approved development control plan. The methodology assumed that, in an uncertain climate, automated data processing would allow the system to respond rapidly to changing circumstances.

In 1977 the DHSS followed up with the 'management plan system'.[16] This report covered the management of the project from the initial feasibility study up to the completion and approval of the scheme design. It dealt with the process in great detail, took account of NHS guidance, and was fully compliant with the procedures that, under Capricode, had become mandatory.

The outcome was the *DHSS Project Model*, a report by the Directorate of Works Development DHSS.[17] It was intended as a demonstration of the application of the development control plan and management control plan sub-systems to the process of developing the design and preparing the documentation for the construction of a hypothetical 548-bed DGH. As such it posed an alternative to Nucleus. By the time it was submitted in 1980, systems and design methodology were no longer in favour. Ironically, the 'product', that is to say the resultant schematic of an acute hospital, proved to be ahead of its time. Twenty years later, overseas hospitals with the same functional arrangement and built form were to be held up as exemplar models for the UK.

At a time when the construction industry was already overcommitted and the future pattern of services was uncertain, authorities looked to industrial building methods for a short-term solution to a pressing problem. In taking over primary care, the health authorities acquired a number of health centres built under Section 21 of the National Health Service Act 1948, maternity and child welfare clinics and the like, that previously had been the responsibility

1.16

Modpac – Relocatable
Modular Building System.
The module shown is
with optional Solarshield.
Architects: Derek Stow
and Partners

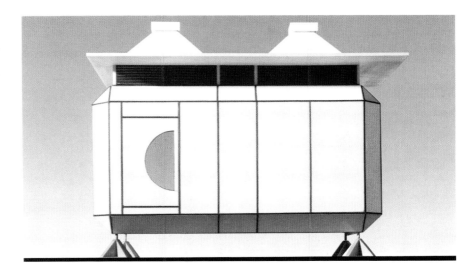

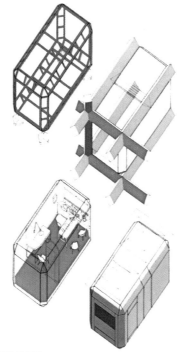

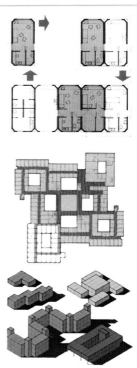

CONCEPT

– To provide a fast, flexible, pre-fabricated modular building
  system, designed to the highest quality specification.

– Maximising the benefits of modern technology in terms of
  materials, design engineering and performance standards.

– Combining all the necessary skills to allow a total service; from
  the assembling of project finance through to site installation and
  commissioning.

– Allowing the space standards, quality and permanence of a
  traditional building with the facility to relocate the building when
  and if required.

APPLICATION

– The system is designed for the rapid provision of front-line
  services, where time is the critical factor.

– The flexibility of the building system allows for the expansion,
  replacement or relocatability of each module.

– Modules can be stacked up to three storeys high providing
  many variations of form and function.

– The integrated engineering services within each module can
  be fitted and factory-tested before delivery, preventing
  delays occurring on site during installation.

1.17
Modular Health
Centre, South Poplar.
Architects: Derek Stow
and Partners

of local government. Usually, these had been designed and constructed using prefabricated systems originally developed for housing or schools programmes. Many local authorities had placed serial or term contracts for their use, with the consequence that schools, magistrates' courts, drug addiction centres, etc. would all be built using the same system. Heavy pre-cast concrete, steel frame and lightweight timber systems were deployed. Systems based on ISO standard freight containers, volumetric systems developed for the hotel market, cassette systems, plug-in sanitary pods, operating theatres and mortuaries, etc. were all available. Examples of all these were to find their way onto hospital sites throughout the country. None was wholly satisfactory. Apart from the Oxford Method, none was healthcare specific.

Derek Stow and Partners were commissioned jointly by the DHSS and the North East Thames Regional Health Authority to assemble a design team and develop a system specifically for healthcare. The resultant system was based on three-dimensional modules of pre-planned activity space which, when assembled within a three-dimensional master grid, automatically formed an infrastructure for the incorporation of environmental engineering services. In order to respond to the dynamics of the particular situation, the system could be implemented by traditional construction methods, as a site-assembled prefabricated system, or as a complex of fully fabricated, engineered and equipped, transportable and relocatable modules (Figure 1.16). UK prototypes were built at South Poplar (Figure 1.17) and the Isle of Dogs.[18] The British Modular Building Consortia (BMBC) was formed in order to make a government-backed bid to provide a total primary healthcare system for the Kingdom of Saudi Arabia, including health centres, polyclinics and local emergency hospitals.[19]

At the time, the NHS was reputed to lead the world in the delivery of healthcare and UK architects were highly regarded worldwide. Architects Co-Partnership, Hospital Design Partnership, Llewelyn-Davies Weeks, and Watkins, Gray, Woodgate International were responsible for important seminal projects in Africa, the Middle East, Asia and the Far East. In particular, the John R. Harris Partnership worked in 15 different countries overseas.

At the close of the decade, after the 'winter of discontent' with its disruption of essential services, the 1979 election saw the inevitable return of a Conservative government, and the publication of *Patients First*, a consultative paper.[20]

The new government announced its intention to abolish area health authorities and grant greater autonomy to district authorities. At the same time Lord Taylor, in the *British Medical Journal* (BMJ), attacked the mega hospital with its inhumane environment, which was the consequential outcome of its dependence on 'the deep plan'.[21] On another front, the Department, concerned with sustainability and the unnecessary destruction of existing facilities, pursued the Nelson Hospital Project as an example of how an existing hospital need not be demolished and replaced but could be upgraded to conform to contemporary standards, serve the local community and support the DGH.

1980s – Rolling back the state: a new strategy for capital investment

The new decade saw a fundamental change of philosophy. Instead of a centrally controlled and comprehensively planned health service, the new government considered that the best interests of the population would be served if those in need of care benefited from an NHS organised to make the most effective use of the resources at its disposal. The lessons of the successful commercial sector should be learnt and the service managed as a business. In 1983 Roy Griffiths, the Deputy Chairman and Managing Director of Sainsbury's, was appointed by the Secretary of State to assemble a team to study and report on organisation and working practices within the NHS. He recommended that a manager, not necessarily a healthcare professional but possibly a person from industry or commerce, should be appointed to every functional unit within the NHS. His recommendations were accepted and incorporated in Circular HC(85)26, issued by the Secretary of State for Health and Social Security in 1985.

Also in 1983, Ceri Davies, a senior architect with the DHSS, carried out a survey of the NHS estate with the objective of establishing the extent to which property was underused or surplus to requirement.[22] The subsequent report recommended firstly, that each area health authority should put a capital value and a notional rent on all of its properties, and secondly, that it should be allowed to dispose of the surplus and retain the proceeds of the sale to fund the cost of upgrading and redeveloping its estate. Ultimately this was to lead to the imposition of capital charges by way of an incentive.

It seemed that the moment had come and that the stage was set for the modernisation of the NHS estate, with its 480,000 beds distributed across the country in some 2,750 hospitals. An established set of procedures was in place and experienced, multi-disciplinary teams of professionals, supported by their equivalent in the private sector and the regional and area authorities, were well qualified to undertake the task. Across the estate, planning studies were undertaken and design proposals were drawn up for projects and submitted for 'approval in principle'. Typical projects of the time were:

- At regional level: proposals for the development of a regional neuroscience service, which involved an option appraisal of development control plans prepared for six major hospitals including three London teaching hospitals.

- At area level: a similar exercise involving five existing hospitals in the Brighton area, proposing the recasting of acute services and their redeployment on two major sites.
- At district level: the development of day and community health centres on the sites of existing local hospitals in order to bring together primary, community and specialist health services.

In the event, the proceeds from the sale of redundant property went to the Treasury and could not be retained to fund redevelopment. With the Nucleus programme taking priority, few of these enterprises proved achievable within the constraints of a region's budget allocation for capital works. The central Department became the Department of Health, ceasing to be responsible for social services. As built, 12 years after its inception, the Langthorne Community Health Centre was much reduced: without the Department of Social Security, with no specialist services and with only seven GPs instead of the intended 14, it represented just 45% of the original project (Figure 1.18).

The projects that did come to fruition were those made necessary in order to upgrade facilities to meet new statutory requirements, for example pathology departments, or to respond to the arrival of new resistant forms of infection, such as HIV, as a result of trans-border migration, for example the 24-bed maternity isolation unit at Barking Hospital. Other projects that survived were those that benefited from private funding from charitable trusts and the like, for example the paediatric surgical unit at Harefield Hospital (Figure 1.19) and the day surgery unit at Kings College Hospital.

1.18
Langthorne Hospital, Community Health Centre.
Architects: Derek Stow and Partners

1.19
Harefield, Paediatric Transplant Unit, Pyramid.
Architects: Derek Stow and Partners

A late flowering

There were other exceptions, one of the most notable of which was Powell and Moya's Conquest Hospital at Hastings where the site, like a vast amphitheatre facing the sea, inspired a highly original solution to the spatial disposition of the functional elements that make up a DGH. Another was Edward Cullinan Architects' much acclaimed Lambeth Community Care Centre, which combined respite and terminal care for elderly people in a 22-bed ward with bays opening onto a continuous terrace, over an open-planned ground floor containing the ambulatory care services, the whole accessible to the landscaped garden in which it was set.[23]

The flagship hospitals

At the close of the decade, the first of what the Conservative government hailed as its flagship hospitals was opened. As a symbol of a new, modernised NHS, Ahrends, Burton and Koralek's St Mary's Hospital on the Isle of Wight was to prove a brilliant demonstration of how the

1.20
St Mary's Hospital, Isle of Wight.
Architects: Ahrends, Burton and Koralek

component elements of the Nucleus system could be deployed to create an efficient hospital with a unique identity that was both exciting and welcoming to patients and staff. The standard linear orthogonal form was eschewed in favour of an arrangement where four linked pavilions of Nucleus templates radiated in a 90-degree arc around a central hub. With its lake and glittering stainless steel façades, it was likened to a giant sundial set in a therapeutic landscape (Figure 1.20).[24]

Energy conservation and the high operating costs of modern acute hospitals were major concerns of the central Department. St Mary's was the first demonstration model of the low-energy hospital; the second was to be Wansbeck Hospital in Northumberland. In parallel, the Department was under way with what was to be one of its last major research projects. Design for Reduced Operating Costs (DROC) was a computer-based study that set out to identify, simulate and measure every activity necessary to operate a DGH of a given design.

It was time for the NHS to redress the mistakes and omissions of the past, to conserve energy, make the best use of the available resources and, with the loss of Crown Immunity, accept its civic duty to take account of the impact that the development of a hospital has on the fabric of the community that it serves. The South East Thames Regional Health Authority published *Shaping the Future*, a review of acute services.[25] Nothing epitomised the spirit of the time more than the Greenwich District Health Authority's strategic review of its acute services and plan to recast its estate.

The objective of the Authority's plan was to make possible the upgrading and modernisation of Greenwich District Hospital and thereby avoid the closure of a building in its care that it

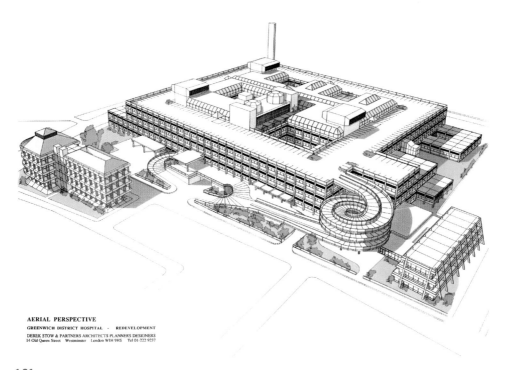

AERIAL PERSPECTIVE
GREENWICH DISTRICT HOSPITAL · REDEVELOPMENT
DEREK STOW & PARTNERS ARCHITECTS PLANNERS DESIGNERS
14 Old Queen Street Westminster London W1H 9HS Tel 01-222 9237

1.21
Redevelopment of Greenwich Hospital.
Architects: Derek Stow and Partners

recognised as an icon of twentieth-century hospital architecture. The strategy was to concentrate the cardiothoracic services in a new unit to be built on the site of a disused cinema in Greenwich adjacent to the DGH, and to transfer the services at the Herbert Hospital to the vacated space at the Brook Hospital. The footprint of the DGH was to be expanded, an extra floor and rooftop car park provided, the main concourse developed as a shopping mall, the external envelope re-fenestrated to allow natural ventilation to the perimeter, and the whole building re-engineered to reduce energy consumption. The London Borough gave its support and granted full planning approval to the proposal. The £45 million project was to be partially funded by the proceeds from the sale of the Herbert Hospital (Figure 1.21).[26]

Overseas, the John R. Harris Partnership, in association with Lee and Orange, were completing in Hong Kong Tuen Mun, the largest hospital built since the Second World War.

1990s – The market rules: deconstructing the system

Another decade and, as had become the norm, the country was to face another reform of the NHS. On this occasion the objective was to be the deconstruction of the existing comprehensively planned and integrated healthcare delivery system and its replacement with a dispersed organism, developed in response to local initiative, and driven by the forces of supply and demand within the 'healthcare market'.

The process of deconstruction was set in train:

- The Department of Health's Directorate of Works was transformed into the NHS Estates Agency.
- The works departments of the regional health authorities were disbanded – with the authorities themselves to follow in due course.
- Hospitals were grouped into quasi-independent trusts to serve as 'suppliers' of healthcare services.
- GPs were to become 'fund holders' empowered to purchase healthcare services on behalf of their patients.

The aim was to create an internal market where the suppliers would compete to win the custom of the purchasers. As such it was the first stage in an exercise in risk management. By devolving the responsibility for managing the estate and delivering the service, the government transferred the risk from the centre to the new local healthcare NHS Trusts. To ensure that Trusts discharged their new responsibilities to common standards of good practice, the NHS Executive's guidance (EL(92)47) required them to identify strategies for estate usage and capital investment. Market testing, benchmarking, affordability studies and business planning were introduced. The *Capital Investment Manual* (CIM) (1994) set out mandatory procedures for the preparation of a business case in support of NHS Trusts' submissions for the funding of capital projects.[27]

In parallel with the government's concern over the management of the estate, that is the 'process', there was great concern as to the effectiveness of the end 'product', that is the resultant healthcare environment. There was growing support for the proposition that design had a positive role to play in the creation of a therapeutic environment for the delivery of healthcare, to the benefit of patient and staff alike. *Better by Design*[28] was published by NHS Estates in 1994, followed by *Patient-Focused Architecture for Health Care* by Peter Scher in 1996.[29] Peter Senior, Director of Arts for Health, which was established in 1988 at Manchester Metropolitan University, led the campaign for the inclusion of the arts, both visual and performing, as a standard provision in the planning of all healthcare projects.[30]

The atrium hospital

In 1993, Sheppard Robson's new Chelsea and Westminster Hospital opened, the second of the government's much heralded flagship hospitals. It replaced the existing St Stephen's Hospital, which itself, in 1975, had been held up as an exemplar for the redevelopment of the urban Victorian hospital. The new hospital was a demonstration model par excellence of what the government sought to achieve under the reformed NHS. Built up to the boundary on all four sides around a spectacular atrium, it exploited the site's development potential to the absolute maximum. The dramatic increase in capacity allowed the transfer of services from other hospitals in the group, and their subsequent closure and disposal. This included the extremely valuable site of the existing Westminster

1.22
Atrium, Chelsea and Westminster Hospital.
Architects: Sheppard Robson

1.23
Mid Kent Oncology
Centre, Maidstone.
Architects: Powell and
Moya Partnership

1.24
Critical Care Centre,
King's College Hospital.
Architects: Halpin Stow
Partnership

Hospital. From the outset, as with the first flagship hospital, provision was made for the inclusion of the arts in the quest for the healing environment (Figure 1.22).

Elsewhere, the positive effect of the reforms and the onus placed on trusts to compete for their share of the potential market spawned a number of specialist units on the sites of acute hospitals:

- Powell and Moya's oncology unit at Maidstone Hospital (1995) (Figure 1.23).
- Halpin Stow's critical care centre at Kings College Hospital[31] (1994) (Figure 1.24) and Planetree Centre (ambulatory care and day surgery) at Whipps Cross Hospital (1997)[32] (Figure 1.25).

1.25
Plane Tree
Centre, Whipps
Cross Hospital.
Architects: Halpin
Stow Partnership

- Avanti's ACAD (ambulatory care and diagnostic) centre at Central Middlesex Hospital (1999).

The negative effect of the reforms, and of capital charging in particular, was to lead to the concentration of services onto the sites of fewer acute hospitals, their overdevelopment, and the closure of local hospitals with the loss of comparatively new community health facilities built under the previous regime. The threat to community hospitals and intermediate care continues to the present day.

The Private Finance Initiative

To increase the funds available to finance the public sector's capital works programme the government launched the Private Finance Initiative (PFI). It had favoured unconventional methods of procurement in the past – design/build and develop/construct, for instance. Under the new system, a private consortium, the special purpose vehicle (SPV), would bid for a contract to finance, construct, service and maintain a new healthcare development to meet the requirements of an output specification issued by the trust. The trust would pay an agreed rent for use of the facility under, say, a 25-year lease, after which ownership of the property would revert to the trust. In 1994 the Treasury stated that no capital scheme could proceed unless it had been tested for implementation under PFI.

An advantage of PFI was that the capital investment in a project would not add to the public sector borrowing requirement. At the same time the government promoted the practice of outsourcing whereby industrial support services, laundry, linen, pharmacy, sterile supply and disinfection, clinical waste, and even pathology services were contracted out to private service providers. The object of these measures was to further involve, and transfer the financial risk to, the private sector (see Chapter 7).

The introduction of PFI had the effect desired by the Conservative government. Nationwide, it acted as the catalyst needed to prompt a wide range of local initiatives. It brought about a number of joint ventures between NHS Trusts and groups active in the provision of private healthcare. The number of 'pay beds' in NHS hospitals had fallen to 3,000, while in Scotland the large new private Clyde Hospital had failed and had been taken over by the NHS.

PFI seemed to provide the opportunity to redress the balance. With private healthcare providers joining the consortia, PFI schemes included private patients' bedded and clinical accommodation, while some of the larger projects depended on the inclusion of patient hotels, medi-parks, etc. for their commercial viability. This upsurge in activity produced many potentially exciting and innovative projects. Unfortunately the vast majority of these schemes, which made heavy demands on the resources of the participants once the preferred bidder had been selected, failed to proceed. The first batch of 15 schemes was approved by the new Labour government in 1997 to a value of £1.4 billion but an assessment of the success of the PFI method of procurement would have to await the coming of the millennium.

The decade closed with the Labour government implementing the Private Finance Initiative that it had objected to when in opposition. At the same time, it put in train yet another set of major reforms of the NHS. A key element of these reforms was a declared intention to move away from the dominance of the hospital as the focal point for the delivery of healthcare, by recognising that, as the portal through which the population accessed the system, primary care should be seen to lead the service.

2000 – Devolution, dispersal and the return of the mega hospital

Come the millennium, true to the 30-year cycle, history repeated itself and, courtesy of PFI, the mega hospital returned. However, during the intervening years the world had changed. The Harness programme of the 1970s had deployed a wholly British product. It was a standardised system, which was designed by UK professionals, and produced by the UK construction industry, with no outside influence. The fresh crop of PFI hospitals were conceived against a background of globalisation. Each is individual and most have an international component in their planning and design, and in the consortia responsible for their implementation. In their quest for market share they are substantially larger.

Anshen Dyer's award-winning Norfolk and Norwich University Hospital has 953 beds compared with a standard Harness hospital's 800 beds. Instead of the three- or four-storey continuous horizontal monolith of Harness, designed to allow ebb and flow in demand between departments, the hospital has been deconstructed and reassembled as a complex of linked buildings containing the separate functional elements that make up the whole. The beds are arranged in 36-bed wards in nine individual pavilions. The rectilinear blocks containing the functional content radiate in a gentle arc which together with the internal planning – the panoptican layout of the theatre recovery ward, for instance – display a distinct North American influence (Figure 1.26).[33]

With its services transferred to the PFI-expanded Queen Elizabeth ex-military hospital at Woolwich, that icon of post-war hospital architecture in the UK, Greenwich District Hospital, its upgrading aborted, stood empty and abandoned as a monument to the past.

1.26
Norfolk and Norwich Hospital. Architects: Anshen/Dyer

In 2001 the government published *The NHS Plan*, which included a commitment to the largest hospital building programme ever to have been undertaken in the UK, with the promised construction of 100 hospitals by 2010.[34]

At the beginning of 2003, Nightingale Associates' £484 million PFI scheme for the 1,212-bed Walsgrave Acute Hospital was signed. Shortly afterwards the then Minister of Health, Alan Milburn, condemned '900-bed big-is-beautiful hospitals', and declared his intention to promote, 'smaller hospitals with 500 or so beds serving catchment populations of 250,000–300,000' – the district general hospital of yore. But in the following year, 2004, driven by a need to assemble an ever larger clinical mass to support an ever increasing investment in high-technology medicine, the mega hospital continued to dominate the scene.

Llewelyn Davies's £185 million PFI 670-bed UCL Hospital was completed. The £827 million PFI scheme for the Paddington Healthcare Campus was awaiting the outcome of the Audit Commission's report into its feasibility. HOK International with Skanska Inisfree's 'monolithic' £1 billion PFI scheme for the Royal London Hospital was in contention. 'Healthcare campus' or 'health village', could it be that the 1970s vision of the 'balanced teaching hospital' was about to be realised?

As proposals for ever larger hospitals came forward, it became obvious that demand was exceeding the capacity to supply, and standards were becoming difficult to uphold. NHS Estates' response was to commission a number of research and feasibility studies with the objective of modernising NHS guidance and rationalising health building design. At the same time, to relieve the pressure on an overcommitted construction industry there was a revival of interest in the 1970s approach to standardisation, off-site pre-assembly, service pods, prefabrication and modular building.

1.27
Cardiothoracic/Neuroscience Centre, St George's. Architects: Broadway Malyan

To further their policy of devolving responsibility, transferring risk, encouraging local initiative and increasing private funding available for development, the government introduced a number of measures:

- PCTs (primary care trusts) were encouraged to provide some services hitherto provided in acute hospital settings – such as for minor injuries, minor surgery, etc.
- The creation of foundation hospitals. Initially high-performing acute hospitals, and eventually all hospitals, were to be allowed independence from the centre, including the ability to borrow capital to fund their own planned strategic development.
- LIFTS (local improvement finance trusts) were public/private partnerships to foster the development of local communities with the set priorities of (a) wealth creation, (b) housing improvement, (c) upgrading education, and (d) enhancing health and social services, including accommodation for key workers.
- DTCs (diagnostic treatment centres). Private healthcare companies from overseas were invited to build and operate DTCs in the UK.
- A&E (Accident & Emergency). A national programme for upgrading A&E departments. East Anglia reported that with a three-week waiting time to see a GP, attendances at A&E had increased by 50%.

As part of the continuing process of deconstructing the monolithic acute hospital, the 'specialist care centre' arrived. Broadway Malyan's 245-bed cardiothoracic and neuroscience centre at St George's Hospital was completed in 2003 (Figure 1.27).[35] Proposals for several other specialist care centres were in the pipeline. These included Health Estates' scheme at the Royal

1.28
Façade of the Richard Desmond Children's Eye Centre at Moorfields Eye Hospital. Architects: Penoyre Prasad

Victoria Hospital in Belfast for an £80 million critical care centre modelled on a variant of the CCC at the Griffin Hospital in Connecticut, and Penoyre Prasad's International Children's Eye Centre at Moorfields Eye Hospital (now completed, Figure 1.28).

As a result of a gathering concern over reliance on outside contractors to provide essential support services, a consequence of the policy of outsourcing, more and more trusts were seeking once again to become self-sufficient. For instance, a self-contained industrial zone was planned at the Royal Victoria Hospital, and another planned to support the 1,500-bed five university teaching hospitals in the Manchester PFI project. Ironically the original industrial zone at Hither Green, which served 3,500 beds, has been demolished to make way for a residential development.

Building a 2020 Vision: Future Health Care Environments had been published in 2001.[36] This report was the outcome of a research study, funded by the Nuffield Trust and RIBA Future Studies, with the object of forming a vision of healthcare and its buildings as they could evolve by the year 2020. It predicted four new strategic settings for patient care:

- the home
- health and social care centres
- community care centres
- specialist care centres.

The report discussed the main issues that should influence the location, design, construction and procurement of this new generation of health buildings. In 2004 this vision had already begun to materialise with the dispersal of services and the arrival of a range of new building types for health and social care.

It is now widely accepted that hospital design should focus on those that it is intended to serve as well as the search for the most efficient disposition of the functional elements, and an interest in evidence-based design has re-awakened. There are today several active catalysts for change in the planning, design and construction of future hospitals: heightened security concerns, the spread of healthcare-associated infections, globalisation and trans-border migration (bringing in its wake the introduction of resistant strains of infectious diseases), the power of consumerism and the continuing march of technology.[37] For example, in order to combat cross infection, the open ward, with its mixture of multi-bed bays and single rooms, may cease to be the norm and, out of necessity, the bed capacity of future hospitals may be made up exclusively of single-bed rooms.

The first 30 years after the Second World War, 1945–1975, saw the construction of a comprehensively planned, fully integrated health and social care service. The following 30 years, 1975–2005, will have seen it deconstructed. Instead of a service delivered under the direction of 15 regional health authorities, the new NHS is an organism made up of some '600 separate organisations, each with its own Chairman, Chief Executive and Board of Directors' (Nick Webb MP). In April 2005, the Agency that was the direct descendant of the NHS Directorate of Works disappeared. NHS Estates has closed, and its staff and database, the latter the product of 45 years of research and development, has been dispersed. Three icons of the old NHS, Swindon DGH, Greenwich DGH and Northwick Park Hospital, have already, or are set to, disappear.

The process of deconstruction appears to be complete. 2005 saw the start of a new era with a new devolved healthcare delivery system, which will spawn a new family of building types. However, ultimately, as in the past, the architecture of hospitals, their location, content and built form, will be determined by the wealth, culture and ethics of the society that commissions them.

Notes and references

1. A. Cox and P. Groves, *Design for Healthcare* (London: Butterworth,1981).

2. Nuffield Provincial Hospital Trust, *Studies in the Function and Design of Hospitals* (London: OUP, 1955).

3. Nuffield Foundation, *Nuffield House, Musgrove Park Hospital* (1967).

4. W. P. James and W. Tatton Brown, *Hospital Design and Development*, (London: Architectural Press, 1986).

5. *Health and Hospitals*, Special Edition of the *Architectural Review*, June 1965.

6. Ministry of Health, *Hospital Plan for England and Wales* (London: HMSO, 1962).

7. Francis, Glanville, Noble, Scher, *50 Years of Ideas in Healthcare Buildings* (The Nuffield Trust, 1999).

8. D. Stow, 'Industrial Zone, Hither Green Hospital', *Architects Journal*, September 1970.

9. T. Howard, 'Mobile Medicine', *Architects Journal*, February 1970.

10. 'Lakeside Health Centre Thamesmead', *Architectural Review,* August 1972.

11. S. Verderber and D. Fine, *Healthcare Architecture in an Era of Radical Transformation* (New Haven, CT: Yale University Press, 2000).

12. *Health and Welfare,* Special Edition of the *Architectural Review*, May 1970.

13. *Hospitals for People* (The King's Fund in association with the DHSS, 1977). Foreword by Barbara Castle.

14. J. Symons, 'Ellesmere Geriatric Day Hospital', *Architectural Review*, May 1978.

15. *Development Control Plan Sub-system* (Report by Derek Stow & Partners in association with the Architects Division DHSS, and F2 Ltd, 1971).

16. *Management Control Plan Sub-system* (Report by Derek Stow & Partners in association with the Architects Division DHSS, Percy Thomas Partnership and William Nicholls Associates, 1977).

17. *DHSS Project Model* (Report by Derek Stow & Partners in association with the Directorate of Works Development DHSS, and Percy Thomas Partnership, 1980).

18. 'Poplar Re-locatable Modular Health Centre', *Architects Journal*, February 1981 and *Building Magazine*, April 1981.

19. P. Buchanan, 'Middle East Modules', *Architectural Review*, March 1981.

20. Department of Health and Social Security and Welsh Office, *Patients First* (London: HMSO, 1979).

21. Taylor, *British Medical Journal*, 31 March 1979.

22. C. Davies, *Underused and Surplus Property in the National Health Service* (Report of the Enquiry, Department of Health and Social Security; London: HMSO, 1983).

23. Department of Health and Social Security, *HBN 1 Buildings for the Health Service* (London: HMSO, 1988). Includes Maidstone Nucleus Hospital, Ellesmere Geriatric Day Hospital, Langthorne Community Health Centre, Queen Mary's Pathology Department and Lambeth Community Care Centre.

24. P. Davey, 'St Mary's Hospital Isle of Wight', *Architectural Review,* February 1991.

25. South East Thames Regional Health Authority, *Shaping the Future* (1990).

26. Derek Stow & Partners, *Redevelopment of Greenwich Hospital* (Report to the Area Health Authority,1990).

27. NHS Executive, *Capital Investment Manual* (London: The Stationery Office, 1994).

28. NHS Estates, *Better by Design* (London: The Stationery Office,1994).

29. P. Scher, *Patient-Focused Architecture for Healthcare* (Faculty of Art and Design, Manchester University, 1996).

30. R. Phillipp, *Arts, Health, and Well-being* (Nuffield Trust, 2002).

31. P. Scher, 'Critical Care Centre, Kings College Hospital', *Hospital Development,* April 1994.

32. P. Scher, 'The Planetree Centre, Whipps Cross Hospital', *Hospital Development,* January 1997.

33. P. Scher, 'Norfolk & Norwich University Hospital', *Hospital Development,* February 2002.

34. Department of Health, *The NHS Plan: A Plan for Investment, A Plan for Reform* (London: The Stationery Office, 2000).

35. P. Halpin, 'St George's Hospital, Cardio-Thoracic/Neuroscience's Centre', *Hospital Development*, September 2003.

36. Susan Francis and Rosemary Glanville, *Building a 2020 Vision: Future Health Care Environments*, Nuffield Trust and RIBA Future Studies (London: The Stationery Office, 2001).

37. Nuffield Trust, *Globalisation and Transborder Health Risk in the UK* (2003).

CHAPTER TWO

Managing hospital change: lessons from workplace design

JOHN WORTHINGTON

John Worthington draws upon a career devoted to understanding the bigger strategic context within which design takes place. Thirty years ago some of the complaints levelled today against hospital design could equally have been levelled against office design: lack of attention to the needs of the users, inflexible and outdated planning, poor coordination of management premises issues, zero architectural ambition, little integration with the city. There has since been a revolution in office design and DEGW, the firm that Worthington co-founded, has been at the centre of it. The idea of the 'New Office' has overturned old assumptions about the use of space by the bosses (expansive) and secretaries (sardine tins) and by people doing different activities at different times. In their drive for environments that are at the same time more convivial and more efficient, organisations have had to work through considerable changes in working culture. Accordingly, Worthington and colleagues have developed an understanding of the briefing process that allows the best intelligence to be released and enshrined in the design.

What are the lessons for hospital design? This chapter is a primer for anyone embarking on any new hospital development. At its centre is the proposition that organisational innovation and building design need to be approached as one integrated project if we are to realise the true long-term value that can come from constructing well-considered environments. The key here is change. A new building embodies change, whether knowingly guided or blindly entered into. Unless the change is in step with inevitable organisational changes, changes that will go on, organisational effectiveness will be compromised. The task, then, is not so much how to manage the process of change to achieve quality in design but how change and design can be integrated as a process where the achievement of organisational objectives by process re-engineering and/ or the development of high-quality facilities are one and the same thing. This places design at the heart of operational effectiveness in a way that is new but increasingly widely recognised. This chapter makes it clear just how the biggest opportunities for success can be won, or lost, in the briefing stages of a project.

Introduction

In an unpredictable world, change is the one factor of which we can be assured. Of the myriad factors that might impact on the way we design and plan our future environment, three themes stand out. First, the speed of change is such that it has become the norm rather than the exception. Second, there is a shift away from the desire to own branded goods to a growing concern for the quality of life, fuelled partly by the greater availability of information through the internet. This is reflected in the interest in health, learning and outdoor pursuits that now absorbs an increased proportion of individual discretionary spending. Third, the clear-cut binary framing of choices, as *either* this *or* that is giving way to a world paradox where the challenge is to accommodate *both* this *and* that. Reflecting on my experience in planning, briefing and designing for the world of work,[1] this paper argues that, if the healthcare building programme is to meet the challenges of the increased speed of change, and a differing set of consumer expectations, there should be a new paradigm for building briefing, design and delivery.

Healthcare in the UK today is in a period of unprecedented change, both in the way the service is delivered and in the buildings where it is accommodated. Following decades of low and unstructured investment, the National Health Service (NHS) is now undergoing the biggest investment programme in its history. The NHS capital investment programme rose from £1.5 billion in 1992 to £3.5 billion in 2003, with further expenditure planned through to 2010. The political goals for healthcare are ambitious, relying on private sector funding and management expertise to deliver results. The size of the programme within a short timescale compounds the challenge.

Further, the NHS, founded on expectations of public funding, is firmly rooted in a culture of the 'public good' and a hierarchical structure of professional and support roles, with well-established procedures that constrain change to reflect different expectations. By contrast, in the manufacturing and service sectors the impact of information and communications technology has stimulated a process of rethinking the organisation of roles and work processes, which has been reflected in new ways of using space and real estate delivery. How far can the lessons learnt in commercial buildings be applied to healthcare?[2]

This chapter looks at the world of work and the approach to briefing, design and property management that has emerged to meet the challenges of effectively accommodating 'new ways of working'.[3] Drawing on this wider experience, three propositions are explored and the implications for the healthcare building programme presented. The first proposition is that time spent in thoughtful briefing and design, which matches organisational innovation to building design, will yield effective results. The second is that a culture of learning through continuous evaluation and feedback is at the heart of speeding up the process and improving quality. Evaluation is often perceived as a post-project auditing process rather than a learning opportunity at the start of the next project. Lastly, it is proposed that experience from the world of office work shows that new building projects, which are conceived in isolation from organisational rethinking, provide limited returns. Case studies are used to show that the greatest chance to deliver sustainable improvements, including driving down costs and improving productivity, comes from an integrated approach that links organisational innovation with building design, coordinated with a change management programme, which in turn leads to a continuous programme of innovation and development.

Current healthcare programme

As part of the RIBA Future Studies, the Medical Architecture Research Unit (MARU) supported by the Nuffield Trust prepared *Building a 2020 Vision: Future Health Care Environments*.[4] In 2002 a summary was published by Building Futures as a precursor to a conference jointly hosted by the Nuffield Trust, RIBA and Building Futures (February 2003) for trusts, providers and their designers. The goal of the event was to explore issues facing the current health programme, in the context of the likely demands for healthcare through to 2020, and to reflect on how other sectors (for example, airport authorities) and countries (for example, North America) are handling the process of designing for change and an unpredictable future.

From the discussions at the conference and MARU's report, six areas have been identified where I believe a willingness to reappraise current procedures could lead to improved design quality and healthcare delivery:

1. **Adaptability** – recognising continuous change as the norm rather than the exception by developing a briefing, design and construction process, linked to a programme of healthcare delivery, which can respond to often unpredictable future needs.
2. **Integration** – achieving maximum success by linking organisational innovation (modernisation) and new work processes (IT applications) to a coordinated programme of building design, delivery and project management.
3. **Change management** – ensuring new building programmes support, and are related to, potential opportunities for innovation in healthcare delivery.
4. **Measurement** – recognising that improvement programmes can benefit from being able to diverge from stated targets, and by matching organisational performance to physical change.
5. **Availability of design resources** – few schools of architecture today have engaged with healthcare buildings, with the result that design talent has not been sufficiently attracted to the healthcare sector. Healthcare design has been perceived as specialised, prescribed and unexciting, with complex, difficult client bodies. Until recently, it was viewed in the way that office design was 30 years ago, as uninteresting and not central to the agenda of architecture. With the explosion of healthcare building work, and the recognition of the similarity of many of the functions in a hospital to those in other sectors (hotels, offices, etc.), health, like education, has presented a new attraction to the design professions.
6. **Procurement** – there is still a gap in current procurement processes, particularly those involving PFI and public private partnerships, between briefing, design, implementation and continuous estate management. The paradox of striving for both market competition and collaborative partnerships is challenging the capacity to improve through shared learning and continuous feedback.

Designing for change

Change is simultaneously both organisational and physical. It is an inevitable process that can be moderated and managed, but not stopped. Most people would recognise the change around them and are not resistant to change as such, but they are, perhaps, resistant to *being* changed. In managing the process, it is important to match the speed of the process to the culture of the organisation, recognising those elements that are cherished and 'fixed' and those that are 'fluid'. Building design strategies that meet the demands of change are reflective of time and the process required to moderate that change.

Designing for change has been central to the architectural debate. Theories vary, from short life ('precise fit') to Alex Gordon's dictum of long life ('loose fit').[5] The 'precise fit' protagonists expound the concept of the 'manufactured container', precisely engineered around specific functional demands and disposed of when redundant; the 'loose fit' protagonists search for a robust building configuration, where the activities and their interior settings are disengaged from the long-life building shell. John Weeks's 'duffle coat' principle,[6] originally conceived for hospital buildings, encapsulates this approach to accommodating change.

More recently, as the disciplines of building design and property management become more interrelated, it has been realised that change can be facilitated through flexibility of tenure arrangements and providing a mixed portfolio of space. Commercial organisations are recognising that they can increase their real estate flexibility by owning as little as 30% of their space as 'fixed', in order to give meaning to the values of the organisation, with the remainder being 'flexible' – 40% (on short lease); or space that can be hired 'on demand' – 30%.[7] Within these conceptual approaches, architectural responses vary.

Le Corbusier's Domino House provided a frame for change and a machine for living. Mies van de Rohe, with his iconic Farnsworth House, was concerned with providing undifferentiated space, which attracted the minimum of intervention. Louis Kahn, by contrast, aimed to create spaces with 'no names', where the unique quality of the spatial experience initiated a response. His Unitarian Church at Rochester, with its well-ordered collection of varying dimensioned spaces, or the Richards Laboratories in Philadelphia, with their 'served' and 'servant' spaces, both illustrate this approach well. Herman Hertzberger, following on from Kahn's work, provides yet another example of a loose fit approach at the Centraal Beheer insurance offices at Appeldoorn. Drawing on structuralist principles, Hertzberger creates a honeycomb of repetitive platforms within a generic discipline of dimensions, which allow a variety of activities and settings to thrive. Paul Rudolph, with his plug-in living capsules, celebrates the 'precise fit' philosophy.

When establishing building briefs, clients and their advisers, mindful of potential future change, liberally call for adaptability, flexibility, and even occasionally agility. These concepts are often used interchangeably, so losing their precision and much of their value.

What then are the differences? *Adaptability* is strategic, allowing for functions to change or expand. It is allowed for through the choice of the dimensions, configuration, and relationships between the different spaces provided. Kahn's search for the bunch of 'spaces with no name', which would comfortably accommodate a variety of functions over time, where a change of name on the door could allow for different uses within, is the architectural expression of adaptability. *Flexibility* is short term, tactical and relies on physical changes. The kit of parts that came together to make the Eames house at Santa Monica allows the flexibility for parts to be changed without disturbing the composition of the whole. A building with *agility* is both adaptable and flexible, with the added ability of rapid response. In a world in continuous flux, it allows for conditions to reverse to the original design. With the miniaturisation of computing and emerging new materials, an architecture is emerging that allows for instantly responsive environments,[8] which will adjust to the changing activities and conditions around them.

In the United Kingdom, the hospital building programme of the 1980s aimed to provide the maximum flexibility of servicing, with the ability to adapt to complex equipment requirements across all spaces. The result was a building stock designed to meet the worst case scenarios. Solutions such as the Greenwich Hospital were an exemplar for total adaptability with 'just in case' capacity – at a price, and with considerable management implications in order to extract the potential. The result is that, 30 years later, the building lies forlornly empty. Learning from commercial office-building experience, the alternative approach might have been to identify the functions requiring complex servicing and those that could use generic, low-serviced, sub-lettable space (for example, ward space). Buildings would become zoned according to levels of complexity of servicing, with the appropriate space types for each.

Integrated procurement and management

The property delivery role is changing from one of providing and maintaining buildings to one of devising comprehensive asset management solutions. The accommodation provided is a combination of the buildings (hardware) and support services (software), with the primary goal of adding value to the patient experience. Buildings have traditionally been viewed as permanent assets, independent of the vagaries of the business, encompassing every element from the structure to the light fittings. Such an all-embracing approach has become increasingly untenable with the rapidly changing demands of modern organisations. The 75-year life cycle of a building sits uncomfortably with the five-year life cycles of much of healthcare technology and practice.

To reflect the increasing speed of change, and manage the inevitable unpredictability associated with the longevity of buildings and the shorter cycle of technological and medical change, my own practice, DEGW, has identified four levels of decision-making:

- Building shell, which has a life span of 50–75 years and consists of the basic structure (foundations, supports, floors, roof and cores). The long-term success in adapting to unforeseen demands is dependent on a few critical design decisions concerning floor to floor heights, configuration and size of floors, depth of space, location of cores and the permeability of the structure.
- Building services, which may have a life span of no more than 12–15 years before they are obsolete. The services adapt the basic shell to specific activities, depending on the sophistication of utilities and environmental control required.
- Scenery, with a life span of 7–8 years the scenery, or fit-out, fine tunes the building to user and functional demands through the choice of the appropriate partitions, finishes, lighting and furniture. While not the major cost element in the overall construction budget, the scenery is often the primary element in reflecting user needs and fulfilling client and user expectations.
- Settings, the final level of decision-making as part of the day-to-day management of the building and adaptation of the scenery to meet continuously changing requirements. With the recognition of the increasing importance of intensifying the use of resources by managing space and time, the continuous reconfiguration of space to match changing operational needs is becoming a central requirement.

The layering of decisions, and the definition of the building delivery process in terms of shell, services, scenery and settings, has now become a recognised approach to commercial workspace delivery. A similar approach has been pursued for hospital design since the 1960s. John Weeks's 'duffle coat' principle[9] and the subsequent componentised hospital building systems (for example, the 'harness' model in the 1970s proposed by the Directorate of Works in the DHSS) reflected such an approach. However, these systems were hardware driven, with an emphasis on improving the construction and maintenance process, rather than reflecting an agile approach to space use and management. As a conceptual model for the healthcare estate in today's rapidly changing world, it may be more appropriate to layer the briefing, delivery and management process to seven Ss – adding site (timeless), skin (25 years), and systems (three years).

Shifting the way we view buildings from the 'particular' to the 'generic' potentially frees our perception of the nature of hospitals and their settings. In the North American sprawling suburbs, day healthcare facilities, undertaking treatment that previously would have been carried out in large hospital complexes, are associated with shopping malls, in buildings that could be converted to commercial use. For those who need overnight care, commercial hotels, with their high standard of service, provide 'bed-spaces'. Healthcare in Europe, due to its funding regime, has been less aggressive in rethinking the paradigm and applying information and communications technology to reduce overheads and improve performance.

DEGW's global studies of the characteristics of building intelligence have shown that buildings that effectively accommodate and use technology are those designed to absorb change and adapt to specific contexts, not the ones with the greatest number of high-tech features. The Intelligent Building studies[10] redefined the intelligent building as one that 'provides a responsive, effective and supportive environment within which the organisation can achieve its business objectives. The intelligent building technologies are the tools that help this happen.' The three layers of building intelligence are:

- Common sense – the intelligently designed building shell that has sufficient capacity to adapt to a variety of functions over time.
- Appropriate technologies – to manage the building, space and business (healthcare) to an appropriate level of sophistication and within its available resources. An excess of features can be as 'dumb' a solution as too few.
- Integrating technologies – to effectively deliver and network the applications. These may consist of technological systems, such as Wi-Fi[11] groupware, etc. or personnel-driven systems, such as a facility management.

The future hospital could be conceived as a network of buildings and locations, some owned, others leased and others simply being the beds at home in the patient's space. The integrating factor is information and communication technology (ICT). The building becomes the frame to support an ever-changing array of activities and their technology. Within the framework, the 'building animator' (facility manager) takes on a new significance as stage setter and director. Managing the hardware (building management and maintenance) may become less important in comparison to managing the experience (events management).

Maximum value may be gained by providing continuously changing and responsive settings that maximise the use of the building and improve user satisfaction and healthcare delivery. Westminster and Chelsea Hospital in London, organised around a central sunlit atrium, has an imaginative programme of art and music events, and a retail centre that is open to the public. Once the institutional 'closed' perception of hospitals is broken, one could envision the hospital as a focus for extended education and associated businesses, and as a major community hub with 16-hour activity (Figure 2.1).

Many corporations today, with a desire to minimise the risk of vacancy, own the bare minimum for representational value and outsource, or lease, the bulk of their requirement. This willingness to overlap functions and share support services has reduced overheads and improved the companies' agility. New paradigms of property management and ownership, which are now possible within the PFI programme, could have similar advantages for the NHS.

The Shell company approached DEGW Twynstra[12] when it was developing a new learning centre for senior management from around the globe. The brief was to provide a centre within an hour's travel distance of Amsterdam airport. The project had to be delivered within a year. Management suggested it could be in a new office building or an old castle. The solution was a deal to share space with Holiday Inn Hotels. Peak times for the hotel were at weekends and the eight weeks of the summer vacation, the very times when the building was not needed by Shell. From Monday evening to Thursday evening Shell used the building and its excellent

2.1
Westminster and Chelsea Hospital atrium

leisure facilities, while the rest of the time Holiday Inn used it as a hotel. Shell, through the use of projected imagery and logos, made it their own. To adapt the building, they built a small auditorium, which at weekends was used as a cabaret theatre by the hotel. Both parties gained, with a saving on overheads and a significant intensification in space usage.

The BBC provides a similar example of effective property portfolio management.[13] As part of their 2020 vision, which was first initiated in 1999, they have outsourced their property portfolio, while keeping control over the quality of design and fitness for purpose. Initially, in parallel to the organisational vision and with the support of DEGW's strategy for 'new ways of working', a series of pilot spaces within the BBC headquarters were constructed and tested through use. These pilots integrated both organisational and building change, ensuring that they were far more than design prototypes (Figure 2.2). The results of experience were then assimilated into design guidelines for the broader property workplace programme. On the setting up of a public private venture the guidelines became a critical component for briefing, evaluation and continuous improvement. The BBC experience suggests that success depends upon an overlapping and integrated approach, where the client/user body keeps close contact throughout the process.

2.2
General view of office

Briefing, design and implementation

At the heart of good design is a clear understanding of the client's needs – a good brief.[14]
However, briefing is not a linear process, but iterative and interactive. Clients only know
what they want when they can see what they can have. Design and briefing are interlocked
and continuous. The process is layered, moving from the strategic brief, which focuses on
organisational decisions, to the project brief, expressed in the language of construction and
prepared by the design team, through to the detailed fit-out and operating brief. At each stage,
requirements and solutions are being tested and ambitions and expectations reinterpreted to

a more precise schedule of requirements. Essential to the continuous process of briefing is the recognition that organisations have an overarching business project – to deliver an effective health service – and within that a number of building projects that unfold over time.

The long-term continuity of the business project allows for continuous evaluation, feedback and learning. Post-occupation evaluation (POE), rather than being viewed as an audit of failures, can be undertaken at the start of the next project in the spirit of learning. Evaluation at the pre-project briefing stage is an integral part of needs assessment, problem framing, option testing and solution searching. This sequence is frequently frustrated by insufficient top management time being allocated at the pre-project strategic decision-making stage, a pressure to appoint teams and initiate a construction project, and a shortage of consultants familiar with strategic thinking. The Private Finance Initiative (PFI), with its potential long-term perspective, should allow for just this integrated strategic thinking, linked with implementation and continuous feedback. However, in practice, the need for competitive procedures and closely defined specifications for performance may hinder the opportunity for collaborative briefing and continuous improvement through evaluation and feedback.

DEGW's experience of working with corporate clients has shown that significant improvements can be achieved through the client being prepared to engage with and manage the continuous process of briefing, with the provider being recognised as a partner and part of the learning process. Inevitably, the expectations of the user and building teams are not always aligned. Users wish to reflect continuous business change, keeping options open to the *last responsible moment*, while the building team, to deliver the project at cost on time, is searching for a clear beginning and end in order to define the project and freeze requirements at the *earliest possible moment*. Both of these expectations are correct: the challenge for the design brief manager[15] is to balance the differing interests.

Continuous building programmes, as exemplified in healthcare, potentially allow for continuous improvement. Each project is no longer a 'white sheet of paper' but can learn from the last; briefs become a combination of prescription and performance. The components of the brief that are prescriptive take what has been successful from the last project and repeat the solution, adapted and refined as necessary. The performance brief selects elements where it is felt improvements can be achieved to reduce costs and/or improve quality, and focuses the design team on solving these issues.

The challenge in managing a serial programme of building is to keep improving, by repeating successes and innovating in areas where evaluation has identified opportunities for improvement. Organisations that have a continuous building programme, such as the British Airports Authority (BAA), have achieved major efficiencies by establishing internal development managers to manage the briefing and feedback process.[16] They achieve continuity through working in partnership with selected professionals and suppliers. During Sir John Egan's chairmanship of BAA, through subjecting each project to a series of value management and engineering reviews, it is estimated that the cost of construction was reduced by 15% and fitness for purpose improved.

Measurement and continuous improvement

In a typical business organisation's operating budget, 65% of the total expenditure is staff costs, with the remainder being 10% for space (rental or amortised), 10% for office technology and 15% for maintenance, heating, administrative services, etc. Traditionally, the role of the premises department was focused on achieving *efficiencies* by driving down costs and using space more intensely. More recently, it has been recognised that greater returns can be achieved for the business by not only controlling real estate costs but also improving the organisation's *effectiveness*. In a knowledge economy, increased productivity may result from personnel satisfaction, improved communication and the ease with which change is absorbed. With a shift to value being generated through innovation, design *expression* is beginning to be recognised as a major driver of organisational improvement. Building design, the settings created and the way the environment is managed convey messages to staff and customers. Evidence is now being amassed, in both the corporate and healthcare fields, showing the impact that design can have on improving business productivity and patient well-being.

The Construction Industry Council, with the support of CABE, has developed the Design Quality Indicators (DQI) to help define and evaluate design through all stages of the process. Its NHS equivalent, AEDET (Achieving Excellence Design Evaluation Tool), can be used to 'help communicate and share values, clarify design strengths and weaknesses and identify opportunities for improvement'.

DEGW, in work for a major financial services corporation, has established an approach to measurement that reviews efficiency, effectiveness and expression in a holistic format. In a world focused on applying knowledge, quantifiable outcomes such as throughput, although the easiest attributes to measure, often have the least importance. Precision and impact are inversely correlated. *Efficiency* measures are quantifiable and directly related to financial savings. *Effectiveness* measures, however, are indirect, depending on the business goals and context. The measures used in this particular project were perceptual covering issues, such as increasing the satisfaction level for critical services, providing real support to busy people, and giving the appropriate range of choice. *Expression* – reinforcing the culture – was measured against issues such as the degree to which the individual environment reflected wider corporate values, and how the shared amenities demonstrated respect for employee values. Each of these themes was matched against six environmental goals reflecting work style, environmental quality, technical infrastructure, and service and amenity. Three conclusions were clear from our study:

1. Benchmarking is meaningless unless directly related to corporate goals.
2. How the facility is managed is as important as the physical design.
3. Qualitative data on how people perceive the environment is as important as quantifiable measures.

If we are to make design work, we need to measure simultaneously how design can cut business costs, add value to the performance and broadcast the appropriate messages. Bad design and lack of attention can become an equal force for transmitting negative messages.

Using space effectively

Information and communications technology has impacted on the workplace by freeing up where, when and how we work. This, in turn, has led to a questioning of space allocation by status and a willingness to reappraise the allocation of space by function and usage. Studies of companies have shown that, typically, staff are only in the office for 60–75% of the time available, and are only at their own desk for 40–50% of that time. Furthermore, individual space is least occupied by senior staff.

A reappraisal of space use has resulted in increasing numbers of firms embracing 'new ways of working',[17] with space being allocated to shared settings and projects, and individuals moving between settings. In DEGW's own London offices we have, by moving to flexible ways of working, increased the number of settings for collaborative work, improved the ease of setting up and managing teams, and added to the variety of work settings available. The recognition of the time that individual workstations were lying vacant has resulted in a greater diversity of work settings and more individual space for those who are in the office for the majority of their time, resulting in 25% improved capacity.

Overlapping and shared use of clinical space in hospitals is well understood. However, there may be opportunities for improved usage and effectiveness gains, by using a more flexible form of space briefing. This form of briefing focuses on providing adaptable building shells, within which space can be allocated, and specific settings can be designed as demands emerge and change. Such an approach of budgeting space to functional zones is in stark contrast to the current procedures of building up a detailed spatial brief from specific activities, with centrally prescribed fixed space standards as the template. Space allocation expresses organisational values and expectations. A schedule of accommodation freezes organisational thinking at a moment in time.

Managing the process of change

Experience in the commercial sector shows that if the way that the building is to be used, and the organisation managed, have not been thought through in parallel, new buildings are likely to have a diminished impact on business performance. Managing the process of change runs in parallel with the process of building design and delivery. A new building is an opportunity, rather than a threat. Our experience is that staff are not resistant to change, but they *are* resistant to *being* changed. A programme is most successful where groups can identify how they work and where improvements can be made, and these outcomes are linked to the opportunities afforded by the new building.

DEGW were the architects of the new Freeman Centre for the University of Sussex where, in tandem with the construction programme, we were able to initiate a process of briefing and change. The new building brings together two research organisations – the Science and Technology Policy Research Unit (SPRU) at the University of Sussex, and the Centre for Research in Innovation Management (CENTRIM) at the University of Brighton. The aim of the new building was to bring together two different cultures and help them to integrate. Using DEGW's envisioning cards, we worked with groups from the two centres in order to understand what each wanted to achieve and the perceptions they held of each other. By getting the groups to work together, we were able to articulate expectations and, through focus groups, develop the types of settings that could support their aspirations and work practices.

These ideas were fed out to the rest of the staff members in a ripple process. Their aspirations were to allow for individuality, within a strong structure and a sense of community. The outcome was an open-plan environment with 20% of the floor space given over to shared enclosed rooms. The space fosters sharing, collaboration and chance encounters, thereby meeting staff members' desire for a strong structure with a sense of community and a sharing of ideas and risk. The building has already shown the ability to adapt and change. However, the 'soft landing'[18] afforded by the programme of continuous briefing and change management sat uneasily with the University estate department's building procurement procedures. It was considered peripheral and outside the prime task of delivering the building in a timely and cost-effective manner.

With current attitudes to PFI bidding, it is difficult to see how a supportive programme of change management can be linked with the building delivery process. However, evidence shows that major gains can be achieved when both physical change and organisational innovation become aligned.

Implications for healthcare

The UK government's commitment to a ten-year continuous building and improvement programme affords the opportunity to build on experience, learn from previous projects, and continuously improve by repeating those elements that are successful and innovating where opportunities for improvement are identified. Experience from the commercial sector shows that major advances can be achieved where clients and their suppliers adopt a culture of collaboration. Are there lessons here for the NHS, and is there room for improvement?

The conclusions drawn are those of one not steeped in healthcare design practice, but with practical experience in other sectors and insights into health service design. These insights have been gained through design panels, conferences, working with the NHS Design Briefing Working Group (DBWG) and DEGW's advisory work with NHS Estates reviewing schemes and advising on briefing. From this experience, I would single out a number of opportunities and threats that face the current hospital building programme if it is to achieve its goal of delivering improved healthcare in buildings that the country can afford and of a quality we will be proud of in the future.

I would single out three areas of opportunity:

1. **Reverse briefing and continuous evaluation**
   With a continuous programme of hospital building, there is already a series of new hospitals built and running. Each could be used as a template, which can be evaluated by those about to build in order to identify what 'works' and where improvements can be made. This information could then be used to prepare a brief. Like 'reverse engineering', the brief works backwards, establishing what can be repeated (prescriptive) and areas for innovation (performance). Evaluation happens at the start of a project, in a climate of learning rather than blaming, and continues throughout the project and on into the building in use. To achieve this approach would, however, require the early involvement of the preferred supplier and their design team. Selection of the preferred bidder by competitive interview, with selection on experience, compatibility and pricing structure, would reduce cost and improve quality through dialogue.

2. **Managing the process of change**
   The long-term success of a project from the users' perspective is sealed by early client involvement and ownership of what the project stands for. Recognising that the design of a new building involves both organisational and building change can show tangible returns. The emerging role of the process manager focuses on managing a continuous

brief, monitoring the users' expectations and orchestrating the move. The change manager, working on behalf of the users, would be appointed by the trust and paid for by the provider. This role has been successfully undertaken by DEGW in two government public private partnership projects – HM Treasury's own offices and the Ministry of Defence.

3. **Continuous partnering**

   The Private Finance Initiative (PFI) was initially seen as a means of minimising public sector risk, by diverting it to those with the greatest experience, while at the same time removing capital expenditure from the public spending balance sheet. The result has too often been complex contractual arrangements based on an expectation of failure, setting fixed detailed requirements years before they are needed, and risk transfer leading to budget protection with design invariably given a low priority. Experience of public private partnerships in the Netherlands suggests a more symmetrical relationship, where each party collaborates on the basis of togetherness, cooperation, added value for all parties, shared risk and return, and collective responsibility. The lessons learned are to create a culture of trust and collaboration and only pass on risks that are manageable to those who are most suitable to manage them. Procure 21, an approach advocated by NHS Estates, shows promise of yielding a more flexible approach to partnership. The first 12 partnerships, all led by contractors, are being actively encouraged to liaise and share in the spirit of 'collaborating to compete'.

There are optimistic signs of change. A wider range of architectural practices are becoming involved with the health sector. These are respected and innovative smaller practices, through the LIFT programme for primary healthcare, as well as more established practices, through a realisation by providers that good designers can provide the competitive edge. The major PFI consortia are collaborating to improve the context, so that they can then compete. 'BE Healthy', a club of the major providers that has developed from the Design Build Forum under the able leadership of Richard Saxon (BDP Architects), is collaboratively exploring how good design and effective construction can add real value to healthcare delivery. Within the hospital service, the Modernisation Agency recognises the impact building configuration can have on frustrating or supporting effective service delivery, and this message is being reinforced by the NHS Confederation. The DBWG's publication for NHS Estates[19] sets out a template for hospital briefing, which stresses the need for establishing a robust strategic building brief, derived from a thoroughly considered strategy for service delivery. The King's Fund programme for local improvements through design has raised grass roots enthusiasm, while CABE's campaign for better and more innovative design has captured the public imagination. Public awareness has been raised and a number of mechanisms for improvement initiated (for example, AEDET and the Design Review Panels). However, the question remains: do structural barriers still exist to achieving real improvement?

My sense is that three hurdles stand in the way of maximising opportunities within the current PFI approach. The first is the use of the 'public sector comparator', which is primarily seen as a way of fixing costs and specification, rather than a vehicle to discuss ambitions and expectations and communicate these to the bidder's design teams. The second is the bidding process. This involves establishing expectations of quality that are reflected in rigid output specifications, which are then put out to tender to several bidders. These bidders then take separate proposals to a design stage before a preferred bidder is selected, which consumes valuable resources and separates the design from the briefing process. The cost of 'blind bidding' must eventually return to the client. The third is an emphasis on performance measures, which focus on more easily evaluated efficiency targets. The emphasis is overwhelmingly on delivery at the expense of innovation. The current systems neglect the nature of design, briefing, use and evaluation as a continuous iterative, interactive process that thrives on designer–user interaction.

The last word

As the span of many individuals' creative working lives reduces and lifespans increase, health and well-being will take on a new significance. As we move away from a society intent upon measuring success by gross national product and the ownership of consumables, towards a focus on the quality of life, it is interesting to speculate on what impact this could have on the NHS and its demands for accommodation. If a fraction of the money spent on marketing consumer products were spent on raising society's expectations for lifelong health, education and leisure, we could see a very different paradigm for healthcare.

Looking ahead to the hospital requirements of the future is at best speculative and at worst futile. However, what we can be assured of is that the nature of healthcare and society's expectations will be very different. Short-termism is not a sustainable option. Our health service is too important to be viewed as a matter of numbers. There is a growing body of evidence that shows that the quality of the built environment can impact on patient response and service outcomes. Hospital procurement procedures should find a way to balance risk and innovation, accountability and continuity, and the short- and long-term perspectives. The challenge is to craft procedures that take a holistic perspective and integrate the management of buildings, space, technology and amenity.

Notes and references

1. For a review of the work of DEGW since 1985, see F. Duffy *et al.*, *Design for Change: The Architecture of DEGW* (Haslemere: Watermark, 1998).
2. The Health Building Futures Conference 'Achieving quality in health care design and broadening the vision', sponsored by the Nuffield Trust, RIBA, CABE & MARU, February 2003, presented a series of papers drawing on experience from other sectors and other countries.
3. Advances in office planning and design, to reflect organisational innovation, and advances in information and communications technology are described in J. Worthington, *Reinventing the Workplace*, (Oxford: Architectural Press, 1997) and F. Duffy, *The New Office* (London: Conran Octopus, 1997).
4. Susan Francis and Rosemary Glanville, *Building a 2020 Vision: Future Health Care Environments*, Nuffield Trust and RIBA Future Studies (London: The Stationery Office, 2001).
5. Alex Gordon, 'The impact of accelerating change on architecture'. Transcript of a lecture in *Royal Society of Arts Journal*, March 1980.
6. Llewelyn-Davies, Weeks, Forestier-Walker & Bor, *Long-life, Loose-fit: A Comparative Study of Change in Hospital Buildings* (London: s.n., 1973). Report carried out within the concept of the long-life, loose-fit, low-energy study initiated by the Royal Institute of British Architects in 1972.
7. J. Worthington, 'Accommodating Change – Emerging Real Estate Strategies', *Journal of Corporate Real Estate* 3(1): 81–95.
8. The Architectural Association runs a Masters programme, 'Emergent Technologies and Design'. http://www.aaschool.ac.uk/graduate/et.shtm

9.   Llewelyn-Davies *et al.*, *Long-life, Loose-fit*.

10. DEGW with Teknibank (Milan) undertook a multi-client study of the Intelligent Building in Europe 1990–1992 (*The Intelligent Building in Europe,* London: DEGW, 1992). This work was continued in South East Asia and Latin America with Arup Communications and Northcrofts. See Harrison, Low, Read, *Intelligent Buildings in South East Asia* (London and New York: E & FN Spon, 1998).

11. Wi-Fi stands for 'wireless fidelity' and is the popular term for a high-frequency wireless local area network (WLAN). It is a way of connecting PCs and other communications devices to each other and to the internet without any wires.

12. S. Stuebing, 'Briefing for Adaptable Use. Case study of the Shell Learning Centre', in Blyth and Worthington, *Managing the Brief for Better Design* (London and New York: Spon Press, 2001), 138–42.

13. In November 2001, the BBC (via its subsidiaries) entered into a 30-year property partnership deal with Land Securities Trillium (Media Services) Limited. The partnership aims to deliver improved and integrated property outsourcing solutions to the BBC's London and Scottish estates.

14. Blyth and Worthington, *Managing the Brief*.

15. The role of the client's adviser, or process manager, as distinct from the product project manager is growing in acceptance. See Wijnen, Gert and Kor, Rudy, *Managing Unique Assignments: A Team Approach to Projects and Programmes* (Aldershot: Gower Publishing, 2000).

16. G. Chick and P. Clarke, 'Partnering workshops get people ready for improvement', *In Context*, Spring 2001. http://www.baa.co.uk/pdf/incontext_5apr01.pdf

17. Worthington, *Accommodating Change*; Duffy, *The New Office*.

18. David Adamson, Director of Estates University of Cambridge, has set in motion a programme of working with the end users in commissioning buildings to ensure a 'soft landing'. DEGW, in parallel with their interior design and space planning services, provide workplace change management services. A. Bell, *Transforming Your Workplace* (London: Institute of Personnel and Development, 2000).

19. Department of Health and NHS Estates, *The Design Brief Framework for PFI Public Sector Comparators at OBC Stage* (2004).

CHAPTER THREE

Financing hospital investment

MICHAEL DAVIS

The financing of the construction and operation of public service buildings features rarely in books about design, in spite of its profound impact on the subject. The implementation of the Private Finance Initiative (PFI) in the UK and its increasing spread worldwide in various forms of public private partnerships (PPP) has huge implications for hospital design owing to the perceived suitability of the PFI for such large, complex and one-off projects. The original reasons for the adoption of PFI in UK ranged from the idealistic to the expedient: from a belief in contractually enshrining a long-term view and in the effectiveness of having a single point of responsibility for delivery; to the questionable practices of off-balance-sheet accounting and finessing of the public sector borrowing requirement. In the event, sheer pragmatism drove the adoption of the PFI. A major programme of investment was badly needed in the UK after years of neglect of the health estate and there appeared to be no politically available method to fund the necessary scale of capital investment without private money. A true single point of responsibility solution proved politically as well as logistically unviable, at least initially, because the delivery of clinical services had to remain in the public sector. So only the responsibility for the construction, financing and maintenance of premises transferred wholly to the private sector. The question marks over PFI relate to fears that the public sector is getting a bad deal, that this is an inherently inflexible arrangement and that design quality will always be secondary.

Mike Davis has a considerable knowledge of the PFI process and its politics and offers insights and pointers for the future, albeit as an advocate of a procurement method that remains controversial. The chapter reviews how the market and PPP processes have developed in response to Government policy to reform the NHS and, at a time of change, looks ahead to the future evolution of the financing, procurement and design of healthcare premises.

Mike believes there is nothing inherent in PFI to cause design quality to suffer. He also observes that the investments that PFI providers make come from savings and pensions and that the financial success of PFI therefore returns value to the public through the health and security of their investment and pension plans. Essentially, whether through taxes and public borrowing for exchequer-funded development or through PFI/PPP-funded development, it is ultimately the same money – citizen's earnings, savings and pension investments – that is circulating and value for money comparisons must take this into account. Looking to future patterns of funding buildings for health, education and other public services, Mike suggests seeing all these as a single asset class: 'Social Infrastructure'. The implication is that PPPs would be formed not just to serve this or that sector but to provide maintained capital assets across services to provide economies of scale and potential co-location benefits together with short- and long-term adaptability.

Introduction

Around the world, countries with ageing or unfit physical infrastructures are in, or are entering, another investment cycle, the catch up. The effect of ever faster development of new technologies, consumer demand and globalisation means that the time between investment cycles is shortening. Simultaneously, healthcare and pensions for retired populations living longer are consuming ever greater proportions of national income. The convergence of these factors means that governments are increasingly looking to private capital and business skills to provide long-term investment and, importantly, to improve productivity and share risk in the delivery of new infrastructure and public services.

Written in the winter of 2007, this chapter reflects on the fortunes of the NHS under New Labour over a ten-year period following their election in 1997 on a wave of optimism and with an unprecedented majority. The decade in review ended in 2007 with a toxic 'sub-prime' lending crisis in the USA triggering the UK's first run on a major bank since 1866. The threat to the UK financial system because of the failure of Britain's eighth-largest bank, Northern Rock, was so great that the government stepped in to guarantee over £100 billion of deposits and borrowings, a sum greater than the cost of replacing the NHS estate. Contributory causes to the international liquidity and solvency problems included financial institutions financing long-term lending by short-term borrowing, buying and parcelling up ever larger bundles of debt and investments in ever more complicated ways and borrowing more against the security of these structured collateralised instruments to be sold on again. The risk and performance of the underlying individual assets became remote, unmanageable and invisible, creating conditions for instability in the global financial markets when, after many years of growth and benign economic conditions, lessons about business cycles, fundamentals and risk had been forgotten or ignored.

The chapter's central theme is that financial markets, domestic politics and the health of the economy control patterns of investment in the NHS estate and that these factors are not isolated from world events.

Traditionally HM Treasury funded public investment by selling long-term bonds – gilts – to institutional investors in return for government promises to repay capital and interest over time. Government bonds are the most secure form of lending because of the sovereign covenant of the state standing behind them. By giving this covenant, current governments commit their successors to taxing future generations to pay back today's borrowing. Historically, once the proceeds of central borrowing had been allocated to build new hospitals, schools and other public infrastructure at a local level it was treated as a sunk cost and, as with collateralised instruments, the value of the investment in the underlying assets was invisible and unmanageable. Yet over only a few recent years much of the information and management deficit has been removed, with irreversible consequences for the future planning, investment and procurement of facilities for NHS healthcare.

Drawing on lessons from UK experience, the chapter ranges widely to connect separate policies and initiatives before moving on to suggest ideas of what this means for the planners and designers of the next generation of hospitals – and other types of community facilities. Technical and political cycles are short and investment commitments are long. Although Mark Twain cautioned that 'the art of prophecy is very difficult, especially with respect to the future', the final part of this contemporary chapter contains thoughts on strategic improvements in the PFI/PPP process and on the development of health and social infrastructure as a distinct class of high-quality ethical assets prized by pension funds and local communities.

Politics and money

Healthcare is arguably the most complex and fastest-changing industry globally. By common consensus the principal forces at work shaping healthcare are new scientific discovery, the increase in information available to patients, the prevalence of poor lifestyles and consequent chronic diseases (obesity, diabetes, mental health …), and the changing role of healthcare professionals. Perhaps the defining characteristic of successful planning and design over the next decade will be how we respond to the demographics of an ageing population and scarcity in the healthcare workforce, the immense potential of genetics, and the threat of pandemics and antibiotic-resistant bacteria. However, in any tax-funded universal system of care what is achievable will always be dictated by politics and the need to balance spiralling demand against capped resources – which means it always comes back to the money.

So what has happened to the money over the last decade? Revenue spending on the NHS in England rose from £35 billion in 1997/8 when New Labour was elected to £90 billion in 2007/8, an average increase of 10% p.a., or about 7% p.a. after inflation. It is forecast to rise to £110 billion in 2010/11 – still a 4% p.a. real increase over the three years, but widely perceived as being a cut.

The King's Fund estimated that 43% of the extra cash had been spent on pay and price inflation and the think tank, Reform, suggested that although funding had doubled in real terms, output measures of activity, quality and access to services only improved by 20–30%. It is clear that over time a tax-funded revenue 'input' in excess of the growth in GDP is unsustainable, and rising demand and improvements in quality will have to be delivered by increases in productivity.

Also, although resources have increased dramatically, there is great public concern that hospitals are dangerous places. MRSA infection rates have remained stubbornly high and outbreaks of *Clostridium difficile* more common. And in spite of significant capital investment the levels of back-log maintenance, an indicator of the safety and condition of the NHS estate, are worryingly high (although not in PFI hospitals where long-term maintenance budgets are ring-fenced with financial sanctions for failure to maintain in good condition).

Besides the absolute necessity to raise productivity and safety levels, the political priority to improve equity and access means levelling out large variances in the allocation of resources between competing hospital trusts (through the national tariff, Payment by Results and 'choice') – and increasingly through strategic commissioning by switching money from the acute sector to primary care and to the areas of greatest need and deprivation.

With the switch of resources away from hospitals, hospital productivity – a reduction in their unit costs and/or improved quality – will need to increase substantially; fewer staff will have to do more with less and do it better, and acute hospitals will have to reduce in numbers and size.

Different governments over many years have tried without success to shift resources away from hospitals, so for this to work now means a new focus on system change at all levels across large conurbations and within localities, and staff having the right tools for the job, the technology and fit-for-purpose healthcare buildings in the right places.

The Private Finance Initiative can be considered a pilot project, with the main programme of reshaping the NHS estate to help reform our national health system as the task of the next decade.

For indicators of why and how this might happen, it is helpful to look back over the past few years at the bewildering array of initiatives, and forward as the combined effect of current policies to reshape the provision of health and social care services progressively make their impact.

Procurement of physical capacity

Since 1997 there have been a range of procurement initiatives and public private partnership (PPP) derivatives to provide new, better-quality physical capacity to refresh the ageing NHS estate and equip it with new technology. However, since devolution some of these became English-only initiatives, as Scotland, Wales and Northern Ireland have not always chosen the same path.

The first programme adopted enthusiastically by New Labour was the Private Finance Initiative for hospitals. This was followed during their second term in office by ProCure 21, the NHS Local Improvement Finance Trusts (LIFT) and independent sector treatment centres (ISTCs); there were also variants for capital funding including the 'prudential borrowing' regime for foundation trusts and a politically astute pilot to use public capital within the PFI. Then in March 2006, HM Treasury stated in its key policy document, 'PFI: strengthening long term partnerships', that the government aimed to further develop two procurement models, strategic partnerships and a Project Delivery Organisation model, that capture the benefits of PFI but were expected to bring other benefits and greater flexibility.

The Scottish Nationalist Party, elected to govern in 2007, had signalled its intent to use the non-profit-distributing (NPD) version of PFI and to create a Scottish Futures Trust that would issue tax-free bonds to provide the long-term finance for major infrastructure projects.

These and other evolutionary PPP variants are described below in some detail to give an appreciation of who controls and who does what, and to illustrate that private capital and private sector management will be the dominant factor in the financing and delivery of new hospitals and health and social care facilities for at least the next decade.

The scale of the programmes to renew UK healthcare buildings since the mid 1990s presents a golden seam for evidence-based research into which clinical models, designs and procurement methods worked or did not, and why. As over 100 new hospitals will have been completed by 2010, opportunities are rapidly being exposed for researchers to study across a broad front the contribution that design and the private sector made to the modernisation of the UK's last major nationalised industry with its 1.3 million state employees.

Risk transfer

While convinced of the need for new physical capacity, the UK government has been driven by the conviction that public authorities are not good at procuring and delivering value for the public capital being invested.

HM Treasury's 2003 Green Book captured the political desire to direct flows of investment so as to deliver the greatest benefit for society. The Green Book carried a hard message about the public sector's systematic failure to deliver complex buildings such as specialist hospitals to cost and on programme, a characteristic that led to the concept of 'optimism bias', as illustrated by the statement that

> traditionally procured non-standard building projects exceeded initial estimates by an average of 51% of capital cost and 39% on programme.

Counteracting optimism bias is a principal reason for governments to adopt PFI-type mechanisms for managing capital risk at both national programme level and local project-delivery level. Besides fixing and pricing optimism bias, PFI has for the first time made explicit the true whole-of-life cost of financing and maintaining an NHS hospital as well as building it. Because capital was historically treated as a sunk cost (yet part of government borrowing to be paid back with interest) and back-log maintenance was accepted as normal, these costs were accounted for in different budgets and the whole cost was hidden from view and accountability. The effect on decision-making was perverse, allowing a false premise to persist that conventional procurement was cheap and flexible.

Of all the recent methods of procuring new physical capacity, it is the Private Finance Initiative that is the largest and the most significant for the future. An appreciation of the characteristics of PFI structures and risk transfer is essential to understanding how it might evolve and improve and merge with other structures to reshape the UK's social infrastructure.

The Private Finance Initiative

At the end of 2007, HM Treasury listed £57 billion of signed PFI projects in UK, with health being the second largest sector for PFI investment after transport; another £22 billion of deals were expected to be signed by 2011. At November 2007, the Department of Health (DH) listed 72 of the larger PFI schemes that were signed or approved totalling £13 billion and six publicly funded schemes worth £500 million.

Under the conventional PFI model, the winning consortium forms a Special Purpose Vehicle (SPV), a company that contracts to finance and deliver the consortium's design to a fixed price and programme and then to insure, maintain and service the facility for an annual service fee (unitary charge) that escalates in line with RPI.

The principle is that the NHS Trust pays a known, fixed cost to occupy for a long period with security of tenure; and that it only pays if functional areas and rooms are 'available' at all times and meet defined environmental standards. The PFI contract puts the private sector shareholders in control of the hospital building, with the PFI developer as the 'client' that appoints and pays the design team. The private sector takes on the risk that the building and its engineering will work with 100% reliability and be maintained in compliant condition for the duration of the concession, typically 30 years, although some are longer terms than this and one of Catalyst's, the Calderdale Royal Hospital, is for 60 years.

3.1
Calderdale Royal Hospital

3.2
New Manchester Hospitals – architect's perspective of the Children's Wing

The SPV has a highly geared, low-cost capital structure. It finances construction and working capital by raising about 10% of total funds from the project's sponsors as 'risk' equity and 90% by way of long-term senior debt. The former is similar to the deposit or equity in a home purchase and the latter equivalent to a low-cost, very long-term fixed-rate mortgage; the difference is that the SPV is the 'landlord' and the NHS Trust the 'tenant', and the hospital building reverts to the Trust at the end of the contract period.

In the hierarchy of risk and return it is the prime contractor for design and construction that takes the first slice and the biggest share of risk, followed by the facilities management (FM) contractor, then the provider of the equity, and lastly the provider of the senior debt. The prime contractor funds the majority of bid costs, principally the design cost, and underwrites the construction price, programme, commissioning risk and building performance. In taking on responsibility for optimism bias (any time or cost overruns), the prime contractor shelters the equity return, and this means it is good business for it also to be an equity investor. That PFI risk transfer is not a mirage was painfully evident at the Dudley Hospitals and the Central Manchester and Manchester Children's Hospitals PFI projects where the design and build contractors each suffered tens of millions of pounds of losses to ensure completion of the construction. In each case, the principal cause was the complexity of managing and taking the risk on multiple phases of decanting, demolishing and building within a constrained brownfield site whilst maintaining the safe operation of the existing hospital.

The DH/HM Treasury standard form PFI contract is a facilities rental agreement where the design of the facility is largely fixed at financial close. As the NHS Trust signs off and accepts the functionality of the clinical design, the SPV provides no warranties that the hospital will work as a hospital; it also bears no occupation or patronage risk and is guaranteed to receive the monthly payments if the hospital is continuously available and meets standards set out in the payment mechanism. The payment mechanism is a penalty-based system with financial deductions from the unitary charge and no reward for doing better.

The senior debt is secured by the cash flows of the SPV, not the value of bricks and mortar. The combination of a fixed design, penalties, no incentives and highly geared structures makes the SPV allergic to any change in its risk profile that threatens its future cash flows. That SPVs are seen as inflexible is a product of the standard PFI contract, where one party's flexibility is the other party's risk or cost. In addition to bringing transparency to the whole life cost of ownership, the PFI contract, through its change control mechanism, makes explicit the cost of subsequent changes to the building to keep it fit for purpose.

Notwithstanding stop–start procurement largely related to general election cycles and the inherent limitations of PFI, by the end of 2007 the government had met the commitment made in the ten-year NHS Plan to procure 100 hospitals in the period to 2010, over 90% by value of which were to be privately designed, delivered and financed under the PFI.

Having met its targets and been judged a success by government, PFI remains the principal means of procuring larger hospitals. As this book's purpose is to promote thinking and debate about best practice in contemporary hospital design, it is necessary to look at how PFI might evolve and address the interests and concerns of future PFI and PPP developers. Under the prevailing rules, architects and engineers can have great influence on PFI developers if their design satisfies some basic requirements:

An operational solution that can be delivered within the NHS Trust's affordability limit, on time and to budget, with hospital spaces that will always be available, that minimises the risk of health and safety and corporate manslaughter charges, and that is environmentally, economically and socially sustainable. It would be a bonus if future flexibility could be designed in a nil cost.

However, the effect of competition, procurement evaluation criteria and 'affordability' means there is little incentive to enable better productivity through good design and so deliver better long-term value if at the same time the initial capital cost is increased and the unitary charge is made uncompetitive.

Credit Guarantee Finance

Two major hospital PFIs were selected by HM Treasury in 2004 as Credit Guarantee Finance (CGF) pilots. Construction of the first, the £170 million Bexley Wing for the Institute of Oncology at St James's, Leeds, was completed in December 2007.

Under CGF, HM Treasury lends low-cost public capital to the DH and on to the SPV. The SPV's bank or bond insurer is paid a risk fee to underwrite the repayment of interest and capital if the SPV defaults. HM Treasury estimates that CGF will reduce the net cost of PFI debt by around 10%, and on the two pilot projects the whole-life savings are £70 million. CGF is still PFI, but with public 'senior' debt.

ProCure 21

HM Treasury concluded that PFI was not economic for single projects below £20 million. It was anticipated that most would be purchased under NHS Estates' ProCure 21 (P21) national framework agreements with consortia led by Principal Supply Chain Partners (PSCPs), the first

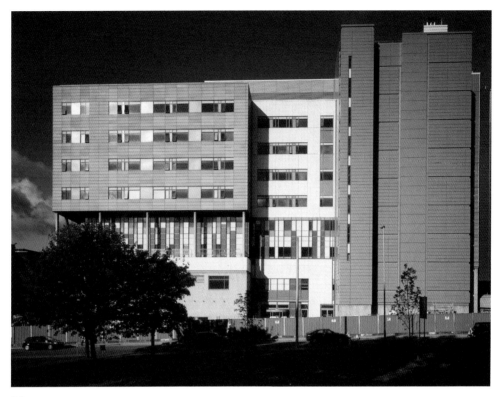

3.3
St James's Institute of Oncology, Leeds –
handed over on time and on budget in December 2007

12 of which were appointed for five years in 2003. P21 is conventionally funded procurement for the delivery of a finished asset to a price and date, but without the long-term maintenance obligation of a PFI contract.

By September 2007, 154 schemes with a value of £630 million had been completed and over £2 billion of potential projects had been registered, the largest being about £80 million; the initial five-year term of the framework agreements had been extended to seven and the number of PSCPs had consolidated to eight.

Independent sector treatment centres

Whilst the creation of foundation trusts heralded the biggest change to the management of the provider side of the NHS, the most tangible evidence of the government's intent to bring about cultural change was the introduction of private sector providers as part of the NHS. In 2003/4, the DH Commercial Directorate centrally procured the first contracts for clinical services to treat NHS patients on a fee-per-case basis in private treatment centres. The programme for independent sector treatment centres (ISTCs) was intended to accelerate the separation of planned surgery from emergency activity, rapidly increase surgical and diagnostics capacity to reduce waiting lists, and introduce choice for patients and competition for acute trusts.

Although the NHS Improvement Plan estimated that the independent sector would undertake up to 15% of procedures for NHS patients by 2008, the deeply controversial programme was scaled back in 2007 and the target dropped. But its purpose had largely been achieved as waiting times had come down, and it demonstrated to NHS Trusts that they no longer had a local monopoly on the provision of elective surgery, establishing the principle that the NHS was set to become the commissioner and payer, but not necessarily the provider of services.

NHS LIFT

The NHS LIFT programme is managed centrally by Partnerships for Health (PfH), an agency of the Department of Health. Each LIFTCo is a privately managed local property joint venture company with private sector majority (typically 60%) and public sector minority shareholdings split between the local PCTs and DH. This contrasts with PFI where the SPV set up for each project is 100% owned and controlled by the private sector. LIFTCos were designed as a means of financing the development of bundles of NHS primary care facilities, initially in deprived and inner-city areas. At the end of 2007 there were 45 NHS LIFT companies, covering two-thirds of the population in England, which had put in place £1.5 billion of investment for 210 primary care facilities.

The shared public/private ownership of LIFTCos is politically attractive, but the model has had mixed success. Its inherent weaknesses are that there are too many parties with a voice and veto and that the individual LIFTCos lack the scale to support sufficient resources to be efficient, effective and to provide value for money. It would seem logical to expect that market forces or DH incentives will lead to major consolidation of LIFTCos, failing which the weak will wither on the vine.

As an indicator of government's wish to see greater collaboration between the NHS and local authorities, PfH was re-launched and renamed Community Health Partnerships (CHP) in 2007. CHP's new goals included working across the NHS and local government to procure and deliver assets for health and social care, with the 'NHS' quietly dropped from the 'LIFT'.

Non-profit distributing

The NPD model was first used by the Labour government in Scotland for schools, before the Scottish Nationalists were elected in 2007. It is PFI with a twist as its structure is designed to regulate the distribution of equity profits to the private sector participants and to effectively cap their investment returns. The SPV uses fixed interest junior debt as risk capital instead of the equity in a conventional PFI structure.

After paying junior debt interest, the SPV distributes any surpluses to a charity associated with the procuring authority to be disbursed for the public good, which may include re-investment into the SPV's assets. Although the board of the SPV is controlled by the junior debt providers, it will also include representatives from the public authority and the charity, who have certain rights of control or veto over management decisions.

Besides confirming their intent to continue using NPD, the Scottish Nationalist government also made a bold political statement about setting up a Scottish Futures Trust (SFT) to raise tax-free bonds to provide a cheap source of finance for public infrastructure. However, under the devolution settlement a Scottish government has no tax-raising or borrowing powers to create or guarantee such a trust without the approval of Whitehall. It is likely, however, that the biggest driver of the shape of the potential SFT will be its accounting treatment under international accounting standards when, in order for the SFT to be off the government's balance sheet, it will need to be under the control of the private sector. If that happens the PFI industry would be involved not as project financiers of single projects but as financiers of batches of investment in multiple projects aggregated such that the scale and spread of risk should achieve the objective of a lower cost of finance compared to the standard PFI single-project model.

Project delivery organisation

HM Treasury has promoted the use of project delivery organisations (PDOs) –also called the risk-integrator model – for large, complex projects that are not part of a programme. This might be for a project where there are long multi-stage construction periods, or where the service requires continuing investment in new capital over a long period and there is a likelihood of material change in requirements over the life of the contract.

The PDO would manage the procurement of the underlying assets and integrate these with the necessary component services (for example, design, construction, IT, facilities management and debt) to provide an overall service to the procuring authority. It would have little or no economic interest in the supply of these commodity elements. The PDO may either operate through contracts or be a well-capitalised special-purpose company capable of incorporating other types of financing and funding streams alongside PFI. It would make sense if it were involved in managing organisational change in parallel with asset delivery; in this case, it would be a dedicated public service business, financially strong to take and share risk, and with robust development, programme and risk-management processes.

Foundation trusts and prudential borrowing

In a move with profound implications for a national health service the government has encouraged all NHS Trusts in England to become foundation trusts. These are independently managed public benefit corporations owned and governed by their members – local people and NHS staff, which share some features of universities and the old-fashioned mutual building societies and cooperatives. It is worth dwelling on the experience of the first few years of implementing the foundation trust policy in order to understand what it will mean and how soon, when every NHS hospital trust becomes a free-standing corporate business with the freedom to borrow and procure its own new facilities.

The first foundation trusts were established as not-for-profit organisations in April 2004 under licences issued by Monitor, the independent foundation trust regulator accountable to Parliament. The idea behind foundations was to give hospital trusts greater freedom to shape their clinical services to local needs, and for the development of their estate to provide better environments for patients and staff. They have a duty to break even financially and can retain surpluses (undistributed profits), trade surplus land and property, and borrow, subject to strict prudential limits set by Monitor. However, core healthcare assets are protected against being sold or mortgaged, and if these assets are PFI hospitals, the SPV will have a guarantee of continuation of the annual PFI payments through a Deed of Safeguard issued in the name of the Secretary of State.

Within the limits set by Monitor, foundation trusts can in theory borrow from banks and, for major investments, raise funds from the capital markets. Although there is a process for a failing foundation trust to be taken over by another, lenders can have no certainty as to how their debt would rank in the event of bankruptcy until the government addresses the politically difficult matter of a statutory insolvency regime. Currently foundations are unable to borrow large amounts on the strength of their own security, leaving the PFI and a Deed of Safeguard with strings attached as their only viable route for a major redevelopment or new build. Therein lies a problem –

a foundation trust can only use the PFI route if it can demonstrate to Monitor that it can reliably forecast and generate sufficient cash flows to service the PFI capital and interest payments over a very long term, which is difficult to do in a fast-changing NHS and under PbR (Payment by Results).

However, that they have learnt to live within their income is evidenced by the financial results. In the half-year to September 2007, 73 foundation trusts reported combined revenues of £15 billion per annum, with 72 of the 73 reporting surpluses running at an average of 2.7%; and during those six months total cash balances rose from £529 million to a startling £1.53 billion.

Foundation trusts are subject to a tougher accounting regime than NHS Trusts – closer to the UK accounting standards (GAAP) for commercial organisations. As the trend is for accounting standards for commercial organisations to become more stringent, rules-based and internationally adopted (under IFRS), we can expect that over time the regime for foundation trusts will follow. Currently a foundation trust's employees are still employees of the NHS. The principle that a corporation's accounts must present a true and fair view will lead to pressure on foundation trusts and other NHS bodies to account for their share of the NHS pension scheme's massive unfunded accrued and future liabilities, and to value and depreciate their assets in a more realistic way. Properly accounting for the cost of a healthcare facility over its useful life and providing cash to fund the actuarial cost of a final salary pension scheme would bring greater transparency to the true cost of running the NHS and be in the taxpayer's interest. These costs would greatly exceed the current level of surpluses being generated, and therefore change how foundation trusts run their businesses and make investment decisions.

Currently, as few foundation trusts that need major investment in high-quality modern facilities can borrow, or afford a PFI project under Monitor's control criteria and the DH capital funding regime, there will be a natural tendency for them to maximise surpluses, hoard cash, stretch the life of existing facilities and undertake piecemeal development. This is swimming against the tide of political policy and public expectation, and it is reasonable to anticipate that something will have to change.

But their role is no longer limited to hospital care, and can extend to primary care. After an announcement by the Prime Minister in January 2008, the Executive Chair of Monitor said:

> Encouraging successful foundation trusts to consider providing new models of primary care delivery is a positive step forward. Commissioners should not be over cautious in taking advantage of strong management teams, clinical excellence, and financial resources where they are available, in order to provide better services for patients.
>
> The drive to greater local decision making and devolved accountability is our greatest opportunity for improving healthcare ... NHS foundation trusts need to ensure the role of members and governors is genuinely meaningful if they are to attract and retain the commitment of millions of members.
>
> ... It is the responsibility of those of us who work in the health system to get the best possible value from taxpayers' spending on the NHS. But good quality care for all is only affordable in the long run if the citizen plays a full role in both preventing and managing chronic conditions.

So it is political policy to encourage vertical integration of acute and primary care provision by local mutually owned public service businesses that will challenge the role and independence of the traditional family GP.

Foundation trusts are at the forefront of a quiet revolution and signal the biggest change in the NHS provider side since its formation in 1948.

Over the next decade and longer, instead of working within the strictures of a monolithic NHS, designers will be working directly or indirectly with a multitude of independent providers of hospital and healthcare services, using a diversity of procurement and financing methods, each stamping its ideas and identity on design briefs.

At least that is the theory, unless DH and HMT decide that so much unpredictable diversity risks destabilising the whole system and its delicate balance of real politics and money and re-establish control by pulling the purse strings again from Whitehall.

Asset-backed investment vehicles

Although not yet widely used, the powers granted to a foundation trust include the ability to invest in bodies corporate for the purpose of, or in connection with, their functions.

If a foundation trust has non-core land or buildings, these may be transferred to a property joint venture with a private sector partner. This asset-backed investment vehicle (ABIV) would be a long-term social partnership, likely to be through a 50/50-owned special-purpose company capitalised by the foundation trust injecting its non-core assets and the private sector partner providing matching value by way of equity or loan stock. The security of the combined assets of the ABIV could then be used to raise debt to develop new assets that earn income by leasing to the foundation trust or third parties.

The ABIV would not take any significant development or procurement risk itself, entering into development management and asset management agreements with its private sector partner, who would assemble the land and obtain all consents and procure and manage the buildings.

The high street

Besides the threat to family GPs from foundation trusts, during 2007 the government publicly encouraged major branded supermarket, pharmacy and health club chains to think about providing general practice and allied medical services in premises convenient for shoppers, commuters and people's places of work, and to open over extended hours. Such 'alternative providers' would already have or would create their own facilities and become an additional source of private finance for the modernisation of the NHS infrastructure. Greater primary care capacity, flexibility and easier access was seen as a way to reduce the burden on overloaded A&E departments in acute hospitals, whilst providing choice for patients and competition for established general practices. GPs have always been independent contractors under contract to the NHS, so the move to encourage retailers into healthcare was not seen as privatisation.

Like local NHS hospital trusts, GPs have in effect been monopoly providers, and having achieved a radical shake up of the acute sector the government appears determined to do the same to general practice within primary care. What is certain is that high-street retailers would bring a new dimension to customer service and consumerism within the NHS and to the design of primary care premises.

Building schools for the future

The connection between healthcare facilities and schools may seem tenuous, but the convergence of policy makes this an area of crucial importance for collaboration between and 'co-location' of public services.

Under a highly significant and strategic partnership model similar to LIFT, the Department for Children, Schools and Families sponsored the Building Schools for the Future (BSF) programme, initially to renew or refurbish secondary schools throughout England through the use of Local Education Partnerships (LEPs). LEPs are owned 80% by the private sector and 10% each by the local authority and the investment arm of Partnerships for Schools (equivalent to the Partnerships for Health). The political objective for this massive centrally managed investment programme is to integrate inspirational design with the best technology to deliver school and community facilities that enable the transformation of educational attainment and improve social cohesion.

Unlike conventional PFI, LIFTCos and LEPs are joint ventures with shared objectives and partnering agreements that provide a structured framework for the planning and delivery of a stream of investment in social infrastructure over a long period. The private sector partner is granted a period of exclusive rights to carry out the property development, subject to the achievement of defined value for money and continuous improvement targets against local and national benchmarks. LEPs, like LIFTCos, are intended to bring the benefits of flexibility, learning and evolution to each of the next phases of a stream of procurements over a medium to long period, whilst retaining the discipline and price certainty of private sector delivery and finance.

Significantly, the BSF 'exclusivity' reward system means that LEPs have a direct commercial interest in helping deliver improved educational attainment, community engagement and even well-being over time. As LEPs mature we should see them working with academics to develop planning principles that link pedagogy to spaces and to be an intrinsic part of the teaching change management process, local job creation and training.

But the scope of the BSF programme will go wider. The government published its Children's Plan in December 2007, which said:

> Families will be at the centre of excellent, integrated services that put their needs first, regardless of traditional institutional and professional structures. This means a new leadership role for Children's Trusts in every area [the target is for 150], a new role for schools as the centre of their communities, and more effective links between schools, the NHS and other children's services so that together they can engage parents and tackle all the barriers to the learning, health and happiness of every child.
>
> ... To deliver world class education and children's services we need world class buildings and use of technology ... unprecedented investment in the fabric of schools and children and young people's services to create schools fit for the 21st century ... [to] produce guidance within the Building Schools for the Future programme to ensure that where possible new buildings make space for co-located services; and set an ambition for all new school buildings to be zero carbon by 2016.

LEPs are well positioned to join up multiple sources of finance and credits arising from the Children's Plan, BSF, housing and regeneration initiatives and NHS Primary Care Trusts, working across agencies to provide any facility relating to education, health and social care, community services, housing and regeneration.

LEPs and LIFTCos are complex organisations and networks operating in complex multi-party public service environments; the early ones suffered from being undercapitalised and under-resourced, a condition described as 'skinny'. As both the LIFT and BSF programmes are high political priorities, incentives, market forces and consolidation can be expected to build up the strength and stamina of the best of the LIFTs and LEPs and give them resources, attitude and staying power.

What is evident is that the evolving goals of LIFT and BSF put these programmes on converging courses, and locally LIFTCos and LEPs will compete (straightforward), carve up territory (anti-competitive) or collaborate (complicated).

The effect of NHS reforms on property

Many of the reforms that will shape the NHS were put into play as a result of the 2001 NHS Plan.

Payment by results

The fiscal mechanism intended to bring together NHS reform and implementation is a system of payment for performance. Payment by Results (PbR) is progressively bringing in standard tariffs of fees for related groups of health procedures payable for the treatment of NHS patients by any approved provider. The idea is that PbR goes hand in hand with 'choice', initially covering surgical procedures and ultimately extending to all NHS treatment and care; money will flow where patients want it to, and BUPA's advertising strapline 'the patient will see you now, Doctor' seemed to neatly capture the government's objective.

With careful calibration and good commissioning, PbR will become the carrot and stick that drive change and NHS healthcare provider performance – and will therefore influence location of new investment. However, good health depends on more than good hospitals. The thrust of policy is to devolve and direct budgets to join up local government social care and public health with NHS community health and mental services to better address the causes of ill health and the prevention and treatment of long-term conditions, and to do that 'closer to home'. Two indicators of the trend to focus on individual care to deliver better outcomes more cost-effectively are the DH's plan to devolve personal social care budgets to people to choose where and how they use 'their' money from the DH; and a pathfinder Public Service Trust to be established in Herefordshire in 2008 under a single chief executive, which will pool the health and social care budgets of the PCT and the County Council to commission integrated personal care packages, working across different types of providers and agencies – effectively using NHS money to keep people out of hospital.

Winners and losers

A hundred new hospitals, greater efficiency and productivity and an increasing role for independent providers bring the prospect of surplus capacity within the NHS for the first time since its formation in 1948. In any event, much of that capacity is in the wrong places and unfit for future purpose, as although the demand in the 1990s for modern facilities had public and political support, in retrospect it preceded the necessary reform of the system.

In December 2005, the English Department of Health published a half-time update on the progress of the ten-year NHS Plan with a summary of what the reforms meant and a timetable for action. It stated, 'The imperative for reform is urgent and growing.' The four planks of the reform agenda were choice and voice (demand-side reform); diversity in providers (supply-side reform); money following the patient (transactional reforms); and quality, safety, fairness, equity and value for money (system management reforms).

The reforms were intended to enshrine the purchaser/provider split, accelerate the redesign of care pathways and shift care out of acute hospitals 'closer to home'. In other words, the historic emphasis on the NHS being a reactive national service for the sick dominated by acute care in large lying-in hospitals was seen as outmoded and undesirable.

Since 2006 there has been much talk of radical reconfigurations. The Royal College of Surgeons thought the number of fully equipped A&E departments could be cut from 200 to 100 and that focusing services in specialist centres meant that although people might have to travel greater distances they would got better care when they arrived. The Institute for Public Policy Research published a paper suggesting that 58 'excess' hospitals should be closed or merged.

Conditions for capital planning

Coherent development and implementation of estate strategies is fraught with dilemmas and conflicts of interest:

- In a fast-changing healthcare industry, the policy of depreciating NHS hospitals over 60 years and locking in to inflexible 30-year PFI contracts looks increasingly unsustainable.
- The need to strategically plan and reshape NHS infrastructure across large areas runs contrary to the policy to devolve decision-making and accountability to individual foundation trusts and PCTs.
- Foundation trusts are asset-owning geographical monopolies with a vested interest in protecting what they have and winning more from others.
- PCTs are not to be providers but independent commissioners of care, not tied to leases or owning property (indicating that a PCT's continuing participation in a LIFTCo is counter-intuitive).
- The speed of the opening up of primary care provision to large retail corporations will be unpredictable, but if patients like the idea the market could be expected to respond with increasing rapidity.
- Where a large area reconfiguration is needed across multiple PCTs, there is no obvious organisation to coordinate planning, programme management, procurement, disposal and capital financing.
- The value of surplus land and property arising from major reconfigurations will need managing in the wider public interest and not in the interest of the foundation trust, NHS trust or PCT that was gifted the public asset in the first place.
- A real squeeze on NHS income will start to bite from 2008/9, just when the need for a new cycle of capital investment takes off.

With luck, and in parallel with strategic commissioning, the DH will shake up and implement a new capital charging system with financial incentives to trigger capital investment across localities, systems and networks in the right things, in the right sequence and in the right places, and then leave the market to respond.

What is certain is that future designs for new healthcare facilities that directly or indirectly respond to all four elements of reform will be required, and a new way will be have to be found to measure 'affordability'.

The following section looks at the implications of the 'what and how' for the planners and designers of the next generation of hospitals and healthcare facilities.

Drivers of future design

'What for?'

That the settings in which healthcare will be delivered will change is inevitable. In his July 2007 report 'Healthcare for London', Professor Sir Ara Darzi, before he became Lord Darzi and Health Minister, reviewed options for the future of healthcare in London and proposed seven places where healthcare might be provided in the future:

1. at home
2. polyclinics – a new type of facility with a far greater range of services than currently offered in GP practices, whilst being more accessible and less medicalised than hospitals
3. local hospitals to provide the majority of inpatient care
4. elective centres for most high-throughput surgery
5. major acute hospitals handling the most complex treatments
6. specialist hospitals
7. academic Health Sciences Centres – centres of clinical and research excellence.

Although extensive public consultation was to follow, the report was an indicator of the thinking that was likely to shape future settings across the capital and its conclusions may have resonance in other conurbations.

These, or similar, categorisations of types of healthcare facilities greatly clarify the 'what for' – and presage the end of the multi-purpose district general hospital.

'How industrialised?'

When looking at types of settings, designers will need to consider the effect of the industrialisation of healthcare processes. The forces for industrialisation include the application of technology and drugs, fee-per-case, national standards, clinical governance and regulation, HTMs and HBNs – and the control of MRSA and bacteria such as *Legionella*, *Pseudomonas* and *Clostridium difficile*. In an age of patient choice and litigation, a provider that can demonstrate that it follows industry best practice is better placed to attract business and to defend itself against claims of clinical negligence. Therefore increasing access to information and league tables of patient safety and clinical outcomes will also drive standardisation.

Places that house the NHS's highly technical diagnostic, treatment, R&D and support processes have much in common with the global pharmaceutical industry's R&D and manufacturing process environments. The NHS and 'Big Pharma' are both in the business of life sciences and Big Pharma is a source of ideas and stimulus for innovation in healthcare facilities process design and safety.

In the same way that big retailers are being invited to provide a customer-focused care package closer to their communities, could Big Pharma start to collaborate with foundation trusts and independent providers to supply programmes of preventative education and cures for chronic diseases with payment linked directly to results? If this conceptually attractive scenario happened it would lead to a reduced need for so many hospitals and hospital beds.

'How compartmentalised?'

Managing infections imported into hospitals and reducing cross-infection is currently one of the biggest challenges facing the NHS. Public alarm over rates of healthcare-acquired infection, the vast hidden cost to individuals and society and the threat of pandemics would indicate a trend towards more compartmentalisation and the ability to isolate high-risk patients and airflows in infectious and infected areas. This trend will clash with ease of access, community involvement and social interaction. Although the safest hospital would be one with no public access, no visitors and all patients barrier-nursed in single rooms, a local balance has to be struck between cost and tougher protocols to segregate people, airflows and waste, and public acceptability.

In the UK we have already seen the first design briefs for new NHS hospitals with 100% single rooms. It is reasonable to predict that, in designing care processes around the patient, infection control and patient choice will also lead to larger, multi-acuity single bed-and-treatment rooms, with a big effect on nursing and clinical models. However:

- Is there sufficient evidence linking the economic case for safer, better outcomes for individuals and society with the higher initial capital cost and nursing and maintenance budgets?
- Where is the rational argument for directing financial flows away from other priorities to designs that achieve this?

'Patients first?'

Whilst technology, national standards, tariffs and regulation will drive standardisation and industrialisation, the effect of fragmentation, regrouping and competition on the provider side is likely to foster diversity in the way healthcare processes are assembled and implemented. Foundation trusts and private sector operators working with good designers and good developers will look to balance the relentless effects of process control and productivity with the human needs of patients, staff, visitors and the community by providing easy access, parking and way-finding, uplifting public spaces, high standards of environmental safety, privacy and acoustics, and natural lighting and temperatures levels that are controllable.

It is possible to foresee the adoption by developers, foundation trusts and independent operators of 'brand standard' approaches to what works for them that will result in safer, better-value, appropriate 'modern' and friendly environments.

'How much?'

Affordability is the PFI term for the calculation of how much the local health economy is prepared to pay for the PFI scheme to support healthcare 'production'. Determining affordability is an imprecise science, which is made more difficult with the advent of competition and payment for results in place of activity-based commissioning.

Whilst it is accepted that new hospitals cost more than those they replace and that for the large, older teaching hospitals the once-in-a-generation site reconfiguration and renewal of worn-out infrastructure and utilities costs even more, unaffordability remains a chronic condition. Although government guidance recognises the value of good design and the contribution of PFI investment to society and the economy outside the hospital, it is difficult to see where this translates into more money at hospital level.

In early PFIs, the annual unitary charge rarely exceeded 20% of a hospital's revenue budget. The Public Sector Comparator, procurement doctrines, risk transfer and lenders' due diligence acted together across the PFI market to benchmark and level up construction prices, life cycle maintenance and FM costs for types of hospitals and their mixes of high and low technical spaces. In 2006, as a proxy for an 'affordability' cap and as a constraint on over-ambitious schemes, the DH introduced a rule of thumb that for new PFI hospitals the unitary charge should be no more than 13% of revenue income. As construction cost is the biggest driver of the size of the unitary charge, this will bring pressure to break away from normalised construction rates and to shrink the building's area. However, this could be counter-productive as it discourages investing in the higher initial capital costs of automation and robotics, circulation spaces and lifts designed to provide rapid radial and vertical transportation, and space for dedicated local stores and centralised service centres, all of which would help minimise the ongoing 30-year cost of FM staff, materials management and logistics.

Similarly, environmental cooling for comfort and well-being will become a necessity under patient 'choice', and together with more medical and diagnostic equipment means greater energy loads and capital costs for mechanical ventilation and cooling and sophisticated building management systems. The financial burden of increased energy demand, potential carbon taxation and a global scarcity and high price of fuel will give great weight to energy strategies, including the positioning and use of external entrances with thermal breaks, solar glazing, blinds and shading, more sophisticated heat recovery and transfer methods, and local generation.

Good PFI design by definition will optimise the '20%' use of capital, energy, operational FM, and life cycle maintenance and replacement costs.

The 13% rule is likely to be a temporary measure as it places all the emphasis on the cost of the building and its FM, and little on what a good PFI design solution might do for the hospital's productivity, or for that matter its sustainability footprint. Looking forward, we can expect to see business case and procurement evaluation criteria being developed that provide incentives for innovation in design and FM service solutions that reduce and make better use of the other '80%'. As the '80%' is mostly staff cost and as demographics will reduce the available workforce over the next decade or two, an economic necessity will in time become an operational necessity as well.

Balancing the cost of high-quality patient environments, clinical staff, drugs, risk and infection, changing function and activity, technology, capital, FM and energy means solving a three-dimensional puzzle of '80/20' economics extended forward over time for which new and more sophisticated financial models will need to be developed.

'How long for?'

As well as answering the 'what and how', society and politicians have to decide how long an individual hospital is to be there for.

During a time of disruptive change it seems illogical to hang on to the past and consider hospitals as icons and long-term assets, yet the NHS depreciates its hospitals over 60 years as though they were 'fixed' assets. Flexible buildings with shorter life cycles are a global trend and it might be better value if NHS hospitals were viewed as short-life shells to be disposed of or rebuilt or sold on for conversion to other purposes as soon as they have helped reform local delivery or are no longer fit for purpose.

This suggests new hospital planning concepts that anticipate the speed with which current clinical processes will be overtaken by new techniques, and which incorporate shorter-term obsolescence to allow rapid changes in configuration.

The political conundrum is that the public are fiercely loyal to 'their' local hospital, and writing off its capital investment and paying off the debt over a much shorter period would be unaffordable under current funding criteria.

Building in real future flexibility is expensive and unaffordable under the short-term discipline of PbR, foundation trusts and balance sheets. However, the same factors mean that an inflexible or obsolete asset that cannot pay its way is a liability. Regardless of the procurement model that is used, an impaired asset is an impaired asset and shorter technological and useful life cycles will bring higher costs of occupation.

There is a case for shaping procurement, design briefs, contracts and funding models to accommodate discrete elements of hospitals having different useful life cycles, rather than assuming the same lifespan for whole hospitals.

However, at a different level, treating affordability as a local issue for individual procurements perversely distorts coherent strategic asset planning and decision-making, with long-term national consequences.

If there is evidence that a higher initial investment in a good design will guarantee better clinical productivity and outcomes at lower cost per case and provide future flexibility then it is reasonable to argue that a more sustainable NHS and local communities will result from something closer to a '70/30' ratio between the income of a hospital and the 'unitary charge' for its use.

Design interfaces

The PFI developer employing the design team and construction supply chain breaks these into a series of professional appointments and sub-contract packages. The greater the number of parties to the design process, the greater the inefficiency and risk of poor coordination, errors and risk, which equates to money. Lessons learnt, repeatability and evolution of what works for a developer and its client trusts should lead to longer relationships with a smaller number of reliable designers in the chain, designing fewer individual elements of new hospitals. This is compatible with the principles of LIFT and the BSF where it can be expected that good LIFTCos and LEPs will continuously improve their brands and suite of design briefs and specifications, to be customised and applied economically to each successive project's unique site, estate and logistics strategy, and to satisfy the provider's care and educational models and processes.

'3-D plus time' design of the structure, spaces, engineering services, logistics, traffic flows and FM services is a virtuous objective enabling:

- computation fluid dynamic (CFD) modelling and 'try-before-build' simulation of process and people flows to identify pinch-points, waiting area congestion, solar gain, wind effect and airflows (useful in determining infection control practice and for the management of room temperatures)
- clash-detection software to improve the layering of engineering services, the sequencing of trades during construction and ease of access for future maintenance
- direct-to-factory ordering to reduce construction cost, risk and time
- 3-D drawings and as-built asset register to reduce commissioning risk and time and improve downstream FM and life-cycle maintenance
- 3-D visualisation to manage transition risk by assisting staff to prepare for and be trained to work in their new spaces.

For this to work, designers and the supply chain need web-based information channels and an integrated design platform with open-access databases. 'Follow the money' might be an indicator of where ownership of these will reside.

Social infrastructure as an asset class

Flexing property

Long-term occupation of many of the NHS's facilities in their present form does not look sustainable or desirable; to survive, health providers will increasingly need to flex in and out of accommodation.

As the local means and settings for delivering healthcare become more diverse, so will the capital stock requirements. We can anticipate:

- clustering of acute, specialist, teaching, science and R&D networks on campus sites adjacent to population centres and transport nodes
- community hospitals and multi-purpose centres – polyclinics – dealing with the walking wounded and offering a wider range of local care for women, children and elderly people, and treatment of chronic diseases; these community facilities will take advantage of new 'dispersal' technologies and will bridge the gap between primary and secondary care.

The shift in structures, resources and financial flows within the NHS will inevitably mean fewer general hospitals able to sustain the safe operation of 24-hour consultant-led accident and emergency departments; and rationalisation of A&E departments across health economies will lead to the politically difficult need to 'retire' or hollow out some DGHs and downgrade them to local or community hospitals, liberating stranded resources to where they can be better used.

Portfolio management

Health, education, urban regeneration and social housing (HM Treasury cited UK social housing backlog maintenance at £19 billion) are separately funded, mostly through taxation. The inability to join up and coordinate capital planning across these systems impedes renewal of essential infrastructure and is a fiscal drag. Managing the tactical retraction and disposal of redundant and unfit-for-purpose estate will be a bigger challenge than the piecemeal acquisition of new buildings that was the characteristic of the past decade, requiring skills sets that are not naturally core to NHS and local government organisations. This leads to the proposition of future 'public' asset procurement and management in portfolio terms across conurbations.

If this is a desirable political objective, there is a compelling case for developing more sophisticated framework PPPs for strategic asset planning and delivery involving multiple users across sectoral boundaries whose needs will vary over time. Instead of LIFTCos or LEPs we may see the emergence of large-scale, regional public service businesses – Local Infrastructure Partnerships (LIPs) – managing underlying portfolios of privately and publicly financed investments.

These would be asset-backed property companies, ABIVs, similar to a well-capitalised LIFTCo or LEP with committed private sector resources taking the development, design and integration risk as a captive PDO.

It may be expedient for the ABIV to become a Community Venture, with the local authority and other agencies putting parts of their estate into the joint venture to create greater scale and opportunity for multi-use development and coordinated procurement of health, education, social care, housing and community regeneration projects.

The idea, and the ideal, is that the long-term focus of the PDO would be the operational effectiveness of its multiple client/partners, aided by expert asset creation and estate management.

A combination of the most valuable features of the PFI, NPD, LIFT/ LEP, PDO and ABIV models would be highly attractive to help join up local government and NHS public service delivery in a coordinated and locally directed way.

Intergenerational compact

Individuals see their pension as a promise to pay 'deferred' salary after they cease productive work. For companies and governments, future pension commitments are growing, unmanageable long-term liabilities that impact their short-term 'profit and loss' accounts, and the government has demonstrated that the NHS no longer needs to own its healthcare facilities and indeed that it would be better if it did not.

With blue-sky thinking, in 20 years' time the UK might see a tax-funded, reshaped and redirected (and renamed) PFI with sufficient scale to link the self-interests of generations of citizens. Through investment in the continuous renewal of our health and social infrastructure, we would ensure better public health and education for the next generation and more secure occupational pensions for the current one.

For private developers, foundation trusts and independent providers, responsiveness, scale, geographical coherence and big balance sheets will come into play as determinants of competition and value. We might expect to see:

- very large Public Service Trusts (PSTs) being formed from joint ventures between foundation trusts and local authority provider arms
- trading of PFI/PPP equity, bringing consolidation of PFI SPVs, LIFTCos and LEPs within counties and SHA boundaries, leading to
- PPP developers engaging in the large-scale planning and property and estate management to support health and social care processes across districts and regions, designing buildings that outlive current service models and providing 'agile' space on flexible terms
- regional asset-backed investment trusts recycling and releasing value from obsolete or redundant property and land and issuing tax-efficient public property bonds to finance accelerated cycles of social infrastructure investment – bonds that would be attractive to trustees of pension funds, with near-gilt security provided by the scale and mix of useful property assets actively and transparently managed in a portfolio.

Conclusion

My proposition is that there is a perfect match between the need for social infrastructure designed and delivered to produce better long-term outcomes and value, and the absolute requirement for long-dated investments with good yields to sustain our pensions system.

A value can be placed on design and quality, but new ways are needed to identify and measure this in a systematic way at macro and micro levels. New 'econometrics' might demonstrate the virtuous circle of public benefit in terms of why 'that' hospital or school should be a priority for long-term lending by a pension fund or local investment trust at 'fair' rates of interest because of a predictable risk profile owing to its effectiveness, adaptability and ability to pay a return on the investment over a long period.

A final thought for healthcare planners and architects and all those involved in the design process:

- Would you risk your savings to pay for the healthcare facility you are involved in designing or delivering?
- Can it can be used safely and productively and attract patients so as to keep up the mortgage repayments over the next 30 years in order to pay your pension?

Appendix – Case studies

Each of the following five second-generation PFI projects by Catalyst Healthcare was an exemplar of best practice in contemporary PFI design and financing at the time it was signed. Some created important project finance market precedents in response to rapidly evolving political priorities to bring about service modernisation and cultural change within the NHS.

Hexham General Hospital

Phase 1

Client:	Catalyst Healthcare/Northumbria Healthcare NHS Foundation Trust
Architect:	Jonathan Bailey Associates
Contractor:	Bovis Lend Lease
Completed:	March 2003
Cost:	£28m
Area:	12,000 m^2
Procurement route:	PFI/design & build

Phase 3*

Client:	Catalyst Healthcare/Northumbria Healthcare NHS Foundation Trust
Architect:	Jonathan Bailey Associates
Contractor:	Bovis Lend Lease
Completed:	Summer 2008
Cost:	£24m
Area:	8,000 m^2
Procurement route:	PFI/design & build

*Phase 2 involved demolition of the original Hexham General Hospital following completion and commissioning of Phase 1

3.4

Hexham General Hospital:

a (top) aerial view showing the hospital building that opened in 2003 to the left of the picture with its distinctive triangular wards, and the new Phase 3 extending to the right

b (left) inside the main entrance atrium

c (above) Easter concert in atrium by children from Sele First School, Hexham

G1000

G800

G900

3.5

Hexham General Hospital – floor plan for the new
Phase 3, due to complete in summer 2008

This extraordinary new £28m, 98-bed general hospital, in the market town of Hexham, was
designed by Jonathan Bailey Associates of Dallas and London and financed by equity and
bank debt. The design supported re-engineering of surgical, medical and nursing practices, and
provided extra large ultra-clean theatres, facilities for laparoscopic and robotic surgery, a unique
circular post-anaesthesia recovery area and flexible-nursing units.

The construction site was exceptionally tight, and the desire to create sufficient internal space
to accommodate a ratio of 75% single en suite bedrooms (a first in the NHS) resulted in an
innovative, compact deep-plan design with a large external perimeter.

The spacious and airy atrium with its central waiting areas has a non-institutional feel,
with colourful sofas and easy chairs, appointment-call pagers, coffee shop, grand piano,
grand staircase and galleries, and rapidly became a centre for the local community to meet
and socialise in after the hospital opened in Summer 2003. HGH is compact, with sweeping
curves, hotel-like finishes and carpets and three triangular nursing units radiating off the central
lift and stair core. Outpatients, the 24-hour emergency care centre, diagnostics, pathology,
pharmacy and therapies are at ground-floor level, with maternity, critical care and the operating
department, with four theatres and circular recovery suite, at first-floor level.

So successful has it been that a major extension was approved as a variation to the PFI
contract and 'Phase 3' will be completed in 2008. This will increase the area of the hospital by
over two-thirds and incorporate an inpatient elective surgical centre, a 30-bed ward of single en
suite bedrooms, an education centre, a chronic disease centre and a large primary care centre.
Within a system where money follows the patient, Northumbria Healthcare Foundation NHS
Trust is confident that such a high-quality environment and efficient design will attract patients
and be self-funding under Payment by Results.

HGH is a model for a small-scale, sustainable multi-purpose patient-centred health and care
system close to its rural population.

Queen Mary's Hospital, Roehampton, South West London

Client: Catalyst Healthcare/Wandsworth
                   NHS Teaching Primary Care Trust
Architect: Devereux
Contractor: Bovis Lend Lease
Completed: December 2005
Cost: £54m
Area: 24,000 m²
Procurement route: PFI/design & build

Queen Mary's is a new £54m compact, integrated community and mental health hospital with rapid diagnostic centre, designed by Devereaux Architects, London. It had a 30-month construction programme completed early in 2006 and was financed by equity and bank debt. The PFI contract services include 'hard' and 'soft' facilities management and this was a pilot project for the government's Retention of Employment model where the majority of the facilities management staff remain employed by the NHS but managed by Catalyst's FM service partner. Provision and financing of medical equipment and its maintenance and replacement is also Catalyst's responsibility.

The development replaced the old Queen Mary's, a centre of expertise in the treatment and rehabilitation of amputee cases, including specialist limb-fitting, and was planned to accommodate the existing mental health inpatient beds and those transferred from Tolworth Hospital. It is 24,000 square metres on four floors constructed on a constrained sloping site and provides 70 inpatient rehabilitation beds, therapies and limb-fitting services on the lower ground floor; a rapid diagnostic and minor injuries treatment unit on the upper ground floor; a 69 inpatient mental health hospital on the first floor with access to large, secure, attractive roof-top courtyards with far-reaching views across London; and offices, clinics and education centre on the second floor.

3.6
Queen Mary's Hospital, Roehampton:
a architect's perspective
b main elevation on to Roehampton Lane

3.7
Queen Mary's Hospital, Roehampton:
a (left) secure mental health garden at first-floor level
b (below) prosthetics and orthotics workshop, also used for
wheel chair modification

3.8
Queen Mary's Hospital, Roehampton:
a (left) walking school where patients learn how to walk again
when fitted with prosthetics
b (below) upper ground floor plan with rapid diagnostic and
minor injuries treatment unit

1. Future Expansion Space
2. Workshop store
3. Integrated Paediatric suite
4. Cafe
5. Support
6. Addiction Treatment Centre
7. Generic Clinic 1
8. Audiology ENT Suite
9. Opthalmology Suite
10. Generic Clinic 2
11. Generic Clinic 5

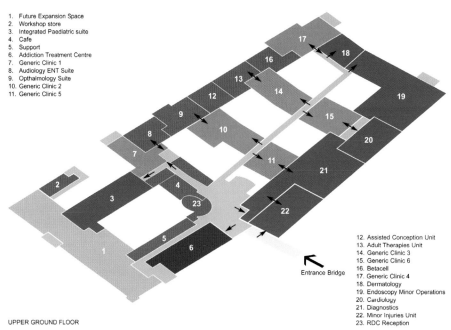

Entrance Bridge

12. Assisted Conception Unit
13. Adult Therapies Unit
14. Generic Clinic 3
15. Generic Clinic 6
16. Betacell
17. Generic Clinic 4
18. Dermatology
19. Endoscopy Minor Operations
20. Cardiology
21. Diagnostics
22. Minor Injuries Unit
23. RDC Reception

Queen's Hospital, Romford

Client: Catalyst Healthcare/Barking, Havering
                                 and Redbridge Hospitals NHS Trust
Architect: Jonathan Bailey Associates/BDP
Contractor: Bovis Lend Lease
Completed: October 2006
Cost: £210m
Area: 96,000 m²
Procurement route: PFI/design & build

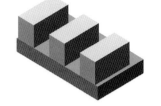

This very large £210m, 939-bed District General
Hospital with healthcare design by Jonathan
Bailey Associates was financed by equity and
mezzanine debt, and a 'wrapped' package of
senior debt comprising a low-cost European
investment bank loan and index-linked,
investment grade bonds. Catalyst provides all
'hard' and 'soft' facilities management services
and medical equipment and its maintenance and
replacement. Like Queen Mary's, this hospital
was also a successful pilot for the Retention
of Employment model for the 'soft' facilities
management services. Queen's is a 96,000 square
metre all new-build hospital with 4,600 rooms on
six levels and four linear accelerator chambers. It
was constructed in 39 months on a contaminated
brownfield site in Romford, to the east of London,
and occupied on time, just before Christmas
2006.

   Selected from six competing PFI bids, the
design solution most closely met Barking,
Havering and Redbridge Hospitals NHS Trust's
requirement for exceptional clinical efficiency
and patient-centred care. This was expressed
through their design brief setting out new clinical
models to be facilitated by a generational leap
in the use of IT – for a paperless hospital with

3.9

Queen's Hospital, Romford:

a architect's perspective showing the four circular towers and
   the low-level areas consisting of diagnostics in the rotunda
   and a ground floor A&E department with theatres above in
   the foreground

b panoramic view taken July 2006

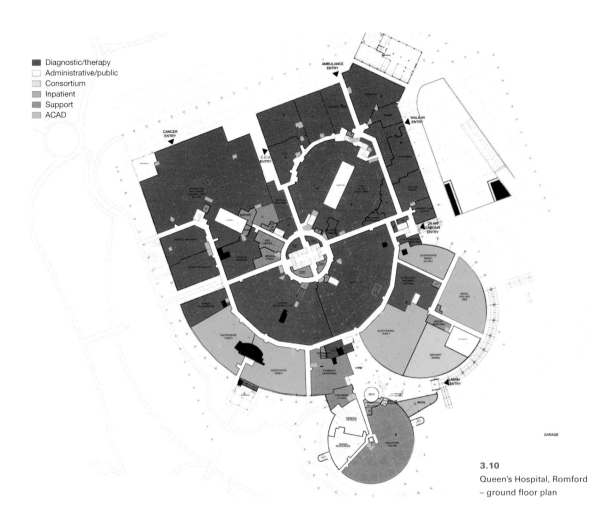

Diagnostic/therapy
Administrative/public
Consortium
Inpatient
Support
ACAD

3.10
Queen's Hospital, Romford
– ground floor plan

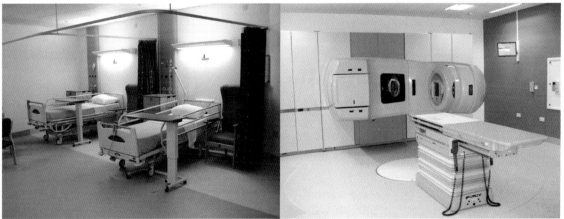

3.11
Queen's Hospital, Romford – a typical four bed ward; b linear accelerator

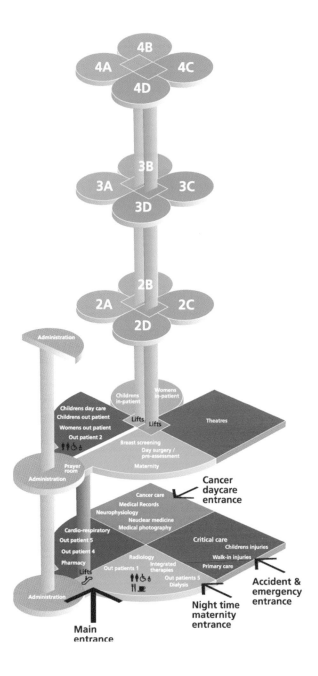

Administration

4B
4A   4C
4D

3B
3A   3C
3D

2B
2A   2C
2D

Administration

Childrens day care
Childrens out patient
Womens out patient
Out patient 2

Childrens
in-patient
Womens
in-patient
Lifts Lifts
Breast screening
Day surgery /
pre-assessment
Maternity

Theatres

Prayer
room

Administration

Cancer care
Medical Records
Neurophysiology
Neuclear medicine
Medical photography
Cardio-respiratory
Out patient 5
Out patient 4
Pharmacy
Lifts

Radiology
Out patients 1
Integrated
therapies
Out patients 5
Dialysis

Critical care
Childrens injuries
Walk-in injuries
Primary care

Cancer
daycare
entrance

Accident &
emergency
entrance

Administration

Night time
maternity
entrance

Main
entrance

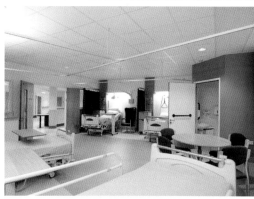

3.12
Queen's Hospital, Romford:
(clockwise from top left)
a schematic layout showing clinical function
b deep plan design reduces the vertical height and number of floors
c the main entrance
d natural light is a feature of the hospital wards
e the spacious entrance foyer

electronic patient records and digital imaging – and a physical design achieving a graduated acuity model of care, strict clinical adjacencies, good separation of patient and visitor traffic flows, short travel distances and future flexibility.

The resulting vertical design with its circular forms, 19 lifts and escalators, and central core and spine for rapid radial and vertical travel has the main diagnostic and treatment areas in an exceptionally deep-plan podium with two main floors of approximately 25,000 square metres each. There are two dedicated 'hospitals within the hospital' with their own entrances for children and women, and cancer care. Four towers of three levels rise above the podium, with central light wells and extensive views; all inpatient areas have natural light and ventilation. The majority of nursing units are designed in two 30-bed semi-circles, comprising six single bedrooms and six four-bed wards, an arrangement that allows excellent nursing flexibility and good observation.

Over 200 Trust staff and specialist advisors, in 70 working groups, were involved during the design process and the exceptional degree of collaboration allowed the Trust's vision to be converted into a unique, efficient and striking design that met the brief to a high degree. That the PFI can also be responsive and flexible was demonstrated during construction, when significant changes to the design were accommodated within the original programme completion date. The changes were helped by the circular form, modular elements and valuable and available 'shell-space', allowing another 60 beds in two nursing units to be provided that, together with a reconfiguration of the high-dependency and coronary care units to create more intensive care beds, enabled the hospital to bid to become a regional centre for neuro-surgery.

The project was selected by *Building* magazine as 2007 PFI Project of the Year.

The Bexley Wing, Institute of Oncology, St James's University Hospital, Leeds

Client:	Catalyst Healthcare/Leeds Teaching Hospitals NHS Trust
Architect:	Anshen + Allen
Contractor:	Bovis Lend Lease
Completed:	December 2007
Cost:	£232m
Area:	67,000 m^2
Procurement route:	PFI/design & build

This PFI can be characterised as a highly technical equipment transaction with a very large single-purpose building designed around it – a £232m, 67,000 square metre regional cancer care facility with 350 beds and 2,400 rooms designed by Anglo-American architects Anshen + Allen. It is a prominent urban landmark, with exceptionally complex engineering and radiological protection arrangements. Completed at the end of 2007, the project was selected as European PFI deal of the year in 2004, being the first PFI where the debt was funded by HM Treasury's Credit Guaranteed Finance facility, an innovative public/private funding hybrid. CGF will save the public sector about 10% compared to the cost of normal PFI senior debt.

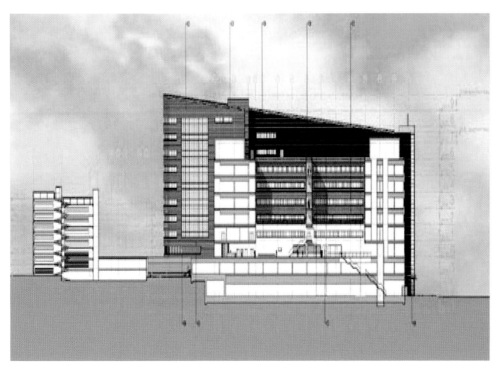

3.13
St James's Institute of Oncology, Leeds – elevation showing the sloping nature of the site and the radiotherapy plinth above which the main building rises

3.14
St James's Institute of Oncology, Leeds – architect's sketch showing the sun path

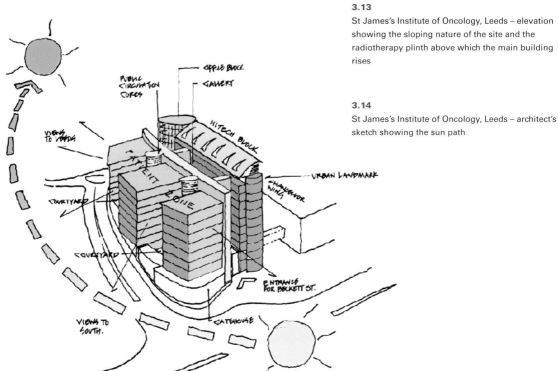

3.15
A new healthcare landmark – the 12-storey St James's Institute of Oncology in Leeds

The new wing provides diagnostic and therapeutic services for non-surgical oncology and specialist surgical services and is a national centre for teaching and research and development. It was constructed on a very constrained, previously developed site requiring extensive excavation and piling adjacent to the Chancellor Wing and the roads and main utility service routes of the sprawling St James's Hospital campus.

It has 12 levels and is divided into three principal zones: a radiotherapy plinth above which the main building rises in an E-shaped footprint with a high-tech diagnostic and treatment zone to the east and patient zone to the west in three vertical elements. A public spine links these together. The E-shape maximises perimeter walls for natural light and ventilation with supplemental cooling by chilled beams. Great attention has been paid to the design of the patient environment, with individual local control over light, temperature and airflows; this was greatly helped by a series of 'Inside Knowledge' plays produced by the hospital arts group Tonic, which articulated the human needs of cancer patients, their carers and specialist nursing staff.

Bovis Lend Lease, the design and build contractor, procured the major medical equipment and underwrote the single-point responsibility and financial risk for commissioning the building together with its equipment, which was a market precedent for health PFI contracts. To manage this risk, Bovis Lend Lease devised a 38-month, two-stage 'build on a building' construction programme. This allowed time for drying of the radiotherapy plinth's dense, magnetite-aggregate concrete shielding to the 12 linear accelerator chambers and for 12-months-early commissioning of eight linear accelerators, two of which are rated at 18 MVa, although the chambers are designed to accommodate Linacs up to 25 MVa.

New Hospitals for Manchester

Client: Catalyst Healthcare/Central Manchester and Manchester Children's University Hospitals NHS Trust
Architect: Anshen + Allen
Contractor: Bovis Lend Lease
Completed: Phased completion to 2010
Cost: £380m
Area: 155,000 m² new build, 110,000 m² retained hospital estate
Procurement route: PFI/design & build

One of the largest and probably one of the last healthcare super-PFIs, this £380m project will create an ultra modern acute and specialist tertiary referral and academic centre of excellence in the heart of the great northern city of Manchester. Built to a design by Anshen + Allen, it is a striking example of how strategic masterplanning and healthcare architecture, complex engineering and construction logistics and the PFI can combine to renew and deliver the transformation of a major teaching hospital's facilities, within its own boundaries, without

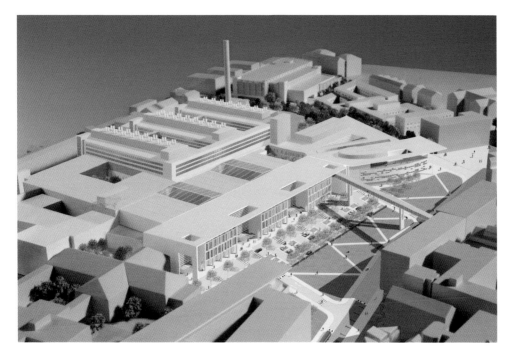

3.16
New Manchester Hospitals – architect's model showing central boulevard and the four hospitals: from the left, the Adults, Eye, Women's and Children's hospitals

3.17
New Manchester Hospitals – aerial photograph taken January 2008

stopping its operation and for a fixed price. The PFI provides for 150,000 square metres of new facilities, the refurbishment of 110,000 square metres of existing estate and the renewal of 100-year-old infrastructure over six years to 2009/10 through 18 phases of decant, demolition, reconfiguration, upgrade or new-build.

Like the Queen's Hospital project, it was financed by equity, a mezzanine loan and senior debt by way of a European investment bank loan and index-linked, investment grade bonds. The PFI contract also provided for Catalyst to take over in July 2005 the responsibility for

3.18
New Manchester Hospitals – aerial photograph taken January 2008

the maintenance and life cycle condition of some 106,000 square metres of existing hospital facilities.

The 'Manchester Joint Hospitals' project will consolidate at the Manchester Royal Infirmary site the Royal Manchester Children's Hospital, Booth Hall Children's Hospital, the Manchester Royal Infirmary, the Manchester Royal Eye Hospital and St Mary's Hospital for Women and Children and new mental health facilities. The new build incorporates some 6,000 rooms, and with existing facilities the campus will provide 1,460 inpatient beds.

In 1906, when the Manchester Royal Infirmary first opened, its island site was organised in a handsome and orderly fashion. A century of change resulted in an inefficient tangle and Catalyst's prime objective was to bring new order to the site through a zoning strategy with:

- a new central boulevard to open up a large green space at the heart of the campus and to provide public transport, cycle and pedestrian access, together with disabled parking and patient/visitor drop-off
- the Clinical Zone to the north of the Boulevard, with the four Adult's, Eye, Women's and Children's hospitals side-by-side. Each will have a separate entrance and identity whilst sharing a block of high-tech diagnostic and treatment spaces to which they are all attached; the wards face south to the green space and sunlight

- a new mental health facility with outpatients department, to the south and east of the island site
- a facilities support zone with the energy centre and base for facilities management services
- up to 3,200 car park spaces
- the Oxford Road Development Zone to the west providing for reuse and infill of the fine original buildings (many being listed), to form a group of non-clinical facilities including education centre, administrative offices, nursery, clinical sciences laboratories and, potentially, space for research, retail, residential accommodation and a medical hotel.

Various means were built into the design to ensure flexibility to adapt to changes in requirements as a result of demographics, new specialisms, equipment, models of care and political imperatives. These include:

- clustering of high-tech diagnostic and treatment facilities in a block structured and serviced to support the specialised needs of these functions and to better enable technology change
- use of standardised rooms and components wherever possible to enable adaptation to shifts in use
- empty shell-spaces, and soft space adjacent to heavy-use clinical areas
- reserving land to the east for the addition of another new hospital, linked to the framework of the base hospitals
- design of research areas to allow for lateral expansion.

When completed, these high-quality new hospitals with their individual identities and associated academic and research facilities all arranged in a more logical and efficient configuration will allow the trust to operate more productively, safely and competitively, and help maintain its position as an invaluable regional specialist centre for decades ahead. All of this had been planned many times before but the sheer scale of the scheme, allied with reorganisations, fluctuations in NHS funding and politics had thwarted the much needed and widely supported development. PFI made it possible.

CHAPTER FOUR

Rebuilding Britain's health service

PAUL HYETT AND JOHN JENNER

Paul Hyett, Chairman of RyderHKS International and a former president of the RIBA, and John Jenner, a founding principal of Greenhill Jenner Architects, have been deeply immersed in designing for the health sector at a time of unprecedented government investment. They have developed a particular interest in the way current conditions and processes impact on the quality of new healthcare architecture. Additionally, both have gained a rare insight into the current state of hospital design in the UK: through their membership of the UK Department of Health's Design Review Panel they have over the last three years seen some 45 projects at various stages of design development.

This chapter sets out important aspects of the context within which the UK National Health Service has embarked upon renewing its hospital estate and goes on, through a series of nine case studies, to examine samples of what is being produced. While Derek Stow in Chapter 1 reviewed the first 50 years of the NHS, this chapter covers more intensely the last decade or so in which, after nearly 20 years of serious under-investment, renewal is taking place in circumstances that are quite different from those of the 1970s – the last time that capital projects on this scale were undertaken.

The distinction between the supply and demand sides is much sharper today than in the NHS of the late 1970s. This, for the most part, follows the global trend of the shifting balance of power and activities from the state towards the private sector. But the changes brought about during the Thatcher years, in particular the creation of the internal market within the NHS with the demarcation of 'purchasers' and 'providers' of services, give the phenomenon a distinctly British character. As regards hospitals as buildings, there is on the demand side an increasingly critical consumer but also a loss of the expertise in design and procurement that is essential to getting the best from the market. On the supply side there exists a construction industry that, concurrent with rapid changes in technological and managerial terms, is trying with varying degrees of success to bring the design, construction and operation of buildings closer together.

Meanwhile, as Hyett and Jenner demonstrate, the electronic communications revolution continues to run its course, as does the shift from a welfare to a consumer-based society. In parallel, ecologically responsible architecture and town planning continue to increase in terms of importance while the concept of the car-based city is subject to ever greater criticism.

This is the background that has informed the authors in their selection of some of the best examples of hospital designs that are emerging today and in the drawing out of key lessons with respect to both process and product for the hospitals that are still in the pipeline.

Setting the scene

As the UK, via its much-loved NHS, advances deep into the biggest single building programme ever undertaken for new healthcare facilities, serious questions arise. How well are we doing? How will future generations view the buildings that we leave? What contributions are we making to this highly specialised sector? Are we applying fully sustainable as well as strategically appropriate designs for Britain's new hospitals?

This book is therefore timely. With some of the new hospital schemes already in operation and others in development, we have enough hard material to sensibly inform a review of progress, and enough projects still to play out for that review to have influence on future buildings.

But no review is meaningful unless the broader context is considered. This chapter will therefore seek to identify and analyse the main developments – technological, socio-political and economic – that are shaping future healthcare services, and in turn the healthcare estate. We will also consider the contractual mechanisms by which the projects are being delivered and through which the completed facilities will be managed.

In this endeavour we seek to complement the important work of Michael Davis (Chapter 3) and John Worthington (Chapter 2). They examine, respectively, the financial models under which most of the new work is being delivered, and the challenges and opportunities that designers face in responding to change. We will also attempt to add a parallel historical narrative that will place Derek Stow's informative review of developments in healthcare design since 1948 (Chapter 1) into a wider context.

As a finale we offer our own view on the questions laid down at the beginning of this introduction: how well, indeed, are we doing, and how *will* future generations view the legacy of buildings that we leave? In short are we – as designers, as a construction industry and as a society – proving ourselves worthy of the challenge that we face? In this respect we offer a qualified but optimistic view, and the case studies that form the second part of this chapter further demonstrate the basis for such optimism as well as some of the inevitable compromises involved in delivering such work successfully.

Impacts on space

The Industrial Revolution had profound effects on architecture and townscape. As well as spawning dense urban conglomerations, it gave rise to a series of tangible products of industrialisation which themselves fostered revisions to spatial arrangements in planning and architectural terms. The steel frame and the elevator enabled high-rise buildings, which in turn enabled greater density – first in America, then in Europe and across the developed world. In parallel, and with the growth of commerce and administrative and social functions, came the growth of service activities such as health and education. This was the late nineteenth-century context in which many, indeed most, of our great teaching hospitals were to be built.

Key among the products of industrialisation, the car has posed the greatest challenge for those who put forward urbanist theories and manage our towns and cities. As a society, we are so wedded to our cars that we demand a city fabric that will permit their maximum use. In terms of the location of hospitals, this has brought an ever increasing pressure to abandon the inner-city sites of old. Those who manage our modern hospitals thus frequently face a siting dilemma: should we release high-value city-centre sites for lucrative redevelopment and move out, or should we stay in those locations for their sustainability benefits (such as public transport), at the risk of alienating the modern car-loving consumer? The car, it seems, has more impact on decisions relating to hospital location and the character of the hospital campus (witness the massive car parks common to many hospitals) than any other single issue.

But despite the profound impact of the car on hospital location and planning, it is the second aspect of modern communication technology – virtual space – that now appears to hold the greatest capacity to affect people/people, people/place and place/place relationships in physical terms both *between* and *within* our future healthcare buildings. Unlike *physical* space, subject as it is to gravity, distance and time, *virtual* space can be limitless in its dimensions: space that is not space – merely a 'system', web or otherwise, providing nodes of opportunity for the exchange of ideas and information. Accordingly, for the last 50 years or so, the architecture and planning of our towns and cities has been increasingly influenced by new developments in information and communication technologies. The 'Communication Revolution' operates at a different level from the Industrial Revolution that initially shaped our modern cities – existing as it does in an intangible and 'virtual' world often beyond human comprehension. Individuals, organisations and societies that embrace this virtual world have exploited its new possibilities in terms of *reducing* intervals of time and the effects of distance, and have often used it as a catalyst for operational change. The architecture for new hospitals must inevitably respond to this new world.

By the close of the twentieth century, the modern 'first world' city had increasingly become a venue for virtual transactions. Commodities are exchanged, ideas are transferred and instructions sent in ever greater proportions in electronic and wireless format. Healthcare is one of the services on which cities and their surrounding populations are inevitably dependent. It also has the potential to become an increasingly virtual service – a fact that will inevitably impact upon healthcare architecture. The modern city is effectively becoming a 'node', connected to other cities and countries in a vast network, and healthcare will increasingly follow suit, providing a network of healthcare delivery.

Virtual space will, ultimately, become the context through which our healthcare services and hospitals are delivered. Its sponsor, modern communication technology, has the capacity to *deconstruct* the hospital as a physical, tangible entity – a concept that John Worthington refers to in Chapter 2. Its impact on architecture and planning will intensify, and it has only just begun to take a firm hold. We need to understand the potential as well as the dangers of virtual space if we are to steer its progress and development effectively. Much as 'telephoning' for a take-away meal distorts the physical relationships between diner and restaurant, the capacity for remote diagnostics and surgery fundamentally distorts the pre-existing *physical* relationships between laboratory and patient, operating theatre and surgeon, hospital and community.

Developments in technology mean that, increasingly, administration departments' record offices are dispersed without geographic boundary and without physical form. This is true of activities as diverse as banking, mail ordering and hospital administration. Already common in offices, 'hot-desking' will become a standard feature of life within the health service as hard documentation is replaced by electronic information banks. These will render the paper-based desk and nursing station obsolete in favour of the plug-in two-way data-docking point. Perhaps ultimately a patient's bed will carry her complete medical history on a coded memory chip which is plugged in upon arrival.

This freedom of location in relation to function has enabled managers to source cheaper labour for many sophisticated areas of activity in many sectors: for example, British Airway payrolls are handled 'offshore'. Surgeons are already advising on operations on patients located in other cities, thanks to 'telemedicine' – which can even simulate physical contact. Will modern nursing follow suit?

Why should any records or administrative operations be based on hospital sites? What, in fact, do hospitals need to contain? Even the walls of operating theatres could disappear as large parts of what was the hospital become virtual, while the remainder evolve physically as components of a disaggregated whole.

It seems eminently feasible for micro-sized 'personal organisers' to routinely incorporate body-monitoring and diagnostic components that offer constant information to a medical centre which, from a remote location, maintains a discreet 'eye' on our health and activities. Will we soon be warned electronically to alter our lifestyles, or be called in, without even having requested investigation, for treatment? Could homes become routine health monitoring/ screening venues as well as diagnostic and treatment units, with the local 'hub' clinic overseen by a regional – but virtual – hospital?

We dare not be Luddite in attitude – new technologies must be embraced with enthusiasm, understood in terms of their potential, incorporated into our work (whatever our discipline!) and used for society's benefit. Hospital departments have the opportunity to become dislocated and even dispersed, as electronic communication enables the establishment of network systems that negate the effects of distance and time.

Issues such as accessibility for staff, quality of environment in terms of staff recruitment and retention, and overheads such as rentals and rates are already steering Trusts towards radical rethinking of accommodation issues. The obsolescence of parts of hospitals (computer halls, switchboards, archive storage), which have been subject to significant influence from the electronic communication revolution, must come under ever greater scrutiny as the revolution proceeds.

In addition to facilities planning, the use of remote communication technologies also impact on facility management techniques. Stores such as Sainsbury's led the way, employing ecological management of individual premises from centralised estate and facilities control centres. Each store's energy use is monitored electronically, and the data are passed at regular intervals to a central computer. Irregular performance, or excessive consumption, results in advice and warnings being sent to the local store manager. As major consumers of energy, hospitals must surely follow suit.

In Chapter 2, John Worthington emphasises the need for *adaptability*, *flexibility* and *agility* in terms of design outputs. The response of designers to these challenges will be increasingly shaped by new developments in communication technologies.

In a world where all established user/building relationships are distorted, designers need to ask how much our concern over the *beingness* of 'being there' will influence healthcare architecture. Will new technologies drive the changes without compromise or will consideration for the human need for firm relationships with real places and real people prevail? Ultimately, where do people prefer to receive their healthcare services?

But in this context a depressing reality emerges: the rate of change in communication technology, and thus its potential to influence the essential nature of our healthcare facilities, is exponential. Against that awesome fact is the reality that hospital development is a very slow business. Typically, our larger hospitals may take 20 years and more from initial planning to handover, of which the detailed design and the construction programme is rarely less than five to seven years. The prospect therefore exists for our new buildings to become increasingly obsolete as a result of the communication revolution – perhaps even before they become operational. At the very least, their suitability and effectiveness for meeting the fast changing demands of medical practice must be constantly in question.

Never before has 'loose-fit' been so critical a condition for long life in terms of hospital design. This necessary 'future-proofing' is one of the greatest challenges facing hospital designers today. Sadly it rarely even flickers on the brief writer's radar.

The consumer-based society: a socio-political rollercoaster

At its inception in 1948 the NHS estate included some of the finest architecture of the nineteenth century, such as the Liverpool Royal Infirmary and University College Hospital (London) – both purpose-built hospitals designed by Alfred Waterhouse. It was his collaboration with Florence Nightingale that had led, in the 1870s, to the evolution of the Nightingale ward which was to remain the main model for ward design in the UK, and extensively overseas, for more than 70 years.

Much of the estate that would serve Aneurin Bevan's new National Health Service would, however, have to function in building stock that was not purpose built (for example, smaller ex-workhouse facilities such as Daventry Cottage Hospital). Furthermore, the wartime approach of 'make do and mend' was carried forward into the culture of NHS estates' management in the form of a wide variety of temporary and converted buildings.

Many ex-military hospitals were employed in NHS service, such as Broomfield near Chelmsford, which also contained a beautiful early modernist sanatorium. With its distinctive narrow wings containing deep verandahs for tuberculosis patients, this complex was, in typical fashion, expanded during the war with an extensive array of single-storey, pitch-roof prefabricated huts housing wards, all linked by flat-roofed 'spine' corridors. Post-war additions included a series of new integrated facilities to provide for A&E, outpatients and radiology, together with one of the country's most sophisticated burns units – a legacy of the specialist skills developed at that site to meet the earlier needs of injured servicemen.

A similar situation developed in many other hospitals across the UK: an initial facility (either purpose designed or converted from other uses) onto which a series of often low-grade additions were built, frequently in the form of temporary surgical and non-surgical wards. This remains the situation at Pembury Hospital near Tonbridge, Kent: poor-quality Victorian buildings surrounded by extremely low-grade huts – facilities that one would expect to find in a refugee camp rather than at a hospital serving one of the wealthiest catchment areas of one of the wealthiest countries in the world.

This, then, was the reality that the NHS faced in the context of a post-war Britain that would for some years struggle under both food rationing and extreme shortages of building materials. And it was against this background that Britain would embark upon one of the most ambitious and extraordinary social experiments in history: the creation of a welfare state, with the NHS as its backbone.

The nascent NHS was organised into regions, which assumed responsibility for the inherited healthcare estate. Over the coming decades some good progress would be made with the development of some new hospitals and extensions to many existing hospital sites (Derek Stow has described this progress well in Chapter 1). The NHS, however, would never embark on the scale of development for new healthcare buildings that was seen in the post-war years within the education and housing sectors.

In consequence, a predominantly ageing building stock, never fully appropriate to the demands that would be placed upon it, faced the increasing dual pressures of improved medical capabilities and an ageing population. The NHS was from the outset thus committed to a process of 'catch-up'; a process that it could never win because the rising demands upon the estate to meet the ever-growing demands upon health services could never be adequately funded. Over the coming decades the healthcare estate would therefore be seen to creak under the strain.

Any ambition to achieve the much-needed expansion and renewal of an estate fit to properly support the work and aspirations of the NHS was finally thwarted by the oil crisis of the early 1970s. This world event triggered the realisation that the ambitions of a welfare-oriented society could not be met within a depressed global economy. But the difficulties were not wholly attributable to Middle East unrest and its wider consequences. Conflicting political ideologies were brought into ever sharper opposition across an increasingly divided nation. Britain consequently entered a period of intensified socio-economic conflict, initially signalled by the miners' strike that brought down the government of Edward Heath in the early 1970s. The colour and creativity, invention and energy, of the 1960s had given way to a decade of strikes, abortive investment in crippled and declining industries, and witless efforts to extend a utopian dream ill-fitted to a harsh commercial world. Yes, the Middle East crisis had impacted on government spending, but the welfare state, as an ideology, had foundered and British socialism appeared to be in terminal decline.

It was against this background that Margaret Thatcher, together with a close coterie of radical Tories, would succeed in shaking the very foundations of traditional English liberal thinking. A heartless reliance on market forces would herald an era of enforced independence and self-reliance. With this would come new opportunities, albeit, arguably, only for the few. Unemployment and bankruptcies hit record levels, negative mortgage equity, evictions and repossessions would destroy families and produce awful and widespread misery, and Yorkshire's newly privatised water company would find itself unable to maintain supplies. Despite all this, Thatcher and (most of) her colleagues soldiered on relentlessly, convinced that the crusade to 'deliver' the British people from the stultifying effects of the 'nanny state' would be rewarded by a renaissance of individual self-reliance, invention and industry.

Thus, by the closing decade of the twentieth century, as Britain moved irreversibly towards a post-welfare consumer-based market democracy, time would finally catch up with the NHS healthcare estate. Put bluntly, it was no longer possible to operate an effective contemporary health service within what was an exhausted, under-maintained estate. The picture was of course mixed, with the standards and scope of facilities varying widely across hospitals and regions, but any serious review of the overall estate would have inevitably concluded that a radical and comprehensive programme of renewal was necessary. The nettle had to be grasped …

There had been exceptions to the legacy of compromise and piecemeal additions that afflicted so much of the NHS estate. Bold, and in some instances, groundbreaking projects remain as examples of a belief in the potential of architecture and design to contribute to the essential mandate of the NHS – excellence in the delivery of healthcare services. Sadly, however, quality new work was all too rare among a generally unexciting programme that included a predominance of bland and modest buildings, which, with grim regularity, revealed the adverse effects of *constraint* on design brief and *restraint* in architectural ambition.

Britain builds again

Suffice it to say that British society has, it seems, seen fit to continue its support for a programme of widespread political and economic reform which is now well into its second decade – under a New Labour government. There have been difficulties, and there has been much friction among politicians, professionals and the wider public as the procurement models for the delivery of state services within a post-welfare consumer-based market economy have been shaped. But in parallel with these developments and with further substantial changes on the horizon, the expectations of our society have developed and grown. Put simply, we have evolved from a nation where the relatively reasoned and restrained expectations of the citizen have matured into the less compromising, more powerful and urgently expressed demands of the consumer.

To meet these new demands within the healthcare sector there have been three categories of response. The first involves the disposal of existing sites and the relocation of all hospital functions within a complete, new, purpose-built facility – as at Worcestershire Royal Hospital, completed in 2002. The second response involves a phased redevelopment of hospital facilities on their existing sites that is so substantial as to represent complete renewal. This process inevitably presents the challenge of minimising any reduction to the quality of the ultimate project that would inevitably arise from the phasing process, as with the example the new Whipps Cross Hospital in north London (currently at planning stage). The final category involves substantial development and/or redevelopment of a part of a site but not on so extensive a scale as to represent a complete programme of renewal as with the new Hope Hospital (now under construction) at Salford. In the latter cases the designers face two further challenges. They must achieve an appropriate ordering of all facilities (both new and existing, internal and external) through rationalisation of the masterplanning and wayfinding arrangements, and they must also achieve an overall visual and experiential impact that is sufficiently powerful to render a positive change of perception in the mindset of all patients, staff and visitors.

But faced with such a massive challenge, what agendas inform the design briefs? What is the extent of such work, and where will it take place? Unsurprisingly, the influences that have shaped, and continue to shape, strategic policy are still in a process of evolution. However, one major consideration has had a particularly radical impact, and that is the ongoing commitment towards satisfying consumers' developing expectations.

Patients have always hoped for modern, clean and efficient facilities, and they have increasingly expected to be treated with dignity in terms of both physical and information-related privacy. For today's consumer/patient, that means a generally more welcoming and stimulating public arena within hospitals with an emphasis on places that will 'lift the spirit', together with an even stronger commitment to single-patient bedrooms among predominantly two- and four-patient rooms. This reflects trends in the US aimed at minimising cross-infection problems, increasing dignity and privacy in terms of patient-based information exchange, and providing optimum encouragement for family and friends to assist in the healing processes through their extended presence and support.

Against that background, too many of our hospitals represent a real image problem for the NHS. New technologies and practice may push the frontiers of medical science, and many of the more recent buildings (delivered before the mammoth current programme commenced) continue to give good service, but overall, a public perception stubbornly persists of a generally poor built infrastructure which is increasingly unfit for service. Over the latter half of the twentieth century there were too many inappropriate alterations and additions. Too many courtyards and landscaped areas were sacrificed to some much-needed and overdue new clinic, treatment unit or waiting area and too many low-grade and wholly inappropriate temporary structures were added, whose life is now extending into its fourth decade or even further. It is undoubtedly true that the work of the NHS, and its ability to advance its service, has been compromised by its estate.

It is in this context that the British government has committed the nation to a massive regeneration programme for its healthcare estate, albeit that financial and political support for this endeavour is contingent on public private partnership (PPP) arrangements. Underpinning the government's zeal for these new forms of procurement are its stated imperatives of integrated supply chains, innovation, best value, controlled capital costs and effective risk management strategies during project delivery.

The pressure has therefore switched from making the case for investment to delivering a level of quality that will yield a worthy legacy in terms of the effort involved. It was in pursuit of that objective that a general government mandate was established to encourage best design, record and communicate best practice, and inform future design agendas. That mandate has also sought to resolve the inherently conflicting demands of the concept of a consumer-based society utilising state healthcare services *within* a modern market-oriented democracy. This socio-political context has profound implications for both NHS Trusts and the designers of healthcare facilities in terms of the nature of the buildings that they are expected to provide.

New goals for new healthcare estates: a 2020 vision

So what, beyond the emphasis on consumerism and a generalised desire to 'lift the spirit' of all those who use our new hospitals, is the agenda that informs the NHS's design aspirations for new hospitals?

As Sunand Prasad has outlined in his introduction to this book, in order to try to draw together some of the widespread dialogues that had taken place about the form and character of future healthcare building, the Nuffield Trust and the Royal Institute of British Architects (RIBA) took decisive action. They jointly funded research that culminated in a report (*Building a 2020 Vision: Future Health Care Environments*, 2001), which recognised that the health and construction industries were each undergoing 'a phase of accelerated change and modernisation', and that future patterns of healthcare would require largely different built solutions.

The study identified broad aspirations that would influence the planning and design of the future healthcare estate, such as the 'development of a holistic social model of healthcare' and 'patient-centred' approaches to care dovetailing with high-quality design. It also broadened the definition of sustainability into social and economic as well as environmental parameters.

The key issues involved in the pursuit of 'a holistic social model of healthcare' were deemed to include living in a healthy environment, access, equity, social inclusion, and new working cultures. Access has especially important design implications, including the physical integration of the hospital within its urban surroundings together with public transport provisions. The new agenda for patient-centred design approaches is also of particular importance. Essentially, it envisions patient pathways reconfigured through managed clinical networks centred around the patient. Thus, in addition to clinical logistics, patients' comfort, convenience and general experience *must* be given high priority in terms of design.

The pursuit of design quality can be described as a holistic endeavour that integrates three factors: functional efficiency and convenience; technical performance of structure, service and fabric; and finally a sensitivity to the therapeutic impact that design can have on the mind and senses. This third factor includes (renewed) aspirations of civic place-making and the clear differentiation of public, social and private spaces.

In addition, the fast growing demands for sustainable, ecologically responsible design bring a host of new challenges. These range from the control of CO_2 emissions and responsible stewardship of natural resources, to whole-life costing of buildings in terms of operational economy as well as capital costs, and the creation of buildings that incorporate the ability to adapt to changing requirements.

In delivering against these various headings, an emphasis was placed within the 2020 Vision publication on the need for a much closer collaboration between the design professions and the clinical service providers. The intention here has been to foster and develop a shared vision relating to innovation in care organisation and a corresponding innovation in the design and delivery of healthcare environments.

For NHS Trusts this can, in part, be simply stated as an objective to develop services and plan new buildings that will work both now *and in the future – a process that* necessitates the engagement of informed client representatives who really value and understand the benefits of good design.

With respect to the architectural profession, the 2020 Vision calls for greater emphasis upon design research, with particular reference to the integration of design and construction processes and the benchmarking of design quality to achieve objective, rather than subjective, assessments.

Clearly, there has for too long been an uncomfortable divide between clinical healthcare professionals and their counterparts in healthcare planning. Now, at a time when both the healthcare sector and the construction industry are undergoing a phase of accelerated change and modernisation, the opportunity exists to re-engage, via a collaborative effort, to define in detail a shared vision for new buildings.

It is anticipated that through such collaboration there will emerge new ways of organising hospitals that respond to the needs of all who use these buildings. Such initiatives should be complementary to the operational changes brought about by innovations in medical practices and the new technologies discussed in the previous section of this chapter. As an example of such changes, ambulatory care centres have already been developed to provide 'walk in, walk out' specialist facilities where treatments can be completed within a day. Further developments anticipated in the 2020 Vision include the 'medical village', with its own separate entrance, organised to confine the patient experience to one part of a hospital site. This would reduce wayfinding problems associated with large institutions and allow for the provision of a more humane environment. An even more radical approach includes the reorganisation of clinical work around patient conditions, thus abandoning the traditional separation of medicine from surgery: for example, a hospital comprising an abdominal centre, a sensory neuro centre, an environmental centre and a mobility centre supported by 'transverse' centres for emergency, laboratory, research, training and administration.

Great emphasis is placed in the report on the accelerating impact of new communication technologies on healthcare practices and facility design (as discussed earlier in this chapter). In particular, remote diagnosis, monitoring and intervention capabilities provide increased scope for care at home and at the primary health centre. The final important message of the 2020 Vision study concerns the location of the facility in terms of the ecological agenda and the urban design agenda – encouraging regeneration of city centres rather than out-of-town development.

In short, *Building a 2020 Vision* provides a blueprint for a consumer-based society in terms of its healthcare services. In so doing it expresses – perhaps belatedly – aspirations and demands that look uncompromisingly towards the future.

Reforms in construction and procurement

Against the influences and aspirations described above, the construction industry is also changing substantially, partly in a parallel response to government preferences for integrated delivery, and partly in response to new technologies. There will accordingly be increasing emphasis on off-site prefabricated and modular construction in pursuit of greater speed, efficiency and economy in assembly as well as better standards of finish. New types of contract will continue the shift responsibilities towards a single point of risk, while the traditional split between design and construction will be continually narrowed. Finally, new forms of financing and ownership patterns will further extend the involvement of those responsible for building (that is, contractor-led consortia). In this respect if they retain ownership and involvement in facilities management, the system should encourage the extended interest of building providers in build quality and operational economy. Such developments also offer opportunities to restructure and redefine the relationships of the builder and the supply chain.

In this context, it is worth examining the background that has led to such substantial change. In particular, we should consider the changing roles of the three main groups of 'players' that are essential to the realisation of any building project: the *Initiators*, the *Facilitators* and the *Officiators*.

The Initiators

As a result of the demise of the individual patron, combined with the reducing scope of welfarist initiatives, the developer had, by the closing decades of the twentieth century, emerged as the principal player in construction development. Increasingly, building projects were initiated and executed by individuals or commercial organisations who would neither own the building nor use it. The Initiators' powerhouse is the property market, which has gradually come to influence the procurement and the character of all building types, from the opera house to hospitals.

But there are inbuilt conflicts in terms of the potential role of private developer involvement in state-sector infrastructure which must be worked through if public private partnerships are to be successful. The objectives of property development relate almost exclusively to the maximisation of profit, with the minimum of outlay, against conditions of minimum risk. The often vast sums of money that are required for this activity are borrowed from pension, insurance and banking funds. However, the financiers and the developers who borrow are not responsible to those who 'own' the money for the way it is used. Accordingly, developers tend to see their business from an entirely different perspective from that of the planner, the designer, the social scientist or the environmentalist.

The product of architecture is thus being redefined in terms of investment return. In the evolution of the design brief, abstract notions relating to security of investment and investment yield now frequently supersede the functional requirements of a building's users. Operating within a largely deregulated market economy where the criteria for success are set by property agents, accountants and bankers, developers have little room for manoeuvre. A system has established itself, but it is one in which no single group has control. Clearly, in providing a major and, thus far generally secure base for the various funds, this system serves the material interest of a large portion of the population. Nethertheless, it has become increasingly evident that the *Initiators* operate within a system that can have a significantly compromising, and occasionally adverse, impact on the quality of our built environment.

The Facilitators

This group includes all those who prepare and issue information relating to a building project (traditionally, architects leading a team of engineers and quantity surveyors), as well as builders. Both of these groups have in recent years been engaged in a process of proactively or reactively redefining their roles, which as a result are being reinterpreted, merged and even transposed. Thus the rules of the property and construction game have been destabilised and the construction industry has undergone the most significant changes it has experienced since the first half of the nineteenth century, when Thomas Cubitt revolutionised its trade practices. With the virtual disappearance of the craftsman from the building site and the rise of the specialist subcontractor, and with the increased adoption off-site manufacturing procedures, builders have inevitably evolved into construction coordinators and contractors.

In parallel, design and build (D&B) has emerged as the preferred model of most developers and latterly local authorities and other state bodies responsible for procurement, such as NHS Trusts. Its rise to prominence was the result of several drivers, including architects and quantity surveyors 'parcelling up' elements of the building and passing the task of detailed design on to specialist subcontractors. At the same time, as a result of the rapidly escalating cost of financing a project, developers were obliged to delay all expenditure (site acquisition and professional fees) at least until they could be certain that a project would go ahead. Severe inflation in the 1970s and 1980s exerted further pressure.

With increasing frequency, therefore, the construction of a building was begun without sufficient information. This led to mounting claims by contractors against the late issue of information by the design team (who were rarely being given enough time to do their work properly). It was in order to protect against such claims that quantity surveyors and developers began to favour the design and build contract. The procurement of full D&B tenders eventually made it possible to divert ultimate responsibility for managing design work away from the architect and supporting design team. As a result the designer's role was, in effect, reduced to that of another subcontractor, and he was often denied any direct contact with the client.

The D&B contract also removes any obstacles to the early certification of funds and improves the contractor's cash flow. Clearly, the closely aligned interests of the developer and the contractors have little to do with social concerns or with the aesthetic qualities of the built environment. Thus, rather than serving the nation, the contracting industry has created the converse situation – one where the population serves the industry by indirectly supplying it with large sums of money through the investment funds (for example, pensions) that make up development finance.

This situation is now progressing towards a much more interesting level where groups of contractors, bankers and facilities management companies come together to form consortia that will maintain a long-term interest in a building project (e.g. a PFI hospital). Their initial selection is based on design quality, economy and efficiency of facility operation in the widest sense of those terms. Privately financed methods of project procurement may have suffered heavy criticism, but the supply market in these areas is maturing considerably and we can expect increasingly sophisticated and worthy projects to emerge – especially in the field of healthcare building.

The Officiators

The remit of local government departments has also seen significant shifts in policy and practice. These include a broad programme of legislation covering environmental considerations, an increase in public participation in the planning process, and the rise of public private partnership in lieu of direct state procurement. In addition, the increased use of Section 106 agreements forces the developer to provide (in return for, or at least as a condition of, planning consent) some negotiated form of planning gain through the provision of building work, or finance that would otherwise be the local authority's responsibility.

When these shifts are considered alongside direct grants, tax benefits from enterprise zones, new regeneration corporations (with immense powers and a questionable level of accountability) and new rolling forms of local planning, it becomes clear that the conditions within which architecture is produced have changed radically during the final decades of the twentieth century. Because planning departments now tend to resort to written policy rather than a (drawn) masterplan, they are no longer directly involved in planning the physical environment, even as an abstract concept. The discipline of 'town planning' has, accordingly, evolved into a social science and rather than having the power and opportunity to take the initiative, the planner is now generally restricted to a reactive role in development.

This is also true of the large offices of state-employed design teams. At their peak they employed 65% of all British architects – the figure is now 13%, and still falling. In the emerging context of privatisation, the state has lost its capacity to design and administer the delivery of building projects through its own departments. As a consequence the development and construction industry continues to change beyond all recognition.

But those who believe that a grand urban plan is incompatible with the free market should look to examples such as the Royal Crescent in Bath or Nash's Regent Street. In both cases there was a masterplan, yet the execution of those monumental set-pieces of exemplary architecture that survive to this day were driven by market forces, with successive portions being built in response to demand. There is no reason why such rich work cannot, and should not, emerge in terms of today's new healthcare estate through the new private finance initiative (PFI) and public private partnership (PPP) consortia.

Seeing buildings as a service

'Lean thinking' within business has led to a realisation among most companies that providing a range of maintenance services in-house is damaging to profits and financial competitiveness, and indeed shows irresponsibility to their shareholders. Modern practice also seeks to direct capital resources towards primary activities. For example, vehicle fleet suppliers are engaged to both supply and service leased vehicles, as today's management would not permit substantial capital to be tied up in the ownership and direct maintenance of transport systems.

When related to the supply and servicing of equipment (cars, computers, even aircraft), such outsourcing arrangements are simple, understood and welcomed. But these concepts have been very slow to develop in areas such as the provision and maintenance of built infrastructure – especially the state-owned variety.

PFIs are, however, at last becoming increasingly common. But there is continuing resistance as the tradition of state ownership of school and hospital buildings remains popular with the public and is preferred by many within the architectural profession. They continue to be deeply suspicious of alternative models of building procurement. The current practice of PFI provides some grounds for such suspicion, but self-interest and ideology also play their part.

But even the most committed 'welfarists' would surely accept that, provided a health service of appropriate quality is free at the point of delivery, it is preferable that the service provider – the Trust – should procure and operate its buildings as economically as possible.

PFI should, at least in principle, enable a much higher proportion of the available health service funds to be used efficiently and exclusively for healthcare, as opposed to the acquisition of expensive property, or for uneconomic building management and maintenance procedures. Its practice should be continually examined to ensure that these desirable outcomes are being achieved.

As the role of its estate departments evolves in relation to new forms of procurement, the health service is increasingly reliant upon output specifications against which design proposals will be developed and measured. This is all the more important within the context of PFI-type delivery, where the relationship between architect and the Trust is dislocated. It is crucial in this new 'landscape' to identify how the brief-preparation processes will be informed and where collaboration between medical experts and specialist designers will take place. How will Trusts be protected against the poor-quality design work that will inevitably arise if such work is passed to firms and individuals of inappropriate expertise, experience and ambition?

As an example of the skills required, let us examine the area of infection control which is currently subject to rapidly increasing research. Effective environmental decontamination relies on appropriate materials and detailing of building finishes, and on the correct arrangement and servicing of spaces. Recent research into tuberculosis outbreaks has revealed that only 35% of UK Health Trusts had *negative* pressure facilities for the isolation of infectious patients. Similarly, control of nosocomially acquired aspergillosis is dependent on high-efficiency air filtration, positive pressure ventilation and frequent room air changes. The skill involved in monitoring spore counts during building work at hospital sites demonstrates the highly specialised nature of this type of building, from both a design and a construction management perspective – not a job for generalists.

Notwithstanding its ability to release capital, PFI's success will be dependent on establishing new and effective collaboration between medical experts, designers, constructors and facility operators – from brief preparation, through design work, to ongoing research and facility management. Hospitals must be developed to meet ever-changing needs, but development must also occur in the way in which we deliver such buildings, in the context of new rules of engagement, new players and new sharing of responsibilities. The future belongs to the Trusts and the consortia who carry among their ranks the appropriate levels of expertise and skill as well as the ability to deploy the new arrangements and relationships to deliver greater value to the public.

Health design: where are we now?

In the preceding parts of this chapter we have considered the enormous changes that together produce the context within which the biggest ever single building programme in healthcare estate design and development is taking place. We have considered the communication revolutions – real and virtual – and their impact on relationships between *people* and *space*. We have considered the social, political and economic changes that have been manifest in the transition from a *welfare* to a *consumer-based* society, which places new and demanding requirements on our healthcare estate. We have also considered the enormous changes within the development and construction industry in terms of the shifts in *roles* and *responsibilities* of its main players, and the new responsibilities that the consumer increasingly expects to be taken on by the private sector.

This, then, is the context in which the current British government, after years of neglect, piecemeal thinking and incremental development, has decided to embark on its enormous programme of revision and renewal of the healthcare estate. It is now necessary to undertake a brief review of the current state of the architectural profession – itself a crucial element of the renewal programme. How is it placed to cope with the challenges it faces in terms of skills, resources, culture and aptitude?

The architectural profession has responded with varying degrees of success to the great changes witnessed since the Second World War. The establishment of the Welfare State led to the formulation of a whole state infrastructure – from hospitals, schools and libraries, to prisons, housing, leisure facilities, and the whole infrastructures of our great nationalised industries. All these organisations had their own architects' departments. By the early 1970s, some 65% of the architectural profession worked for public bodies and young architects anticipated long careers in the state sector, engaged as it was in large-scale, complex and sophisticated building programmes.

The state offices were *big* offices. At the peak of the programme, some 85% of all hospital work in the UK was delivered through NHS architects' departments. Major private firms such as YRM, Llewelyn-Davies, RMJM and Watkins Gray did excellent hospital work but they were the exception. Most large commercial firms were unsuccessful in securing state sector work and their portfolios, and therefore their knowledge base and experience, were generally restricted to commercial work.

The fact that 60% of the profession today work in practices of five people or fewer, and 80% work in offices of ten or fewer, would have been inconceivable to architects employed within the vast state offices of the 1960s and 1970s. There are proportionately many more architects in Britain today, but they have, in collective terms, less influence. Put quite simply, in the post-Thatcher years the architectural profession's 'state sector' resources have been decimated. But we should see this as a period of transition – it is not a situation that we should presume to be static.

We do not propose calls for a reversion to the state as the principal employer of architects; indeed we acknowledge the many disadvantages of that system (although we would wish to highlight the many great achievements and contributions that have been and, in some cases, continue to be made). What is important is to recognise that over the last three decades the state sector resources in terms of healthcare building (where much of the specialist design expertise resided) have been largely dismantled. As a result, the architectural profession's current capacity to deliver healthcare facilities has been much compromised.

In turn, private commercial practice has not yet expanded adequately to fill the gap, and small practice cannot possibly meet the challenges. The UK's architectural profession is, in consequence, now inappropriately structured – there are currently far too many small (private) practices, and nowhere near enough medium and large ones. Too much of the profession's knowledge base, in many specialist sectors such as hospital building, has either been lost or is in the wrong place – namely, in small practices. This results in wasted talent, missed opportunities and, commonly, a failure on the part of many architects tasked to design hospitals to respond adequately to the challenges before them. All too often, and however outstanding their design skills, the existing big architectural offices lack the appropriate specialist experience.

The demand in terms of delivery targets for healthcare is immense. The government has called for some 100 new £100 million plus hospitals – all at once! That represents some £50 million of architect's salaries per year during development – or some 1,700 healthcare architects. Who will deliver them? These projects need experienced teams of 25 or more architects operating within offices of 100 plus people – the concept of single-project offices is unworkable and commercially naive. But with 60% of its membership in firms of five or fewer, the UK's profession is hardly in good shape to cope with these new demands or, indeed, the opportunities that arise from them.

A new way forward....

Hospitals are for people ... Because they are hospitals, their buildings have to be large ... But our architects and designers understand today that they must do their best to achieve buildings that fit into their surroundings ... And perhaps even more is possible ... by their careful design ... [these buildings] should make a positive contribution to the recovery or comfort of their patients.

This quote comes from then Secretary of State for Social Services Barbara Castle's foreword to the publication *Hospitals for People: A Look at Some New Buildings in England* (1975). It is astonishing to note that way back in 1975 a Minister was urging clients and design professionals to consider how hospital buildings might address the relationship of the building to the site ... respect the experience of staff and patients and explore the potential to be therapeutic. Astonishing because a review of the contributions made to the healthcare estate of England over the following 20 years would suggest that, with relatively few exceptions, those responsible for building work took little note of the aspirations Castle so eloquently set out. (This is an opinion echoed by CABE – the Commission for Architecture and the Built Environment.)

As reported in *Building a 2020 Vision: Future Health Care Environments*, evidence of the disappointing quality of, and general lack of interest in, hospital design can be found 'not only from the buildings themselves' but from the fact that 'few hospitals have received architectural awards'. It is also correct in saying that healthcare buildings are rarely featured in the mainstream architectural press, and that this building typology is 'not commonly the subject for design projects in schools of architecture'.

The authors went on to offer a series of explanations for this sorry state of affairs, which included the following: firstly, that hospitals are considered to be highly sophisticated technical environments with an abundance of regulatory controls; secondly, that the organisation of the space is complicated as a result of having to respond to the needs of three groups of users – patients, staff and visitors; and lastly, that low fees have deterred architects.

These are rather curious conclusions, as it could be expected that the sophistication of requirements, and the general complexity of hospital design problems, would make this genre of buildings particularly interesting for designers. Furthermore, for much of the post-war era the majority of hospital work was carried out by state-employed architects – a group that were not, as salaried employees, much affected by fee levels. Anyway, financial returns have rarely been a deterrent to intense competition among architects for worthwhile architectural opportunities.

Nevertheless, it seems to be generally true that there has been little evidence of interest in hospital design within the architectural press or in schools of architecture. With the notable exceptions of the work of MARU (the Medical Architectural Research Unit) and the current research of Professor Bryan Lawson's team at the University of Sheffield, serious consideration of hospital design has been conspicuous by its absence. One reason for the past lack of interest and progress in hospital design may be that in the era of highly centralised government control, as epitomised by the Nucleus Standard Planning and Design System, it became difficult for architects to innovate and develop new design ideas.

Either way, the authors of *Building a 2020 Vision* were seemingly correct in concluding, while acknowledging exceptions, that the majority of buildings developed for the NHS did not 'succeed in attaining either the depth of architectural thinking or levels of innovation found in other building types'. This disappointing fact contributes to the current concerns about the compromising effect that poor quality, in both the design and the condition of today's NHS estate, has on healthcare outcomes.

This, then, was the context in which the first wave of new (largely PFI) hospital projects planned in the last months of the twentieth century would be considered. Sadly, albeit with good reason, there has been widespread criticism of much of the work – and rightly so. However much money is poured into the healthcare estate, achieving design quality is of critical importance. The government must therefore ensure that public money is well spent irrespective of whether it is in the form of capital investment, or ongoing public revenue commitments under PFI and PPP arrangements.

In recognition of this, former Secretary of State for Health Alan Milburn stated in November 2001:

> to ensure that good design is embedded within the NHS healthcare building programme
> ... design proposals in future will be reviewed by a panel led by NHS Estates and The
> Prince's Foundation, CABE and others, at the earliest stages of the procurement process
> before a preferred bidder is chosen.

This statement heralded the formation of the Centre for Healthcare Architecture and Design at the Department of Health's buildings agency, NHS Estates, with the remit of reviewing all major capital schemes and, through such reviews, influencing better outcomes. The importance of Milburn's words cannot be overstated, and in pursuit of the intentions he so clearly set out, the Design Review Panel is now fully integrated into the business case process.

Members of the panel include renowned academics, professionals, advisers, enablers and researchers who meet periodically for training workshops. The panel is carefully selected to ensure, on the one hand, that no conflicts of interest exist in relation to the assessment of any particular scheme, and that in each review members bring to the table an appropriate range of complementary knowledge and skill. The intention has been to produce a culture of constructive collaboration with the Trusts.

Projects are initially reviewed at the early stages of the design development where the Trust produces a conceptual scheme that is a physical representation of its design aspirations, and a demonstration of the capacity of the site to accommodate the proposed buildings. This provides an early opportunity to explore the design constraints, problems and opportunities of a site, and the Design Review Panel input (DRP1) at this stage can be of critical importance to later outcomes. A further review takes place, which gives opportunities for influencing design quality as the proposals are developed and refined.

Examples of this process, illustrating a selection of projects currently under development, were included in *Tomorrow's Hospitals,* published by the NHS in 2005.

Conclusions

Despite our best efforts and intentions, as management systems and medical practices and technologies advanced during the life of the NHS we had lost, somewhere along the way, the

ability to appreciate what senior nurse Sarah Waller describes as the 'totality of experience' –
a totality that puts 'place' and physical context firmly alongside treatment and care as critical to
successful outcomes. Or as Waller so elegantly puts it: 'Places for mixing, places to be alone or
with loved ones, places to do, places for stressed staff to find calm, for distressed relatives to
find composure; places for exhausted patients to find new strength.'

In response to such critisms, and as will be evident from the case studies that follow,
enormous effort is at last being made to ensure a 'humanising' of new hospital environments.
The need for an appropriate quality of space planning – in the widest sense of that term
– coupled with a need to ensure that this quality is maintained once the building is in use, is, at
last, becoming properly recognised.

In pursuit of these objectives, some trusts are giving their staff training so that they can
contribute more fully to the design development of new facilities. This involves training in
awareness of the value of design, the processes by which better design is delivered, and the
qualities by which better design is identified. Such training also enables staff to contribute
more fully to the ongoing maintenance and effective use of facilities during the operational life
of the project.

How well are we now doing?

- **From a welfare state to a consumer-based society**
  Those involved in the design, development and management of new healthcare facilities
  need to continue to develop an ever better understanding of the dynamic context in which
  they operate. Britain's socio-political character is changing and, while the intent remains to
  provide healthcare services free at the point of delivery, the demands of an economically
  more independent and successful society have raised the bar. The modern consumer
  demands more in terms of choice and standard of facility.
- **New forms of engagement**
  The design professions need to better understand their roles and responsibilities under
  the emerging procurement routes. Architects in particular must address new obligations in
  relation to their position within the supply chain, while contractors should further embrace
  their expanded long-term responsibilities to the real clients – the building's users.
- **The value of design**
  Efforts to raise awareness of the potential of design among the medical profession and
  public must be intensified. There is still much to do here. More must be expected in terms
  of building performance and the potential of architecture to offer new possibilities for the
  delivery of healthcare services.
- **Evidence-based design**
  Lessons must be drawn by *all* concerned with the delivery of new healthcare facilities
  from the research work currently in progress (e.g. Roger Ulrich/Brian Lawson).
- **Be encouraged ... be positive ... be optimistic**
  The challenge is enormous but, while there have been setbacks and disappointments,
  strength and encouragement must be drawn from the success stories. New and better
  facilities are being created, and the conditions for those who seek treatment, those who
  visit, and those who work within our healthcare buildings *are* improving.
- **Environmentally responsible design**
  Only lip service is being paid to this agenda – we must do better. We are the first
  generation to *knowingly* hand the planet to our children in a condition worse than that
  in which we inherited it. Buildings generate 48% of the CO_2 emissions that are wreaking

increasing havoc with the world's eco-systems: that is a shameful legacy. Hospitals are among the most unsustainable of all building types, and government has a major responsibility to demand better.

So, how well are we really doing? Well, we are 'on the up', but there is much room for improvement and for wider aspirations to inform the healthcare rebuilding programme. There should be no let up in our efforts – our patients and those who love and serve them deserve the highest quality of hospital environments.

Notes and references

1. Susan Francis and Rosemary Glanville, *Building a 2020 Vision: Future Health Care Environments*, Nuffield Trust and RIBA Future Studies (London: The Stationery Office, 2001).
2. NHS Estates and the Department of Health, *Tomorrow's Hospitals* (2005).
3. *Hospitals for People: A Look at Some New Buildings in England* (1975).

Case studies

As described by Derek Stow in Chapter 1, the National Health Service invested heavily in the theory and practice of hospital design throughout the 1960s and 1970s. An extensive body of guidance in the form of Health Building Notes and Health Technical Memoranda was produced. Though in need of updating, it remains unsurpassed as the UK's most comprehensive and well-researched body of knowledge on the functional fundamentals of hospital design. Alongside the ongoing production of guidance documentation there was continuous experimentation with design both within the Department of Health's in-house architects' teams and within the select group of private architectural practices that were engaged with healthcare work.

The focus was on process, logistics and economy as indicated by the names of some of the innovations – the 'Harness Hospital', the 'Best Buy Hospital' and the 'Nucleus Template'. Only occasionally, as in the work of Powell and Moya at Wexham Park, did architects directly address non-medical aspects of the patient's experience. Design was overwhelmingly seen from the provider's point of view.

And so it is that perhaps the greatest difference between the approach to hospital design in the NHS today and that of the previous era of hospital building springs from a shift of power from the supply side of healthcare to the demand side. This appears, for example, as the 'consumerism agenda' in governmental parlance. For design and construction teams the new approach manifests itself as 'patient-focused design' or 'therapeutic design'. Despite this, and while there is widespread agreement that the environment *can* play a significant part in the therapeutic process – capable of both enhancing and inhibiting healing – there is much variation in the extent to which the patient's experience is addressed within the design processes and outputs. But good progress is being made and the case studies below describe nine of the most 'thoughtful' projects of the recent period of hospital building. The recognition of the experiential significance of the environment does not in any way reduce the importance of functional solutions to the issues of clinical/medical process, logistics and economy. Indeed the pace of change guarantees continuous and intense attention to the technical and functional realm of hospital design. As stated earlier in this chapter, key components of change today include rapidly developing technology; the impact of IT both on this and on the ever burgeoning administrative component; and changes in the regulatory and legislative context such as the increased attention to safety and security. Indeed change, and the need for hospitals to be adaptable to developing medical practice, is itself becoming a key driver of design. Logical and elegant design strategies that deal with all these matters are therefore the subject of constant search, as illustrated in the case studies. However, most hospital buildings are being built on sites already occupied by the hospital they will replace or extend, and existing buildings all too often restrict design options and compromise outcomes.

Contemporary briefs for new hospital buildings place considerable emphasis on clinical adjacencies, and often demand a quantity of accommodation not easily fitted onto the site. These priorities can lead to deep plan designs that rely upon expensive, highly engineered and energy-demanding mechanical and electrical installations for environmental control. At the same time they create artificial conditions that, except in the most highly technical spaces, may unnecessarily compromise patient, practitioner and carer comfort. The recent intent to introduce more natural light and ventilation has led to spatial concepts such as courtyards, malls, arcades, atria and covered streets, all of which can also enrich circulation arrangements. At its best this disaggregation of space serves to moderate or break down the sheer physical bulk of hospital buildings to a human scale.

Given that many hospitals have the population size of small towns, recent developments in their ordering and organisation have been much informed by the discipline of urban design. It is accordingly common now to hear references to squares and piazzas and to the 'hill town', the 'village green' and the 'health village' in the context of hospital planning. However, such approaches are usually more demanding in terms of space and can be difficult to effect on very restricted sites.

The urban analogy also holds another as yet unrealised promise: towns and cities increasingly contain extraordinary examples of the ability of certain types of built form to accommodate complete changes in the purpose to which a building is put (e.g. Victorian industrial buildings and even churches converted to luxury inner-city apartments). Many are saying today that the general hospital as understood for the last 150 years, starting with the 'lying-in' hospital, is obsolete. And yet there is a clear need for such hospitals in the immediate future, and the poor condition of the estate of the NHS continues to require replacement. How can we design modern health buildings and campuses that may ultimately be turned to a quite different use in the future? And what can we learn from the history of cities in this quest? In this context one further challenge must be addressed within most hospital design: how can the facility as a whole be successfully integrated into the surrounding urban fabric in both physical and architectural as well as social and economic terms?

The case studies (as listed below) which conclude this chapter address a variety of these issues:

1. The ACAD (Ambulatory Care and Diagnostic) Centre, Central Middlesex Hospital, Park Royal, Brent, London.
2. The BECaD (Brent Emergency Care and Diagnostic) Centre, Central Middlesex Hospital, Park Royal, Brent, London.
3. City General Hospital, Stoke on Trent, Staffordshire.

4. University Hospital Birmingham, Birmingham.
5. New Oncology Wing, St James's University Hospital, Leeds.
6. The London Breast Care Centre, St Bartholomew's Hospital, London.
7. Kings Mill Hospital, Sutton-in-Ashfield, Nottinghamshire.
8. Evelina Children's Hospital, London.
9. Norfolk and Norwich University Hospital, Norwich.

The ACAD (Ambulatory Care and Diagnostic) Centre, Central Middlesex Hospital, Park Royal, Brent, London

Client:	North West London Hospitals NHS Trust
Architect:	Avanti Architects
Contractor:	John Laing Construction
Completed:	1999
Cost:	£12m
Area:	8,000 m^2
Procurement route:	Traditional

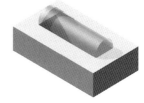

Typology: Predominately Atrium/Galleria over Street

Although day surgery and outpatient treatment departments have featured in the healthcare provision of the NHS for many years, the Ambulatory Care and Diagnostic (ACAD) Centre at Central Middlesex Hospital, North West London, is believed to be the first purpose-designed and stand-alone ambulatory care facility to be built in the UK. Designed in 1995 and opened in 1999, the ACAD Centre established a prototype for the new wave of diagnostic and treatment centres (DTCs) now being developed throughout the country.

In order to understand the architectural response it is necessary to look, if only briefly, at the clinical model underpinning the ACAD concept. Combining recent philosophies of patient-focused care and the need to rethink the conundrum of shortening waiting lists in an age of increasing demand, the ambulatory care principle is that routine elective care should be separated from acute and emergency services and organised within its own specific environment with dedicated scheduling, rapid diagnosis and interventionary procedures. This enables patients requiring routine treatments to be processed independently and economically, thus avoiding all the uncertainties, cost and disruption associated with the conventional mixing of clinical pathways through the main hospital.

The ACAD building, in effect a hospital without beds, seeks to translate this concept into architectural terms. As the name suggests, the key idea is the ambulatory basis of patient movement, and the armature of the plan is the 90 m triple-height pedestrian mall, which connects all parts of the facility and imposes a sense of legibility by exploiting the most precious resource available to an architect – natural light. A continuous roof light and large glazed screens that enable waiting areas to overlook planted courtyards also allow sunlight to permeate deep into the interior and maintain a strong sense of connection with the outside world.

To one side of this thoroughfare lie the consulting and pre- and post-intervention suites; to the other are ranged the diagnostic imaging facilities and theatres. The building section stacks these functions according to their servicing and technical characteristics – the high-tech floors on one side with their intensely serviced and sealed environments and rooftop plant rooms

4.1
ACAD north-east elevation

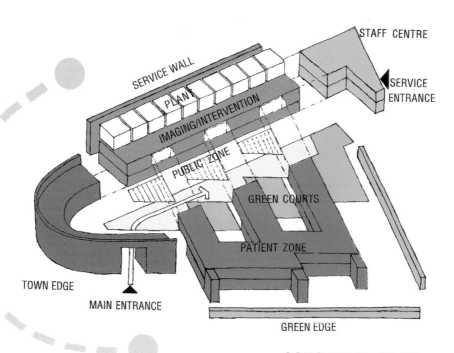

CONCEPT DIAGRAM

4.2
Diagram reflecting simplicity and ease of use

above, and the low-tech floors with their more cellular suites of conventionally serviced rooms on the other. At the first-floor level a series of bridges connect the respective stages of the patient 'journey' in a typical treatment episode from preparation, through surgery, to recovery.

Using these basic organisational principles, the building is tailored to the circumstances of its site – a seemingly awkward 30/60 triangle bordered on the west by a brutal industrial feeder road, and on the south by the residue of pre existing buildings, including elements from the hospital's origins in the old Willesden Workhouse. (These buildings have now been partially cleared to make way for ACAD's younger cousin, the BECaD Centre.) However, this disparate context provides an effective setting for the building's differing functions. Flanking the highway, the high-tech section offers a protective barrier against the worst effects of noise and pollution (though offering easy access for plant replacement), while the consulting and recovery suites overlook newly created landscaped courtyards and gardens. The triangle thus reconciles the geometry of the hospital with that of its neighbourhood, the widening footprint of the plan perhaps even suggesting the open offer of healing and improvement in the quality of life that it makes to those it serves.

The building also addresses its context at each approach – the entrance prow proclaiming the centre to Park Royal and containing reception, café/restaurant, office and conference facilities, and the rear housing staff rooms and service facilities adjacent to the internal hospital road. The choice of materials is likewise related to building context – panelled cladding and a protective undercroft on the outer 'industrial' façade, with a warmer palette of brick and blockwork, timber and render on the inner elevations.

Driven by an intensely aspirational client team, the ACAD Centre makes a dramatic step-change in the delivery of elective care services in an area historically scarred by underinvestment and deprivation. Architecturally, an attempt has been made to redefine what a modern hospital *can* be and what it *can* feel like: light, generous, elegant and even classless. Overall, this project represents a serious endeavour to counter both the anonymous institutional character of much recent design and also the contrived domesticity that is so often, and mistakenly, used to camouflage it.

4.3
a   Reception – airport-style check-in desk
b   Well-lit mall with supernumerary signs
c   Each waiting area has a high quality of
    views and light, and is related directly to
    courtyards of differing designs

The BECaD (Brent Emergency Care and Diagnostic) Centre, Central Middlesex Hospital, Park Royal, Brent, London

NHS client:	North West London Hospitals NHS Trust
Architects:	HLM Architects and Avanti Architects
PFI client:	Bouygues UK
Hospital handover:	March 2006
Site completion:	January 2007
Cost:	£80m
Area:	28,000 m²
Procurement route:	PFI

Typology: Predominantly Low Rise, as opposed to Hybrid

If ACAD spearheads a revolution in the elective sphere of NHS healthcare, the Brent Emergency Care and Diagnostic (BECaD) Centre represents an equivalent attempt to reinvent the organisation of services in the traditional district general hospital. Developed by the same client, the North West London Hospitals Trust, and located directly to the south of ACAD at the Central Middlesex Hospital site, the BECaD Centre aims to re-engineer and rationalise the intractable problems of acute and emergency services.

With elective care functions now effectively housed in ACAD next door, the sequel building seeks to apply the same principles of patient-focused care to the processes of assessment, triage, major surgery, trauma, intensive care, etc. – differentiating the respective admission streams in such a way as to facilitate an integrated and tailored clinical response, thereby avoiding the conventional 'shuffling' of patients through a range of separate departments to effect the whole treatment episode. The redefinition of treatment protocols and associated retraining of clinical teams that underpins the new model of care formed a crucial part of a client–staff programme prior to occupation of the new building, and were the key drivers in developing the brief for the design team.

Significantly larger and more complex than its earlier cousin, the BECaD adopts a different organisational diagram – a cruciform with courtyards – but equally exploits the benefits of natural light, spatial generosity and the focus on specific views to achieve an equivalent legibility and sense of order. A lofty central forum is located at the crossing of the cardinal axes of the building. The north–south route connects the entrance with reception, the main circulation core and beyond to ACAD; the east–west route runs as a spine through open courtyards to link all sections of the building. Other locational markers are provided by the cylindrical staff pods that punctuate the spine and register the special importance accorded to good accommodation for clinicians who are, after all, at the heart of the quality service that the centre aims to deliver.

Unlike ACAD, which was traditionally procured, BECaD has been built under PFI, though this is not unduly apparent in its appearance. The architectural language is slightly simpler, as befits a larger building – tile and coloured render forming the principal external fabric, with fenestration organised into a series of linked zones that effectively 'scale' and 'order' the façades. An extensive canopy, part covered, part openwork, throws a delicate 'web' across the building at roof level and conveys a sense of lightness to set off the geometric solidity of the volumes below.

But BECaD also makes another contribution to innovative design: its southern edge takes the form of a generous and welcoming crescent that will form part of an eventual major new

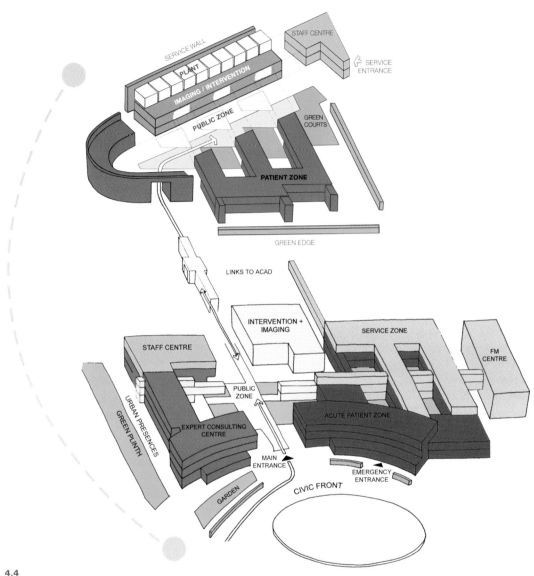

4.4
ACAD–BECaD – the clarity and organisational simplicity in ACAD is reflected and
developed in the planning of BECaD to ensure a logical and legible hospital

urban space when the residue of redundant hospital buildings is cleared. Despite its glamorous-
sounding name, Park Royal, even with the regeneration investment that has occurred over the
last decade, has continued to lack any distinct identity or urban quality, consisting largely of bland
warehouses and soulless industrial distribution centres. A vital design ambition of the BECaD
project was to exploit the opportunity provided by such a large building to create a new urban
centre for the district. The circus that will be formed when the lower section of the site has been
redeveloped will provide a transport centre and strategic focus for the whole neighbourhood and
register the significance of the new hospital as the largest public resource within it.

4.5
a   Atrium north – view on entry to BECaD
b   Atrium south – view from the second floor looking over the triple-height space

Taken together, therefore, the achievement of ACAD and BECaD should provide a powerful rebuttal of the two criticisms most commonly levelled at the current hospital building programme – that existing care models are only being re-accommodated and not re-engineered, and that the massive wave of investment is providing little benefit in terms of design quality and urban place-making. Not only should the combined development offer a radical clinical prototype for the hospital of the twenty-first century, but its built form will provide a bespoke and distinctive contribution to the civic identity of its locale.

City General Hospital, Stoke on Trent, Staffordshire

Client:	University Hospital North Staffordshire NHS Trust
Architect:	RyderHKS International
Contractor:	Laing O'Rourke
Completion:	2012
Cost:	£250m
Area:	106,000 m²
Procurement route:	PFI

Typology: To be completed

This design represents a serious exercise in combining a high-quality patient experience with operational efficiency, architectural coherence and good urban design. When completed, it will constitute the most significant built component in the rationalisation of healthcare facilities within

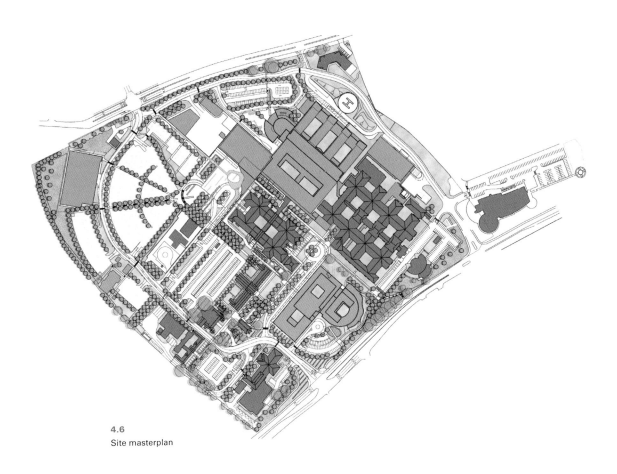

4.6
Site masterplan

North Staffordshire. Associated projects, being carried out by the same team, also include maternity and oncology provision at the same location together with a community hospital in north Stoke.

The design allows for the consolidation of services currently provided across three sites to be concentrated onto a single urban campus. Previous logistical problems involving patient and staff movements between the various sites will be eliminated.

A masterplan has been developed which has a clear and straightforward rationale. Car and public transport movements are all to the northern side of the site. Thus patient, visitor and staff arrival is immediately separated from the emergency and service traffic which is located to the southern side using different site entries. The site will accommodate all necessary car parking eliminating the previously required transportation of staff from remote facilities by bus.

The existing site contained a fairly typical collection of buildings developed piecemeal over the preceding 170 years. These ranged from listed early Victorian workhouses through 1950s wards to 1980s Nucleus templates. These buildings were thoroughly analysed for their historical context and their potential functionality for future healthcare needs.

The listed buildings are all retained, although some insensitive additions will be removed. Their setting will be transformed by the creation of a new 'parish green' onto which they will face. They will be converted for administrative use.

Most other buildings will be demolished as the development progresses including the service elements of the Nucleus buildings. The Nucleus wards and operating theatres will be retained

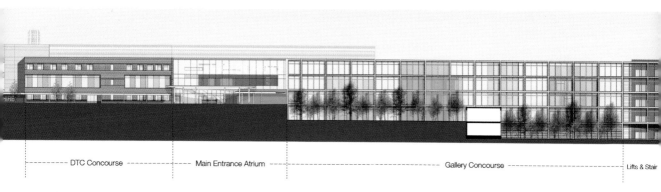

4.7
Main entrance and gallery elevation

and refurbished. The major new building will attach directly to these retained clinical buildings to permit internal circulation across the campus for the first time.

The heart of the new building, known as 'The Hub', contains the central diagnostic and treatment departments. This pivotal location enables these principal facilities to be shared by both outpatients and inpatients. This simple design strategy has led to economies in the amount of diagnostic and treatment facilities required on the site as well as associated efficiencies in staffing and operation.

The main entrance to the hospital buildings will be across a large public piazza into a three-storey glazed atrium space which is immediately apparent from all public car parking and arrival areas. This is the beginning of an effective approach to 'wayfinding'. Connecting to the atrium is a full height glazed gallery rising to five stories as the external ground levels fall away. The gallery provides access to all outpatient clinics; node points and entrances are colour coded and visible before visitors even enter the building. The gallery and atrium overlook a linear garden designed to provide a contemplative space as well as further aiding passive wayfinding.

The main Hub facilities are situated at the lower levels where the deep plan space can be exploited as these departments generally require mechanical ventilation. Upper levels are reserved for the outpatient clinics and wards where natural ventilation and views can be best provided. The wards are located on the southern side where, by virtue of their height, they gain long distance views across the valley beyond. They will also be visible from long distance and their architectural form and articulation has accordingly been developed in the light of this broader urban context.

Wherever practicable natural ventilation has incorporated and mechanical systems are designed to minimise the use of non-renewable energy and permit reclaim. Specifications have been developed requiring the use of sustainably sourced materials.

The site landscaping has been carefully considered. The perimeter of the campus is to be planted with a dense woodland mix to provide a degree of identity and separation from the surrounding streetscape. This will provide a habitat for birds and other wildlife. Car parking has been broken down into small cells with clear directional walkways to avoid dominating the landscape. Nearer to the buildings the landscape becomes more formal and gardens and other spaces are being developed for patient and visitor use. The site is designed to be generally permeable and accessible.

The overall masterplan provides simple and clear provisions for future expansion. The buildings themselves are designed to permit straightforward internal conversion for different use in the future.

University Hospital Birmingham, Birmingham

Client:	University Hospital Birmingham Foundation Trust
Architect:	Building Design Partnership
Phased completion:	From 2009
Contract value:	£627m (value includes separate mental health facilities for Birmingham and Solihull Mental Health Trust)
Area:	137,000 m², with circa 1,213 beds
Procurement route:	PFI

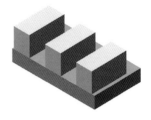

Typology: To be completed

The new teaching hospital will be one of the largest in the United Kingdom. It replaces two existing hospitals (the Queen Elizabeth and Selly Oak) and will accommodate the vast majority of the Trust's activities. The remainder will be undertaken in retained building stock connected to the new building by a glazed overhead link. Overall the design seeks to create an efficient and flexible building that is focused on the needs of the individual patient, visitors and staff. Through this new scheme the Trust hopes to be able to operate its innovative patient-focused model of care fully for the first time.

The hospital has been designed from first principles, considering the experiential perspective of the user and the functional perspective of the operator in parallel. The architects, being a multi-disciplinary practice, were in a strong position to incorporate lessons learned from a wide range of disciplines and projects including masterplanning, landscape, transportation, retail, leisure, offices and education. This approach extends beyond the bounds of the hospital itself to a comprehensive masterplan for the wider healthcare campus. At the heart of this campus a new park will be incorporated on the site of Metchley Roman fort. The new hospital, the existing medical school and a new transport interchange will all address this major public space.

The site for the new hospital comprises the main surface car park for the Queen Elizabeth Hospital. To allow work to begin without the loss of parking spaces, new multi-storey car parks have been scheduled as advance works, releasing the site for construction at the earliest possible date. In order to reduce the normally adverse visual impact of such 'accommodation', these car parks have been set within the natural slope of the site and are terraced in profile. In addition, their elevations have been conceived as collages to break down their bulk and to integrate them into the campus landscape using a palette of materials including cedar boarding, planted screens and stone gabions.

Typologically, the new hospital is a variant on the podium and tower form. Diagnostic and treatment space is located in an extensive three-storey podium, offering maximum flexibility to accommodate future changes in clinical practice and technology. This podium is divided by wide bands of landscape that run north–south, assisting orientation and providing daylight and long views.

Wards are located in hollow, elliptical towers that sit over the podium. These towers are bisected by glazed link bridges and have an asymmetric roof profile to maximise sunlight penetration from the south side. Wards are relatively shallow plan to allow good daylighting and natural ventilation. Cores shared between the wards provide separate lift connections for patients and staff, clean supplies and waste disposal. Visitor access to wards is by lifts rising from the main entrance to glazed public routes at upper levels which lead to individual ward reception areas. The main entrance canopy wraps up and over this visitor lift tower, providing a wayfinding clue while also 'tying' the podium and ward towers together visually.

4.8
Main entrance and aerial view

The design has good clinical adjacencies and is very compact for its overall floor area, minimising walk distances and allowing clinical staff to spend more time caring for patients and less time moving between departments. Vertical integration by lift enables staff with specialist expertise of particular disease groups to work in both outpatient departments and wards. This allows patients to receive continuity of expert treatment by as small a number of different people as possible. In turn, this also promotes the standardisation of diagnostic and treatment protocols and thus the delivery of clinical best practice to patients.

Clinical accommodation has been rationalised into a series of standard templates that have the flexibility to cope with a wide variety of activities simply by a change in furniture and equipment. Standardised semi-elliptical wards provide 36 beds, comprising 16 single rooms and 5 four-bed bays. Patient rooms have good daylighting with low window sills that offer views of the surrounding parkland and residential areas from a sitting or lying position. Another template for standard wards is split into three clusters, each of 12 beds, but flexible enough to create wards of 24, 36, 48 or 60 beds. In order to minimise staff walk distances, shared facilities are located at the apex of the ward and lift cores are located at each end.

Outpatients 'check in' at reception points in the outpatient atrium, a light environment with long views, access to the outside landscape and real coffee! They are called down to the 'gates' of individual clinics on a just-in-time basis. The outpatient department follows a standard linear template, allowing different-sized clinics to be run from waiting areas at each end.

Accident and emergency has a separate entrance on the north side of the building at first-floor level with dedicated imaging facilities and direct lift access to main imaging, theatres and critical care. Theatres (located directly opposite critical care, thus providing rapid access to life support systems for unstable patients) are arranged around a central open plan area where

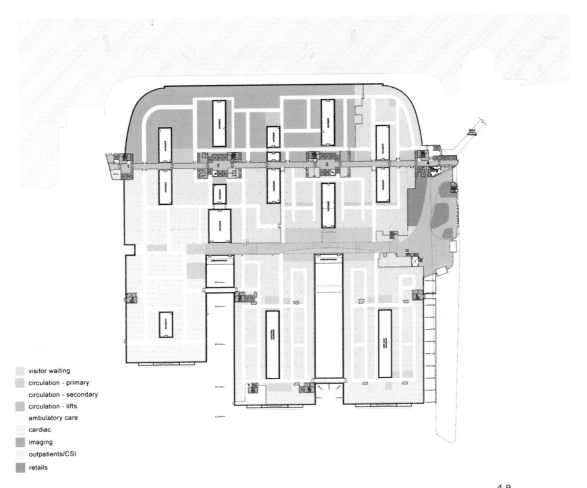

visitor waiting
circulation - primary
circulation - secondary
circulation - lifts
ambulatory care
cardiac
imaging
outpatients/CSI
retails

4.9
Ground-floor plan

patients will recover with the benefit of daylight and screened views. Day case theatres for more routine surgery are located at ground-floor level adjacent to outpatients.

The hospital's teaching role is central to its activities. The education space is, accordingly, fully integrated with clinical accommodation in the podium to facilitate quick access for students working in wards and departments.

The masterplan for the project creates pedestrian and cycle routes that follow landscape 'corridors' through the campus, connecting playing fields to the north with the new park and an area of trees and grassland to the south. A loop road round the edge of the campus connects to building entrances and car parking, achieving a pedestrian-friendly heart to the complex.

The geometry and massing of the new hospital responds to the grain of the site, its stepped form mediating between the urban scale of the existing hospital buildings to the north and the suburban scale of the adjoining residential area to the south-west. The massing of the hospital is characterised by the soft elliptical plan form and sloping roof profile of the ward towers. The combination of these towers with the lift cores between them provides a varied silhouette to the hospital in its position on the horizon. The hospital is clad in smooth, white, storey-height cladding, relieved by varied blocks of colour.

The design takes advantage of the site's south-facing slope to separate the service entrance, main entrance and accident and emergency entrance onto different levels, simplifying access arrangements and the internal organisation of the hospital. Extensive use of ribbon glazing provides good daylighting, with flexibility to cope with future changes in clinical planning. Internally, good use is made of colour and natural materials to create an intimate human scale and ambience for smaller spaces.

The masterplan and building design is intended to promote intuitive wayfinding. The intention is to reduce reliance on signage by using the form of the building, colour and art to guide patients through a hierarchy of routes to reach their particular destination. These routes form an elegant 'skeleton' that will allow separation of the different flows of visitors, patients and staff, and supply and disposal. This is important to the achievement of privacy and dignity, ensuring that patients are not overlooked by the public, inpatients are not mixed with outpatients, and patient routes are not mixed with waste-disposal routes. At the 'meet and greet' point in the entrance, patients are able to see the outpatient atrium and the public lifts up to the wards. Primary circulation routes naturally daylit lead from east to west to guide patients to departmental reception areas that are signalled by their coincidence with points of architectural significance.

The main entrance is immediately obvious to patients, whether arriving by train, bus or car. The drop-off point is optimally located adjacent to both the car park and the reception, making it easy for relatives or friends in cars to drop off patients safely, park close by, and return to the reception area as quickly as possible. Patient and visitor car parking is situated in a multi-storey, long-span, flat-slab structure to minimise the distance to the main entrance and maximise convenience, visibility and security.

The ground-floor main entrance incorporates shops, cafés and large-scale art installations, softening the psychological contrast between the patient's everyday environment and the clinical realm, which is usually only entered because of illness or injury.

New Oncology Wing, St James's University Hospital, Leeds

Client:	Leeds Teaching Hospitals NHS Trust
Architect:	Anshen Dyer
PFI consortium:	Catalyst Healthcare
Scheduled to open:	End of 2007
Cost:	£172m
Area:	66,650 m², with 366 beds and 2,250 rooms
Procurement route:	PFI

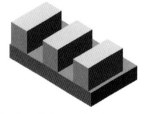

Typology: To be completed

The Trust is replacing an existing facility and bringing together several fragmented services from different locations to create one of the largest cancer centres in Europe. The new wing is a stand-alone complex on a brownfield site that forms part of the St James's Hospital campus near Leeds city centre. This 'hospital within a hospital' will provide a very wide range of services for centralised and expanded cancer treatment within the Yorkshire Cancer Network.

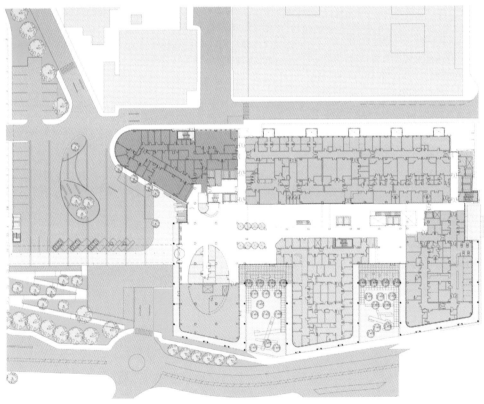

4.10
Model and plan of St James's Hospital, Leeds

This project is, in consequence, an example of a city centre healthcare development at a high density. While the location gives patients better access to services, the inevitable compromises in terms of site area and context have presented considerable design challenges.

The principal architectural challenges presented by the site, and the schedule of accommodation have been:

- organising 66,650 m² of clinical and support space on a site, the area of which is only 15,300 m² – this creates a very high plot ratio;
- reconciling the inevitability of a large, tall and densely planned building with the necessity for creating a genuinely therapeutic environment that responds to the needs of patients and their carers;
- identifying and achieving the potential for using this scheme as a catalyst for re-establishing a sense of order on an otherwise ill-connected and poorly planned hospital 'campus' and creating a new set of connections with the existing buildings; and
- dealing with a steeply sloping site with a level difference of 9 m between the highway – Beckett Street – at the south and the northern boundary of the site within the St James estate.

The New Oncology Wing will be as large as many district hospitals and contain an unusual concentration of highly specialist clinical activities. It will dispense very powerful and inherently frightening courses of treatment yet also provide sophisticated counselling, consultation and highly supportive nursing. One of the principal design issues has been to strike the right balance between providing comfort and respite and achieving a high level of technical care.

The architect's response involved the creation of a well-ordered and legible set of component 'parts' which are zoned horizontally and vertically. The resultant design is a hybrid example of the galleria model based on a linear glazed public street from which the clinical areas are entered.

A high-tech spine of diagnostic and treatment facilities, laboratories, offices and research accommodation runs north–south, and is set against an E-shaped block of three peninsular wings that form the patient zone and accommodate outpatient, day case and inpatient activities. The spine and wings are connected by a glazed galleria that runs the full length of the hospital, linking the main entrance at the north with a secondary entrance off Beckett Street at the south. The galleria contains all the New Wing's public spaces and the three banks of public lifts that serve the upper and lower floors.

The peninsular ward form that has been adopted is seldom used in the UK because of the difficulties of satisfying the hospital fire code (HTM81). Significant work was undertaken at the detailed design stage in fire-engineering a fully compliant solution. This form was adopted to:

- break down the massing of the building into a set of strongly modelled components that mitigate the impact of the high density of accommodation required within the brief;
- provide all the patient bedrooms with views onto open-ended courtyards with a high proportion of the rooms gaining distant views of Leeds city centre and the horizon beyond;
- open up the galleria to views beyond the hospital's boundary; and
- create a simple wayfinding solution by serving each of the wings with a dedicated bank of public lifts.

The patient zone has also been broken down vertically into three distinct layers: a solid two-storey base, clad in brick and timber, for radiotherapy services; a middle band of two glazed storeys of ambulatory activity; and an upper layer of three storeys of inpatient accommodation. The high-tech spine slopes from 10 to 12 floors in height.

It is clear that the design cannot overcome all the problems caused by such intense development on a constrained site but it appears to have created a cogent and well-ordered building.

The internal planning provides intense horizontal sequences of clinical activity. The whole radiotherapy department, with all 12 linac chambers, simulators, consultation, support and planning, is located on a single floor. All the surgical beds, the theatres and the intensive care unit are co-located on an upper floor adjacent to their counterparts in the main hospital. An entire floor is dedicated to haematology, combining outpatient, day case, inpatient, laboratories and research within an integrated unit.

Waiting spaces (and access to them) are located adjacent to the garden courts. In addition there are terraces on the upper floors. Wayfinding is very intuitive since each of the wings is served by a dedicated bank of lifts that are accessible to patients and visitors, entrances to which are located in the galleria's public spaces. The peninsular ward solution is only made possible by connecting all the wings at every level with a hospital street that runs the length of the building, looking into the galleria/lightwell and, on the upper floors, out towards the central Leeds skyline. The location of the goods and patient lifts at opposite ends of this street achieves a high level of segregation between service traffic and public circulation.

The design of the external envelope above the base plinth of masonry construction is unusual in that it will be constructed from a type of fully unitised factory-fabricated system more commonly associated with commercial buildings of high quality. The capital costs of this system are higher than those of traditional construction but are more than compensated for by significant savings in construction time and reduced scaffolding requirements. The size and scale of the building suggested a range of complementary materials. The ward floors of the peninsular wings are clad in copper while the ceramic-tile ambulatory floors below are glazed in curtain walling. The high-tech spine is clad in zinc and aluminium rain-screen panelling.

In conclusion the design strategy has translated well into the finalised scheme, although the detailed design of many of the clinical spaces has suffered from an overly specific brief that has ignored opportunities to create generic plans or sets of spaces, and has treated every department as a very separate entity.

The London Breast Care Centre, St Bartholomew's Hospital, London

Client:	Barts and The London NHS Trust
Architect:	Greenhill Jenner
Completed:	2004
Cost:	£13m
Area:	2,792 m²
Procurement route:	Traditional

Typology not applicable. Refurbishment.

This project, small by hospital standards, is a rare example of the conversion of a historic building to modern NHS medical use with the incorporation of an exceptional artistic programme. The conversion has been achieved through an unusual planning approach which, by placing most of

4.11
Exterior and interiors of St Bartholomew's Hospital

the circulation against the external walls of the building, has created pleasant and outward-looking public areas. These areas are further enriched with specially commissioned art of a commendably high standard. The project arose at a significant moment in the development of thinking about *how* we deliver healthcare and the consistent aim, both in clinical conception and physical realisation, has been to produce an exemplar for the design of patient-focused health facilities.

In particular, the art programme, developed by the Trust's in-house arts project, Vital Arts, together with an independent curator, provided the user/client group with a focus for refining their ideas about the brief and the proposed service. In response to patient and staff hopes that it would not feel or look too much like a hospital, Greenhill Jenner Architects secured 3% of the budget for contemporary art. Seven leading artists were commissioned to create works under the theme 'Anywhere but here', which had been inspired by patients. Running throughout the public areas of the building, the artworks are intended to comfort and 'uplift the spirit' of those who use the building – the aim being to create a positive healing environment.

The £13 million refurbishment of the Grade I-listed West Wing, which forms part of the architect James Gibbs's eighteenth-century Italianate piazza at St Bartholomew's Hospital, was one of the early projects in a wider ongoing £1 billion PFI redevelopment. The project converted what had previously been an old ward block into a world-class centre of excellence for breast cancer, creating a one-stop clinic equipped with the latest state-of-the-art digital diagnostic equipment for outpatients from across north-east London. The project, financed by means of a charitable appeal, was completed in September 2004, on budget and on time.

The building – part of a spectacular architectural ensemble that gives the hospital its special identity – was ingeniously adapted to deliver twenty-first-century medicine without compromising its important historic features. The existing timber structure was retained and the original joinery and plaster features restored. New contemporary features in glass and steel complement but do not physically engage with the original fabric; treated like oversize pieces of furniture, they sit within the external walls, not touching them.

The transition from a historical to a contemporary theme starts in the ground-level public spaces where the greatest number of original features have been retained. Thereafter, and progressively up through the building, the architectural language takes on an increasingly clinical aesthetic: on the second floor, the inserted elements containing central consultation rooms read as single rectilinear volumes in oak-veneered enclosures: on the third floor are diagnostic enclosures filled with digital mammography, ultrasound and biopsy equipment, clad in grey plastic laminate. As a means of addressing the important issue of wayfinding, the incorporation of clearly definable contemporary medical facilities within the restored shell of the old building was an early strategic design decision. It has proved to be extremely effective.

The intensive patient and staff consultation during early design stages resulted in several specific features, including a separate exit for patients for reasons of privacy and sensitivity in the event that they have received particularly distressing news; changing facilities and gowns so that patients do not have to undress and dress repeatedly between tests; a patient information/ resource room; yoga and relaxation courses; and a shop offering professional fittings for lingerie and swimwear appropriate for women who have undergone surgery for breast cancer.

The design team was appointed in the autumn of 2000, following which time the brief was developed iteratively in a process involving managers, clinicians, support staff and patient groups. The construction project was tendered during May 2002, with work starting during November 2002 under a traditional contract that placed overall responsibility and management of the construction with the client and the design team. The project was completed during April 2004, three weeks ahead of programme and within the contract sum.

Kings Mill Hospital, Sutton-in-Ashfield, Nottinghamshire

Client: Sherwood Forest Hospitals NHS Trust
PSC architect: David Morley Architects
Consortium architect: Swanke Hayden Connell
Consortium: Skanska Innesfree
Completion date: 2010
PSC capital cost: £175m
Capital investment
    by Preferred Bidder
    at FC: £300m

PSC typology: Predominantly Low Rise, as opposed to Unbundled

Healthcare activities at Kings Mill began during the Second World War when an American service hospital was established there. Many of its single-storey barrack-like buildings are still in use for patient services. The site subsequently underwent several episodes of major development between the 1960s and the early 1990s. New development spread eastward onto available land, and in one case to the south where a free-standing women's and children's centre – the Dukeries Centre – was built in the 1960s. The present configuration is characterised by long travel distances between departments along extensive hospital streets. Wayfinding, both from the site entrance to the various entrances and within the complex, is poor. Patient services are dispersed in a manner that does not support efficient delivery of care. For example, women's and children's services are spread across the campus, with many in the now run-down Dukeries Centre and others in distant locations.

The site, of approximately 54 acres, lies in a green swathe between the towns of Mansfield to the east and Sutton-in-Ashfield to the west. To the south, opposite the entrance, is a reservoir – a former gravel pit – after which the landscape rises to semi-wooded hills. To the north, agricultural

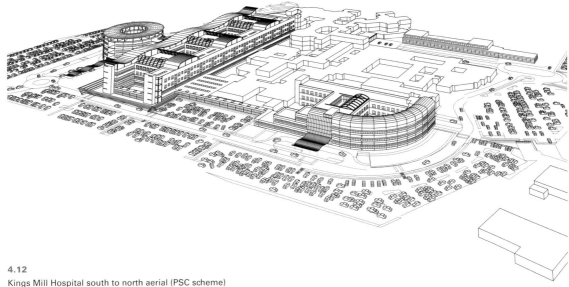

4.12
Kings Mill Hospital south to north aerial (PSC scheme)

137

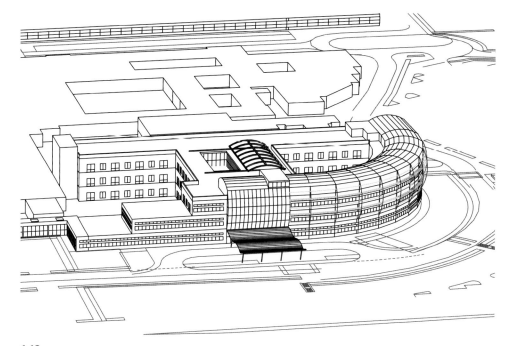

4.13
Entrance (PSC scheme)

fields rise to an escarpment and outlying neighbourhoods of Mansfield. The Trust is the biggest local employer in this former mining area, and the expansion of the hospital will reinforce its importance to the neighbouring communities.

The brief

The Trust had high and wide-ranging aspirations for the redevelopment of Kings Mill Hospital. The site was to be reconfigured as an efficient, clearly organised campus with strong civic presence. Services were to be co-located in new departments, principally in new buildings but also in some retained estate. Key elements of the clinical plan were a new women's and children's centre, a new DTC, an expanded education and training centre, an expanded and remodelled emergency care centre, 288 new acute inpatient beds in new high-quality wards, and a further 288 beds in upgraded retained wards. The existing theatre/X-ray/ICU complex located at the centre of the site was to be retained with minimal change.

The procurement process

The procurement of Kings Mill Hospital is notable because a new step was introduced into the PFI design development process. That new step saw the introduction of the 'Exemplar Design' – a method whereby a 'client side' architect and design team work with the client and other stakeholders early in the project to develop the brief and a conceptual design outside the time constraints of the PFI bidding process. The resulting exemplar design is then made available to the bidders as a benchmark of quality that they must equal or exceed. The concept was pioneered by the Northern Ireland Health Estates under John Cole, its director.

The exemplar design is a logical extension of the Public Sector Comparator (PSC) exercise which, in theory, should have been used to decide whether value for money would be better achieved by a public or a private finance route. Unfortunately the PSC was rarely carried through as a rigorous design exercise and reference schemes all too frequently received little design thought. The adoption of the Design Exemplar methodology at last offered the possibility for the client commissioning a major hospital development to make thorough preparations before going out to the market under PFI. Such opportunity was woefully lacking in the first waves of PFI projects.

On this project the client's extensive understanding of the design issues, its access to excellent designers, and a general raising of standards that was made possible by the exemplar exercise appears to have increased the quality of submissions and the quality of client judgement in selecting the winning bidder. Thereafter the successful PFI consortium greatly improved on the exemplar design because it was able to remove some of the constraints that the exemplar designers were working under.

The design response – PSC design exemplar

The design solution was arrived at through an option-appraisal process which explored all of the permutations for placing new clinical facilities around the retained surgical–diagnostic core and other retained facilities. The preferred design places a major new clinical facility – Block 1 – to the north of the core, and a new women's and children's centre – Block 2 – to the south. This arrangement achieves all of the key departmental adjacencies, and establishes a new main entrance at the north-west corner of the site. A third component – Block 3 – is placed to the east of the existing main entrance, and this brings all FM services under one roof adjacent to a new service yard. The location for Block 1 (which contains the DTC, education and training, main entrance and new inpatient wards) makes sense in terms of phasing, as this area is relatively clear of existing buildings and services. With the completion of Blocks 1 and 3, the site for Block 2 can be cleared and the development completed with a minimum of phasing and decanting. A key Trust requirement has been that clinical services move only once – that is, from their existing to their final locations.

The new site layout is based on a loop road principle with two entry points. This provides clear navigation around the site to the main and other entrances. Parking areas are distributed around the loop to the outside so that the visibility of buildings and entrances is not obscured by cars. Landscape is used to give specific characteristics to entrance zones.

Building typology for the principal new-build elements – Blocks 1 and 2 – was considered in relation to clinical suitability and site constraints. A key issue has been the need to accommodate both wards and outpatient clinics within the same template – for example, within Block 1 clinics occupy the two lower levels while wards are on the two upper levels. This is because the depth of the development site released around the surgical–diagnostic core has been limited by its proximity to the site boundary. To the south of the core, single-storey retained estate occupied the one potential development zone that could have accommodated a greater depth of development. It was this opportunity that the PFI consortium was able to exploit (see below).

A courtyard template was selected for its ability to support both inpatient wards and clinics. Detailed studies suggested that a 28.8 m × 28.8 m courtyard contained by four storeys would provide a good level of illumination at the ground level and also good daylight values to

4.14
Main entrance and single bedroom

surrounding rooms. This was improved by raking back to fourth floor and setting back plant rooms, which effectively formed a fifth floor. The floor plate depth between courtyards is also 28.8 m × 28.8 m, which was demonstrated to support back-to-back 24-bed wards and a wide range of DTC clinics. Along the edges, the template slims down to 14.4 m. The hospital street always runs along one edge of the courtyard so that it has external views and access to landscaped spaces at ground level. The template works well for both Block 1 and Block 2, even though the clinical planning requirements within the latter are much more varied – paediatric and obstetric inpatient and outpatient services. At the south-west corner of Block 2 the template has been modified to a curve to respond to the site geometry and views.

The design response – PFI consortium

Both bidders carried out initial analysis to identify the advantages and disadvantages of the three possible 'seams' along which new clinical facilities could be connected to the retained core. Their conclusions were different from the PSC (and from each other's), and both were made possible by the increased removal of existing estate to the south of the surgical–diagnostic core, an option that was not available to the PSC because of the constraints on public-sector funding.

The unsuccessful bidder placed their main new block to the west of the core, and their women's and children's centre to the south. The constraint of site depth was significantly more onerous to the west than to the north. This factor meant that they were unable to develop a block typology that comfortably integrated wards and clinics, and access to both. Courtyard sizes were compromised, and this adversely affected natural light levels. Furthermore, the western zone had severe phasing and decanting implications, rendering the implementation of the scheme more complicated than the PSC.

The preferred bidder, hereafter referred to as the Consortium, adopted a much bolder strategy – the complete removal of existing accommodation to the south of the core. This opened up huge potential, in terms of both site reorganisation and building typology, as a result of the increased development site width and depth. However, it was initially considered a risky approach, as the high capital cost could render the scheme unaffordable.

In terms of site organisation, the Consortium design has been based on the principle of separation of public and staff/service access prior to entry to the site. The site is zoned accordingly, with the public spaces, parking and new main entrance to the south, facing the reservoir, and the staff parking/access and service areas to the north. Vehicle movement between these zones is access-controlled to maintain staff parking capacity. Hence the scheme's utilisation of the two site entrances is very different from that of the PSC design, with correspondingly contrasting site zoning. It should be noted that this strategy has relied on a larger land take to the south of the site, and a more compact new-build development. The solution plays down the separate identity of the women's and children's centre. However, the numerous advantages clearly outweigh this initial limitation.

The building typology developed by the Consortium architects was, in their early proposals, similar to the PSC. A key difference, however, was that they brought the DTC clinics and other non-inpatient services (women's and children's) outboard into a two-storey building that stands in front of the six-storey courtyard block, a move that was made possible by the geometry of the development zone they had 'freed up'. Hence they were able to develop a floor plate for the clinics that is tailored to the needs of their particular uses – waiting reception areas and many small cellular spaces requiring natural light, and floor plate flexibility to respond to changes in clinic size and type.

The six-storey block, as noted above, was initially based on the PSC template, specifically replicating the ward layout, which the nursing teams liked very much. However, as the ward design developed, another major design initiative was adopted: the enclosed courtyard configuration was opened up to the south, and the template transformed to a series of 'T's. This has enabled all bedrooms to be provided with a view to the south, rather than only a third of them as in the PSC (with two-thirds looking onto the courtyards).

Notwithstanding the undoubted benefit to quality of outlook from bedrooms, the new 'T' template imposes a much more linear layout for each 24-bed nursing unit, and less flexibility to integrate single and four-bed rooms. Positioning of and observation from the two nurse bases became a long-standing issue for the nursing teams. The Consortium eventually reached a satisfactory configuration with the nurse bases located at each end of the unit (each end of a linear array of bedrooms) with only the isolation room around a corner away from direct observation.

The template developed for the DTC and other clinics was based on 'fingers' of linear two-storey blocks with top-lit semi-landscaped spaces between. This arrangement has provided a high level of flexibility and excellent patient orientation. The design is considered highly innovative, providing a distinctive environment suited to the principles of rapid and 'hassle-free' access implicit in the DTC concept.

Evelina Children's Hospital, London

Client:	Guy's and St Thomas' NHS Foundation Trust
Architect:	Hopkins Architects
Completion:	2005
Cost:	£41.8m
Area:	16,500 m^2
Procurement route:	Design and build

Typology: Predominately Atrium/Galleria over Street

This building reflects the client's determination to obtain the highest-quality design and involved an RIBA design competition – the first and, so far, only such competition for a hospital building. The result is an imaginative and skilful response to a very constrained site. A huge conservatory embracing the upper three of six levels forms the social heart of the building and is key to the overall design, affording magnificent views and allowing daylight to flood all the way down to the wide, axially planned concourse on the ground floor. Specially commissioned artworks help to make the environment as *unlike* a conventional hospital as possible.

One intent of the competition was to give a fresh view to hospital design. Never having designed a hospital before, and working with a specialist hospital planner (RKW Healthcare), the architects set out with the aim of improving the patient, staff and visitor experience. They have transposed their experience in other building sectors to respond to the need for functional efficiency and adaptable layouts while at the same time creating spaces for social interaction – 'a place for people'. Throughout, structure and services are flexible, and prefabricated components have been used as much as possible to give maximum opportunity for future changes. Natural materials, ventilation, daylighting and external views have been used for their ecological and health benefits. Circulation spaces rather than corridors have been incorporated where possible to minimise the institutional hospital feel. Continuing this theme, and to simplify wayfinding, each storey is colour coded and artist-designed images have been used for signage.

Typologically, Evelina Children's Hospital is a variant on the atrium form combined with the device of placing three ward floors above three treatment and diagnostic floors. The lower three levels each consist of two parallel blocks either side of a concourse (forming the 'floor' of the atrium) while on the upper three levels the westerly block is replaced by the conservatory, in effect extending the atrium to the very edge of the building. The result is that there are unusually large amounts of daylight in the building and fantastic views out, with the added bonus of additional space being provided that was not conceived in the brief.

The Guy's and St Thomas' Charitable Foundation decided to contribute a major capital grant towards the construction of the new children's hospital with the significant qualification that architectural quality and innovation must be achieved in the design. The brief required a new building to accommodate all 'inpatient facilities' for children served by the Trust to be provided under one roof for the first time. This included a new, rapid diagnostic centre speeding up the diganosis and treatment of unwell children.

The competition organisers invited a shortlist of practices to take part in return for an honorarium. Designs were put on public display for comment and, following interviews, the preferred design team was selected to develop the scheme design to RIBA work stage E. The team was subsequently novated to the chosen contractor.

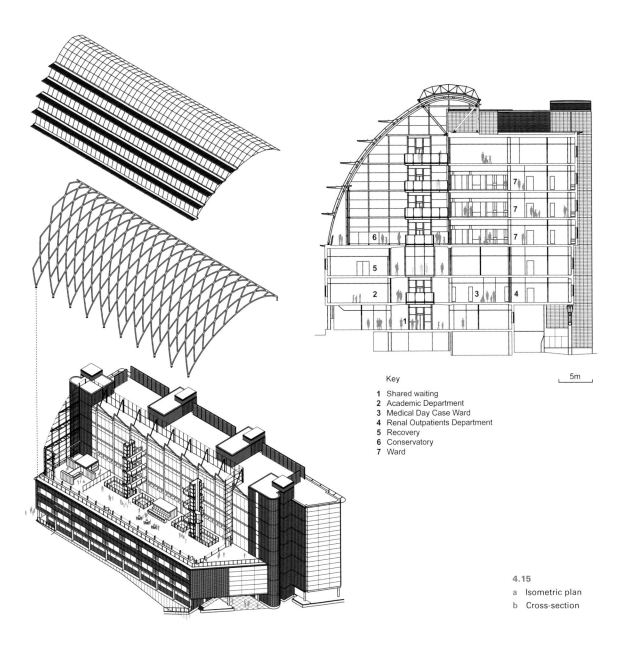

Key   5m

1 Shared waiting
2 Academic Department
3 Medical Day Case Ward
4 Renal Outpatients Department
5 Recovery
6 Conservatory
7 Ward

4.15
a   Isometric plan
b   Cross-section

The site provided a logical location in which to extend acute facilities, of which the Evelina was a part, and the design responds clearly to the site's proximity to the Archbishop's Garden in neighbouring Lambeth Palace. The grounds act as a landscaped focus in the heart of an intensely urban backdrop and, in a very nice touch, this, the largest private garden in London apart from that at Buckingham Palace, has been made available for day use to families and children at the Evelina.

The atrium houses the Evelina school and a café, and provides a meeting space for patients and family, as well as an occasional performance area. Because it admits huge amounts of

4.16
Exterior of Evelina Children's Hospital

natural light, the conservatory provides a therapeutic and healing environment that responds to its young patients' identified needs for a space that is not 'like a hospital' and which affords them the feeling of being outside in the fresh air even when that is not possible. Because it collects solar warmth in winter and can be naturally ventilated by stack effect in summer, the atrium helps to regulate the indoor air-quality as well as offering relief from hospital routine and treatment.

Entrances to the wards open immediately onto a reception and play area and are opposite the boldly coloured glazed passenger lifts that rise through the atrium from the lower concourse. The wards have open-plan social and day areas overlooking the conservatory, while single rooms face north on the other side of a strip of nurses' stations and service areas. The number of medical and surgical beds can be expanded or contracted in response to varying demands. The architects have introduced highly transparent glazed screens and partitions, even around theatres, where privacy when required can be achieved by the use of louvre blinds within a double-glazed panel. This pursuit of openness and transparency makes maximum use of the light and views provided by the conservatory and is an integral part of the building's appeal.

With its clear, rational, plan and section, the building is very 'legible' and easy to navigate. Orientation and wayfinding are aided by the floors having been 'themed' in terms of interior design: the ground floor has an ocean theme while those above are, in turn, arctic, forest, beach, savannah, mountain and sky. This concept is continued into the lifts by means of relevant symbols on the lift buttons.

Community interest throughout the design process has been key to this project's success. As an ongoing commitment to consultation and patient involvement, the Trust has established a children's board that, among other things, selected and chose furniture and assists with the ongoing management of the hospital school.

The recently completed spaces for setting down and the public entrance to this significant building ensure that patients do not have to use the busy Lambeth Palace Road. The addition of a covered walkway joining the new building to the main hosptial, and the refurbishment and cleaning of the main hospital's eastern elevation (which forms the 'rear' of the Evelina building), have greatly improved the relation of the new architecture to the old campus. In doing so the project team has set the highest standards in terms of detailing specification, build quality and architectural ambition.

4.17
Interior of Evelina Children's Hospital

Norfolk and Norwich University Hospital, Norwich

Client:	Norfolk and Norwich University Hospital Trust
Architect:	Anshen Dyer
PFI consortium:	Octagon/Laing O'Rourke
Cost:	£180m
Area:	100,000 m², with 953 beds and 4,500 rooms
Procurement route:	PFI

Typology: Predominantly Unbundled

This new hospital replaced an old and dilapidated facility in the centre of Norwich through the culmination of a long programme of estates' rationalisation. The decision to relocate to a greenfield site on the outskirts of the city was pragmatic: much of the hospital's patient catchment area is rural and dispersed throughout Norfolk and north Suffolk, to the extent that encouraging, through location, the maximisation of public transport usage was not considered to be a significant goal. The site is adjacent to the University of East Anglia and its burgeoning science park, which offered enhanced opportunities for the hospital to engage in education and research. Most importantly, the size and location of the site enabled the Trust to create a model hospital within a masterplan that was uncompromised by site constraints.

The resulting design is outstanding for its clarity of concept, made possible by its greenfield setting. However, the 'out of town' location also generates some transport difficulties and inevitably increases reliance on private care usage. It also, arguably, represents a missed opportunity in terms of town centre regeneration and the further exploration of the challenges of incorporating contemporary large-scale hospital projects within the historic fabric of the city. The location, size and disposition of the site has encouraged a relatively pure model of hospital planning to be adopted within an uncompromised architectural solution upon a specifically created campus. The link between the clinical planning and the completed building has an architectural clarity that elevates this project to exemplar status. The project was the first PFI hospital scheme to reach contract stage and the largest of the first wave schemes. Thus the completed NNUH provides an excellent opportunity to assess the strengths and weaknesses of this procurement method, the soundness of client preparation, and the design capabilities of the profession.

The new hospital serves a population of 480,300 for secondary and 900,000 for tertiary care. The initial brief was based on 701 beds. During the late design stage the number was increased to 850 beds and a further 100 were added during construction when it became clear that the earlier bed numbers had been based on a level of 'migration' of care from the DGH to primary/ intermediate care that could not be achieved.

The hospital is organised on a very clear matrix pattern, setting out three distinct zones of clinical activity – ambulatory care, diagnostic and treatment, and inpatient accommodation – which run in parallel banks of accommodation from east to west. Clinical groupings cross these zones from north to south and create identifiable centres for women and children, inpatient surgery and medical specialties. The three bands of clinical activity have been designed differently in terms of form, depth of plan, and column grid to respond to their separate and quite distinct functions. The detailed planning of the clinical areas has managed to retain and reinforce this initial diagram.

4.18
Norfolk and Norwich University Hospital inpatient entrance

4.19
Norfolk and Norwich University Hospital exterior
and interior

By creating specific clinical groupings, this model also allows multiple points of access, obviating the need for a single entrance and a monumental atrium or gallery. The principal points of non-emergency access have been placed at the north for ambulatory care and the south for inpatient accommodation. These major entrances at the north and south are connected by two atria that run the full width of the hospital and are, in turn, connected laterally by hospital streets. The three parallel zones of the matrix follow the curves of the site's contours – a geometry made possible by the two wedge-shaped plan forms of the atria.

The northerly band of outpatient and ambulatory care functions is located in three-storey interlinked pavilions that maximise the perimeter in their plan form to exploit natural light and ventilation.

The central band of diagnostic and treatment facilities contains non-clinical support services and the cancer centre at its lowest level, with imaging, day case and emergency care on the next level, and the theatres and critical care above. There is a clear gradation of clinical activity from 'hot' emergency care at the eastern end to the more planned activities of the west. This band is open-ended and capable of expansion.

The southern band of inpatient accommodation is arranged in four sets of linked ward pavilions of three and four storeys in height, creating a rational model and rhythmic set of architectural forms.

The triple banding in this matrix has a number of distinct advantages over the more common separation of the hospital into two clinical components – patient zone, and diagnostic and

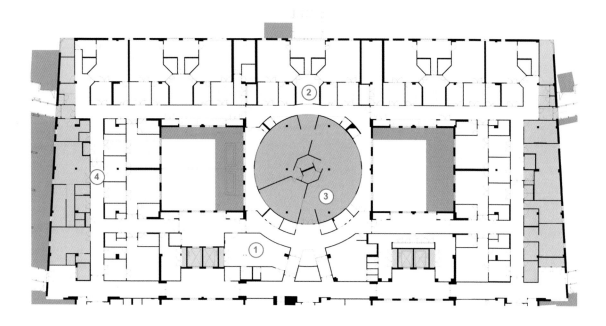

Inpatient Surgery

1   Pre-Op Holding
2   Twin Theatre Suite
3   Post-Anaesthesia Recovery
4   Anaesthetic Department

4.20
Norfolk and Norwich University Hospital plan: surgical theatre suite

treatment – arranged either as a D&T plinth with wards above (the French 'plateau technique') or a D&T spine and separate patient zone often joined by a galleria or atrium. The matrix model is more function-specific and adaptable without losing architectural form, allows the inpatient accommodation to stack without compromise, and achieves a richer mix of elements.

Internally, the atria offer a quality and scale of space that are appropriate to a hospital environment in their proportion and their detail and avoid the retail mall/airport associations more commonly experienced in modern hospitals.

The internal design of the ward pavilions works very well in terms of layout, legibility and positioning of staff bays and the external views from internal areas, and brings an American 'ambience' to the scheme with the patient rooms wrapping around a central support zone. The full-height windows within the bays look south over the landscape.

Externally, the architects have used a calm and understated palette of materials without resorting to ruthless repetition or mundane pragmatism. Brickwork with punched openings predominates, offset by white attic window sections and the curtain walling of the glazed ends of the atria. The pyramidal roofs of the ambulatory and ward blocks are clad in stainless steel and set up a rhythm that reinforces the notion of the hospital being a series of linked pavilions. There has been extensive investment in the landscape of the hospital campus, which, when mature, will provide an excellent frame for these well-scaled buildings. (The Hospital Trust invested in planting 5,000 trees when the site was purchased, demonstrating real commitment on their part.)

In conclusion, the architecture of the NNUH displays an ambition that sets it apart from other first-wave PFI hospitals. It lies on the right side of that fine line between intelligent sobriety and banality and, in the main, achieves its aims.

Some issues for further consideration

Context

Wider awareness is required in terms of the 'Triple E' agenda (economic, environmental and ecological sustainability): the need to plan work through more careful collaboration with wider interest groups – for example, with local bus companies, and with the relevant highways departments, in relation to issues of accessibility and public transportation.

Understanding the potential opportunities and problems of a site

It is important to think clearly around the relevant local authority's development control plans and consult the local development plans. Initiatives should be posited in the context of a 10-year review with further horizons at 15 and 20 years. New building proposals within established hospital sites should also be seen within an existing setting that is qualified in terms of the planned future retention or redevelopment of adjoining building stock. How will this stage of the hospital's redevelopment relate to, or accommodate, future anticipated, but as yet unplanned, phases? The creation of a meaningful (even if loose) long-term masterplan is encouraged to avoid the inevitable compromises that arise from poorly planned incremental development.

- A wider policy of seeing building proposals within the context of their setting among other buildings both existing and planned should be encouraged.
- New work should be planned within a comprehensive larger architectural 'landscape'.

For these reasons, it is particularly important that all proposals are based on a thorough analysis in terms of a site's essential characteristics including *long views* to and from the site.

The common tendency to compromise long-term outcomes through short-term constraints should be avoided (for example, the compromising of the design quality of new buildings through the retention of existing facilities which will soon become redundant).

Massing and scale

Great care is needed in the development of design briefs – whether for the centralisation of hitherto dispersed facilities onto one large hospital campus or for the dispersal of a variety of functions into smaller district facilities. Avoiding over-development – with respect to both the amount of accommodation proposed for a site, and the relationship of the proposals to the surrounding areas in terms of mass and scale – is crucial.

This latter comment relates particularly to suburban areas where proposals have themselves taken on a suburban character leading to low-rise sprawling campus arrangements. Better to consider more compact buildings, where appropriate, over basement car parks than to set low-rise facilities among a vast sea of car parking.

Generic character

The drive towards single, and often huge, deep-plan buildings, with a heavy reliance on artificial light and environmental servicing, appears to be led by a demand for immediate clinical adjacencies.

However, it is clear that the 'deep plan agenda' would benefit from further challenge and research. This means, firstly, the exploration of models that provide adequate and appropriate adjacencies while incorporating more external courtyards and landscaping; and, secondly, a prioritisation of essential adjacencies within otherwise more dispersed and independent buildings.

Movement and people processing

How people access hospitals is a key concern. Sophisticated 'receiving' and 'processing' arrangements are required. In this respect lessons can be learnt from airports (Stansted), railway stations (Paddington and St Pancras) and arcades (Leeds and Milano Galleria), where multiple entrances and a wide range of receptions for different information and destination requirements exist. Wayfinding is easier in such facilities, and ambient temperatures (with local adjustment) can be set to suit both stationary (waiting) and moving conditions.

It seems, therefore, that within our new hospital buildings issues of 'inside' and 'outside' need to be explored more carefully through alternative models that allow for deeper penetration of the facility before screening and processing of patients and visitors begins in earnest. 'Halfway houses' comprising colonnades and part-covered courtyards may offer interesting solutions.

Overall, it seems that a closer collaboration and better understanding is required between the four main groups who drive hospital design briefs and design outcomes – clinicians, medical planners, architects and estate/facility managers.

Internal environments

There is a greater need for:

- internal rooms to have access to outside space (e.g. terraces off wards);
- natural ventilation in rooms and waiting areas;
- better wayfinding and improved development of identifiable 'nodes' (i.e. recognisable places within the matrix of circulation);
- adequately sized light wells and courtyards in which landscaping can flourish;
- planning to take advantage of interesting views; and
- avoiding excessive light contrasts/solar gain problems through inappropriate use of atria and glazed links.

Ecological sustainability

In the wider architectural field there has been some refreshingly innovative work in this area, and awareness of the importance of this issue is clearly growing.

However, with respect to new healthcare buildings, there has been too little evidence of any in-depth approach to ecologically responsible design. Lip service is all too often given to the agenda of ecologically responsible design with little or no evidence of its being applied to design or specification.

For our children's children's sake, we must do better now ...

CHAPTER FIVE

European hospital design

SUSAN FRANCIS

Susan Francis, a UK architect who has devoted much of her career to researching health environments, identifies three major themes running through the best current continental European thinking on hospital design: the relationship of the hospital and the city; the belief that the environment can play an active therapeutic role; and the rapid developments in technology, including IT. She identifies a number of recent hospital projects that point to the future, particularly in the first two of these areas. There is a growing realisation that the more overtly architectural concerns of place-making and of design as a response to feelings rather than only physical function have been neglected in hospital design. As a result, healthcare efforts have been denied some powerful means of promoting healthcare. Accommodating modern technology remains of paramount importance, but there is at least a considerable track record of innovation in building design – one that is being sustained in hospitals such as the Marzahn Hospital in Berlin with its wholehearted embrace of the digital future that is already here.

A major side effect of the rapid development of technology is the raised importance of flexibility and adaptability. There is widespread concern that hospital buildings built today will be obsolete unless design can somehow enshrine an unprecedented agility. It is clear that adaptability as understood to date in hospitals cannot possibly cater for the healthcare future anticipated by many, including Francis in her work with Rosemary Glanville on 2020, *Building a 2020 Vision: Future Health Care Environments* (London: The Stationery Office, 2001), which envisages a greatly reduced role for today's hospital. Instead, we have much to learn from the way cities survive and thrive through wholesale changes in society and the way certain traditional buildings appear capable of serving radically different functions through their thus extended lives.

Introduction

Hospital design in Europe has a rich and varied history and an understanding of the link between hospital designs and their socio-political context is hardly new. Despite the differences in culture, healthcare systems and regulations for infrastructure investment, the trends in design principles are becoming increasingly similar with greater emphasis emerging on the relationship of hospitals to the town or city, the importance of the healing environment and the impact of technological developments on the processes and the buildings that house them.

The link between the socio-political context of hospitals and their physical form is articulated in a comparative study of hospitals from seven European countries.[1] Historical developments, from monastic infirmaries through to modern hospitals, show how changes of emphasis in social and economic factors and developments in medical science are reflected in the physical design of hospitals.

The development of hospital form is illustrated from medieval hospices as places for care and charity, through the growth of science and medicine provided in machines for ventilation and public health, and the emergence of the modern technical hospital with its emphasis on functional efficiency, to the contemporary concerns for the healing environment and integration of hospitals into the city fabric. The movement of ideas and trends across Europe is captured in a set of building typologies and illustrated chronologically through exemplar projects from each country.

The increasing emphasis on the importance of the individual and a view of the patient as a citizen temporarily hospitalised is acknowledged. This is concurrent with the development of the hospital as an arrangement of compact, multiple volumes interwoven into the urban fabric. The pre-eminence of natural light and the logic of networks is generating an internal organisation around the public spaces, which accommodate the interface between the city and the hospital, and the patient/citizen and the medical community.

The potential of architecture as one of the key instruments to improve the functioning of hospitals is another current concern. An international chronology of hospital design developed in the Netherlands analyses hospital architecture as part of a drive to develop an evidence base for design with the intention of reintegrating hospital architecture into contemporary debates on architecture in general.[2] Acknowledging the interface of medicine, management and design in a wider social and political context, the study includes an extensive illustrated survey of European and American designs for hospitals from the nineteenth century to the present day. A database of European projects illustrating examples of good practice and identifying design quality indicators has been commissioned by the Design Working Group of the EU Health Property Network (EUHPN), a group of bodies representing governmental organisations across Europe.[3] The database aims to develop a common understanding and language by which to compare and appreciate designs from different countries.

This chapter does not aim to give a comprehensive account of historical or contemporary hospital design in Europe but rather to select projects that illustrate key design issues, namely the integration of the hospital with the city, the humanising of the environment, and technical sophistication and sustainability. Examples are drawn from the Netherlands, Norway, France, Sweden, Germany and Belgium.

A brief summary of key aspects of the health system in each country and reference to trends in building infrastructure in selected countries in Europe give some background. The main design issues are discussed, and this is followed by brief descriptions of each project presented by country.

Selected European health systems

Understanding how health systems operate is a complex subject in its own right. This short summary merely sketches out key aspects of the systems that affect the design of the buildings for the six selected countries. Information has been drawn largely from discussions at the EUHPN and a publication giving comparative data on healthcare systems prepared by the

EU Observatory on Healthcare Systems,[4] and a study of inpatient accommodation identifying European case studies.[5]

There are two main systems by which the overall healthcare service is financed in Europe: social health insurance and taxation, sometimes referred to as Bismarck or Bevan systems respectively. The healthcare system in Sweden is financed by taxation and is relatively decentralised; Norway is funded through taxation with some payments; Belgium is financed through both tax levy and insurance contributions; Germany and the Netherlands are financed by social insurance contributions combined with private insurance for high earners; France is highly centralised and funding is based on social health insurance for universal coverage with a mixture of public and private providers.

The Netherlands

There are three main elements to the Dutch healthcare system: public universal insurance for so-called exceptional medical expenses, which include long-stay care, mental health, etc; compulsory social health insurance for low-income earners and voluntary private health insurance for high-income earners; and voluntary supplementary insurance open to all. The system provides for the whole population and is funded from sickness funds and private insurance companies.

Most hospitals are private, not-for-profit organisations whose budgets are fixed by the government to ensure compliance with government policy. The government plans and approves capacity and distribution of services. Nearly all hospitals include outpatient and inpatient facilities. The providers of diagnostic services are all private organisations and they may be located in either ambulatory or secondary care settings.

Primary care is provided largely by GPs who are mainly independent and are the central gatekeepers to the system. Insured persons are free to register with the GP of their choice. The Netherlands has a high proportion of care for the elderly in nursing homes and psychiatric and medical hospitals.

Sweden

The responsibility for health and social care in Sweden is mainly devolved to the county councils, and long-term care is devolved further to the municipalities. The state is responsible for overall policy-making and supervises health services. The majority of funding comes from county council taxes (municipal, county and parish taxes) supplemented by grants from the national government.

Patients can choose their first contact care providers: they can choose between primary care centres and hospital outpatient departments, and can also choose to use a private physician or clinic as first contact care. Ambulatory care is provided by a mix of public (salaried) doctors, private doctors and hospital outpatient departments. Basic diagnostic and laboratory services are provided within primary health centres, and more specialised services in public hospitals.

Germany

The responsibilities for health are shared between the federal government, the local regions, or *Länder,* and corporate bodies (representative bodies of the professionals, the providers and the insurers). The overall legal framework is set by the federal government and the local regions are responsible for hospital planning and investment. Each region produces its own standards. The healthcare system is predominantly funded through social health insurance contributions.

Ambulatory care, including both primary care and outpatient secondary care, is provided by office-based physicians. There is almost no outpatient activity in hospitals. Polyclinics for day treatments, diagnostic services and consultations offer almost all specialties with a range of technical equipment including MRI scanners.

In Germany patients are free to select a doctor of their choice and there is no gatekeeping system.

France

Healthcare is predominantly funded through social health insurance contributions from employers and employees and tax revenues. Healthcare is purchased and paid for by health insurance schemes and the government and is provided by private (self-employed) practitioners and public and private (non-profit and for-profit) hospitals.

French patients can choose both their primary care doctor and their hospital. They can visit any GP or specialist practising privately or working in hospital outpatient departments, without referral.

About half of all primary and outpatient care is delivered by doctors, dentists and medical auxiliaries working in their own practices. Outpatient diagnostic and laboratory services are provided by specialists in private practice and hospital outpatient departments.

Norway

The health system in Norway is funded mainly through taxation. In addition, patients pay a nominal fee for each consultation or visit, which has a fixed ceiling for those in need of significant amounts of hospital care.

All hospitals are responsible to the Ministry of Health and Care. They are funded through fixed budgets from the county. Individual private clinicians are contracted to the hospitals and private clinics for specialist and acute medical care. GPs provide primary and home care.

Belgium

Healthcare is provided by both public and private sectors. GPs, dentists and specialists have their own private practices. Public bodies organise and finance preventative and curative schemes such as school and occupational health, outpatient, mental and prenatal health.

Patients can choose their health insurance company, GP, specialist and hospital. Payment is mainly on a fee-for-service basis and is largely financed through compulsory health insurance.

Hospitals are owned by the private sector (mostly not-for-profit) or the public sector through social assistance centres run by the communes. Hospitals receive investment subsidies that require them to conform to standards set by the Ministry of Health.

Building infrastructure

The ways in which authorities control and influence the building or use of infrastructure vary across Europe. This can be measured in three ways: the extent to which the property is owned by government or others; who bears the cost of building and maintenance of infrastructure and the way these projects are financed; and to what extent authorities use planning and regulatory or incentive measures to control quantity and geographical distribution of, and costs involved with, infrastructure.

In a study of selected EU countries (Belgium, Germany, Sweden, Austria, UK, Denmark, Spain and France), the findings show that in six out of the eight countries the government owns more than 60% of the healthcare property.[6] However, in Belgium and Germany the government owns less than half the infrastructure; and in the Netherlands the government does not own any of the healthcare infrastructure since it is owned by non-profit-making trust foundations. The UK and Sweden have the highest percentage of property owned by the government. In the two largest countries, Germany and France, about one-fifth of the bed capacity is operated by private-for-profit hospitals.

The extent to which government authorities contribute towards the costs of infrastructure varies widely: it is almost nil in the Netherlands and France, but 100% by provincial authorities in Denmark. In Germany, Sweden and Denmark, hospital infrastructure is in many cases completely financed by the authorities provided the hospitals comply with certain rules. (It is similar for 94% of the hospitals in the UK and for all hospitals located in 10 of the 17 autonomous regions in Spain. In these countries, public private funding is more common.)

The findings show that countries that finance their health property investments through taxation are looking for other funding sources, mostly through public private financing initiatives. The way this is done varies across Europe and in a sense the systems are becoming more similar in the way that health infrastructure is financed and procured.

Trends in hospital design

There are three key design issues that are currently being widely developed in Europe: the integration of the hospital into the city, the humanising of the environment, and the increasing sophistication of technology in communications and sustainability.

The hospital and the city

One of the key issues for the planning of hospitals is location – many of the hospitals designed in the late twentieth century were concerned with reorganising services to make a comprehensive service in one place, and through rationalisation they brought many services onto one site to improve safety and efficiency. This is one of the underlying principles of the general hospital. With major redevelopments this often entailed rebuilding on new sites away from the city centre. It was an approach that had many advantages, not least that it enabled the construction of new buildings to take place with the minimum of disruption to existing services, provided adequate room for expansion and avoided many of the inevitable compromises entailed in developing existing constrained sites. This rationale led to the development of out-of-town campus sites that required special transport, extensive car parking – for staff and patients – and the dislocation of a major public building to a place remote from the city centre.

With the recent shift in thinking about urban regeneration and city centre renewal from a broader planning perspective, there is a move away from the out-of-town campus locations to the consideration of city centre sites. This is part of a broader emphasis on urban revitalisation, sustainable transport, and greater density permitted in urban locations. It has given rise to the

5.1
Aerial view of St Olav's Hospital, Trondheim

idea of planning hospital locations in inner city sites where the hospital is part of the city and the city part of the hospital.

Hospital buildings are becoming more fragmented in nature, with buildings broken into smaller volumes that correspond to and acknowledge the texture of the local neighbourhood. St Olave's Hospital in Trondheim, for example, is designed as a series of pavilions that are similar to the city centre blocks, making it like a medical city within the city as a whole.

The Hospital in Groningen in the Netherlands has extensive public space including facilities for shopping, conferences and entertainment. The building is more permeable as it opens to become part of the city amenities. It offers a civic space to be enjoyed by local people as part of the city rather than as a hospital.

The setting for the Riks Hospital in Oslo is a city square with a tower to denote the main entrance. Similar in layout to an Italian town square, it provides a civic and public place where

5.2
Entrance to Groningen Hospital
5.3
Entrance to Riks Hospital, Oslo

people can meet and gather, just to sit and watch, as they go in and out of the building. It makes a dignified entrance to the building with a positive connection to the outside while also giving a clear approach to the front door.

In contrast, the approach to the De Bijtjes rehabilitation hospital in Belgium, converted from a manor house, is formal and grand. The entrance is through extensively landscaped grounds leading to the historic building. It is imposing but charming and offers a proud setting for the hospital. The new extension is gracefully planned to offer good wheelchair access for patients and visitors and makes full use of the landscaped park that surrounds the hospital with its ornamental lake and woods. Clearly the landscaping is an important part of the setting and patients are encouraged by the design of the hospital to enjoy it to the full.

The Bretonneau Hospital in Paris, now a nursing home, includes a series of new pavilions that complement the existing buildings and correspond to the scale and form of the surrounding city blocks. On the outside, the blocks fit tightly with the building line, creating a taut boundary between the hospital and the street. On the inside, charming gardens make secluded spaces between the carefully crafted blocks, bringing together old and new.

The Georges Pompidou Hospital in Paris is designed to join together two key parts of the locality through the hospital mall. In this way, the hospital has become a connector rather than a building that divides the neighbourhood. The overall form of the hospital is broken down into blocks of varying heights to give it a sense of scale that acknowledges the surrounding buildings.

The Isala Clinic at Zwolle in the Netherlands follows a similar pattern of disaggregating the hospital into many parts. It has further developed these formal aspects of the design by generating an organic form and texture that provide a unifying treatment for the overall development. It is unusual and inventive, and by pulling apart the hospital into several blocks joined by glazed walkways, the design enables the planning to be efficient while also bringing natural light to and permitting views from the inside.

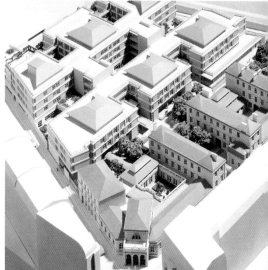

5.4
De Bijtjes Rehabilitation Hospital, Belgium
5.5
The Bretonneau Hospital, Paris
5.6
Georges Pompidou Hospital, Paris

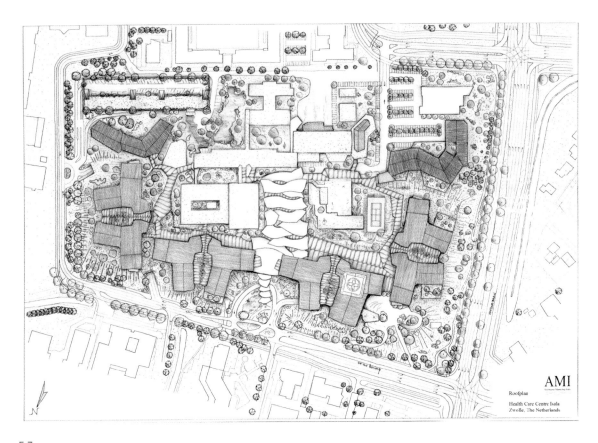

5.7
The Isala Clinic at Zwolle

Humanistic environments

The notion that the environment can contribute to the healing process is now well understood
and the extent to which this is so has become the focus of significant international research
studies. First impressions are known to be important in setting the tone of patients' feelings
about their experiences in hospitals, and architecture plays a major role in creating a good and
positive ambience.

The street at the Riks Hospital not only performs an essential function in terms of logistics
and functionality but is also a positive and uplifting place where people meet informally to
exchange information about staff and patient matters. Designing the street to have places
of contrasting atmosphere avoids the sense of monotony that the length might otherwise
engender; linking the themes to the external surroundings helps to further establish the building
in its local setting.

Common to many of the hospitals is a clear hierarchy of spaces that distinguishes between
formal public spaces and confidential private spaces for clinical treatments. Entrances give
onto malls, atria or streets of significant scale and formality to provide space for shopping,
information and cultural events. It is this generosity of space that breathes new life into the
hospital and connects the scientific endeavours to a more holistic and humanistic sensitivity.

The entrance to Bollnas Hospital in Sweden is made obvious by the vernacular decoration of the surfaces. It leads onto a main circulation space well lit by natural light to which the double-height volume gives importance. Informal places to sit are created here using curved seating to create intimacy. A library open to the main circulation provides a remarkable facility for patients, visitors and staff who can withdraw into the high-backed settles to enjoy reading.

The open day space within the ward at Norrtalje Hospital in Sweden is a surprising and delightful gesture. Creating social spaces where people can carry out ordinary activities helps to normalise the environment and support people in discussing their circumstances. Also, the creation of a larger space open to the ward corridor helps to connect the internal world to the outside, especially where the bedrooms have closed doors.

Creating an internal environment that is stimulating to the senses is a common theme. Theories drawn from anthroposophic principles of colour and texture have been applied in a sophisticated way at Norrtalje Hospital. The delicacy of the pastel paint colours in the wards, the distinctive and stimulating flooring patterns in the intensive care units and the decorative panels in the lift lobbies create special places refined according to their function but within a unified design concept.

Many of the European hospitals have integrated arts programmes, and countries such as Norway and the Netherlands have a commitment to allocating a percentage of the overall budget to the arts in public buildings. With the opportunity to develop the arts programmes as part of the design process, the buildings are able to incorporate the artwork to achieve design aims such as easing intuitive wayfinding.

The hospital in Groningen invited designers to compete for the internal decoration of the outpatient clinics. Each was of similar layout and they now have themed decor to complement their functions. The cardiology clinic, for example, has bright red sculptural lights in the shape of hearts. It is both clever and fun, and helps to distinguish and identify otherwise identical clinics.

Technical sophistication and sustainability

An overriding concern of modern hospital development is ensuring that buildings can respond to future change. Flexibility and future-proofing are not new ideas but there are now some additional requirements. As well as having to grow and change, hospitals may need to be 'elastic' and be able to flex in various parts, and perhaps overall, and become smaller over time. These ideas are driven both by developments in medical science (for example, the potential for more ambulatory care through less interventional and more sophisticated techniques) and through management (for example, the possibility of centralising and standardising certain functions while devolving others to a more local place or to a different organisation).

Flexibility is being considered at several levels:

- at the level of the site, for the overall building site plan to be able to extend or contract;
- for the structure, to allow for internal changes to the volume of the building with minimal disruption;
- for spaces of a similar kind, such as beds and consulting rooms, to be clustered together to enable flexible management of the room uses;
- to standardise more room sizes and reduce the overall number of room types to enable different uses of the same volumes over time;
- for the management of space as a resource, not territory, so that rooms are designated by activity rather than to individual practitioners.

These ideas are ever more important for a health system that is undergoing rapid and unpredictable change.

The endeavour to make paperless and filmless hospitals is being pursued across Europe and the availability of equipment and systems is within a European-wide market. However, the levels of investment and priority for these installations vary from one project to another. The integration of IT systems for information, communication and diagnostics is affecting the overall planning of the hospitals by giving greater emphasis to networked links than to physical adjacencies. It is possible that some administrative and support services can be efficiently provided off site, that conventional requirements for proximity between departments can be relaxed, and even that the overall scale of the hospital can be reduced. The introduction of robotics to assist with logistics has been developed in some European hospitals. The separation of flows for supplies from that of staff and patients often leads to basement floors with mechanised distribution systems in robotic tugs for anything from food and linen to drugs and equipment.

Each country has its own regulations determining space standards and construction. There are variations between them driven by historic and cultural sensitivities. While there is, for example, an overriding trend to provide more single rooms to meet consumer demands and greater expectations of privacy, and improved standards of infection control, the size of bedrooms and clustering of shared wards does vary: the preference for multi-bed arrangements in Sweden is for three, in Germany for two, and in the Netherlands for four.

Several of the hospital wards have staff bases or workstations that are open to the corridor. While this is not especially new for the UK, it does seem to be a recent development in several European countries such as Norway and Sweden.

Sustainability has yet to evolve fully in hospital design and some European countries are leading the way. There is a general commitment to energy saving with judicious use of mechanical air handling, combined heat and power systems, and a greater emphasis on natural light and ventilation. The recycling of materials is further developed in Sweden where specification of floor finishes, for example, has to take into account future disposal.

Hospital projects – Case studies

The Netherlands

Groningen University Hospital (AZG)

Architect:	Original architect: Kruisheer, then Kleinjan; Patijn during the final stages
Client:	AZG
Date:	1997
Area:	232,000 m²

Groningen is a university hospital combined with the faculty of medical sciences of the University of Groningen. The hospital provides general, specialist and tertiary care, including organ transplants, neonatology, clinical genetics, complex neurosurgery, IVF, child oncology, renal dialysis and trauma.

5.8
Groningen Hospital entrance

5.9
Groningen Hospital reception

The original hospital building dates from 1902 and was a pavilion structure with each speciality housed in its own building. Discussions about re-organising the hospital started in the 1950s. The first concept for the new building was to make a series of separate clinic buildings around a centralised diagnostic and treatment core. However, in the late 1980s the concept changed and it was decided to make one building, to cover over the bridges and to extend the front. This reduced the number of entrances from 59 to one. Over a period of 17 years the hospital has undergone a total renewal on the same site. Further changes are being undertaken to the underground car park and bunkers for radiology.

A new organisational concept for the hospital, which will cluster medical specialties to work in interdisciplinary teams, is currently being reviewed. Recently, 200 multi-disciplinary working groups have been considering how to reorganise services and space. This is expected to result in, say, four or five small hospitals within the overall complex.

The hospital is one of seven university hospitals in the Netherlands. It is exploring new relationships with small hospitals nearby and thinking of linking special services to keep the small hospitals open.

The key intention of the design of the hospital has been to make a 'city within a city'. The covered streets that lead to the nursing units and clinics include a shopping alley, café, supermarket, bank and gift shop. The building is used for conventions and many other functions as well as the hospital. The public foyer is open and transparent, making a visual connection with the street. It is located on a city centre site and offers facilities to those working and living nearby.

There is a logical separation of users by floor: service streets underground, with automated pharmacy; public streets at ground level; professionals and patients on four floors above.

A competition was organised to select designs for each of the outpatient clinics. Each clinic was designed by a different interior designer to give variety and identity.

Isala Clinics at Zwolle

Architect:	Architectenbureau Albert and Van Huut BV
Client:	Isala Klinieken
Date:	In development
Area:	125,000 m²
Planning:	Nijst Idema Burger

A new hospital is being developed to provide general care for the immediate locality and specialist care for a wider area, with training for assistant physicians, housemen and nurses. It will accommodate 1,100 beds and provide general services, neonatology, heart surgery, dialysis, neurosurgery and fertility treatments.

The Isala Kliniken resulted from a merger in 1998 of two hospitals in Zwolle: the municipal Sophia hospital and the Catholic hospital De Weezenlanden. It was agreed to build a new hospital on one site, with a nursing home attached. The Sophia hospital site was chosen for its accessibility and potential for expansion. Some of the existing buildings will be retained.

The aim is to develop an innovative non-academic hospital in which the organisation is shaped around patients, reducing waiting lists, increasing places for specialist education, and increasing nursing and medical specialists. It aspires to be an employer that offers a stimulating working environment.

The new hospital is being planned around diagnostic groups (heart and lung, head and sense, parent and child, internal medicine, surgery, elderly) with three support departments (including information and HR). There will be six core groups whose managers will form the management team for the hospital. The organisational and medical organisations will be integrated with a medical manager, general manager and care group manager.

Alongside organisational developments, there are changes in attitude and a shift from technical aspects to an emphasis on relationships. The organisational design is based on streamlining the primary process, creating local power, stimulating horizontal cooperation, using result-oriented cooperation, minimising rules and procedures, and maximising information systems.

5.10
North elevation

5.11
Individual block

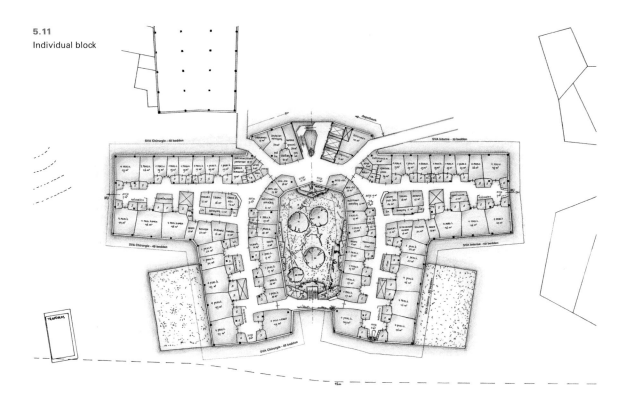

5.12
Cross-section of block

SECTION C-C

Central Hall

A design competition was held among four practices who presented scale models and rough designs. Staff and local residents were asked for their comments. The preferred scheme involved the collaboration of two firms, Albert and Van Huut and Nijst Idema Burger. The latter have a broad experience of working in hospitals and a particular expertise in streamlining the logistical processes. The other practice specialises in organic architecture and has developed banks, offices and nursing homes in this distinctive style.

The design has been developed on organic principles to follow the organisational ideas. It is intended to make people feel at ease in the building 'by blending aspects of scenery, urban building and architecture as much as possible'. Human scale and the relationship with nature are key elements of the design and will be achieved by planning around the functional units – like small hospitals – centred on certain groups of patients. Views onto the interior gardens from the rooms and corridors will give a sense of connection and transparency. Other facilities will include cafés, advice centres, post office and bank facilities, a fitness centre and an auditorium. There will be a hotel for patients receiving day services who need, for social reasons, to stay overnight.

One third of the beds will be in single rooms for privacy and the rest in four-bed rooms. The space at the bed has been designed to allow for equipment such as wheelchairs to support the independent mobility of patients. An increase in the provision of bathrooms will also improve safety and independence.

The hospital plan involves four major accommodation blocks that are linked to one another and existing buildings by corridors. The logistical relationships are based on planning priorities in both horizontal and vertical directions, safety, fire risk, and identification of likely needs for expansion and change. Computer models were used to test propositions and develop the optimum relationships. It is expected to be a paperless hospital.

A key design principle has been to devise a plan that breaks up the hospital into smaller parts, helping to give a sense of direction, connection with the outside and places for contact. The design process is perceived as a catalyst for change – both organisationally and physically.

Norway

Riks University Hospital, Oslo

Architect:	Medplan Arkitekter
Client:	Statsbygg
Date:	completed 2001
Area:	136,000 m^2

The Riks University Hospital is a highly specialised tertiary referral and teaching hospital that includes research and teaching activities involving the University of Oslo. The majority of referrals come from other hospitals and the hospital provides a specialised service for conditions and treatments that are rare and complicated. It provides a national service for organ and bone marrow transplants, advanced neurosurgery, and treatment of children with congenital disabilities. It provides regional heart and paediatric services.

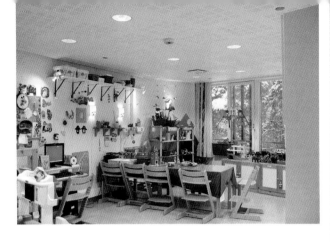

The site of the hospital moved after 100 years to be closer to the University at Gaustad in Oslo. The site was chosen for its close proximity to the main city ring road as well as links to public transport.

A design competition was launched in 1990 and was won by Medplan – a collaboration of practices with varying skills and expertise in hospital architecture. The key design principle behind the competition was the creation of 'the human hospital', meaning a building that inspired confidence and safety for the users – patients, staff and visitors.

The design uses the site's natural qualities to create a horizontal hospital with human scale, easily recognised building volumes and plenty of daylight to all residential and working spaces. The hospital respects the original buildings, and takes advantage of the views from the site and the connections to the surrounding woodlands.

The overall volume is divided into separate buildings that are linked together by a 'hospital street'. Most of the circulation between departments is horizontal, providing efficient logistical relationships. There are four main buildings: one for the treatment of patients, one for inpatient wards and bedrooms, one for research and laboratories, and one for women's and children's services.

These volumes are connected to the main street, which provides a series of squares and spaces for exhibitions that change in their nature and design along the street: from more urban themes closer to the city to more rural themes nearer the woodland. The street is modulated in width, giving a variation in ambience and making

5.13
Riks University Hospital children's playroom
5.14
Hospital 'street'
5.15
Entrance to Riks University Hospital from above

places at the circulation points where there are entrances to departments and clinics. It is top lit, and cranked to give a sense of surprise. The street is the most important space in the building for communication and social exchange. Orientation and spatial identity are clearly helped by the integration of art into the design, reducing the reliance on signage for wayfinding.

The entrance at the centre of the building is marked by a tower and resembles the arrangement in Italian towns with a plaza and landmark. The spaces immediately outside the entrance are enjoyed in good weather by patients, staff and visitors. The entrance to the women's and children's building is like an arcade announcing a different part of the hospital.

The building has been designed to provide flexibility in a number of ways by bringing together in one place similar functions, such as laboratories, wards and treatment buildings. In the treatment building, facilities for surgery, radiology and polyclinic treatments are assembled on separate floors. Within each building, departments may expand and contract as demand for space changes. Over the highly technical departments, there are interstitial technical floors to enable access with least disruption. In bedrooms, change of use between basic care and intensive has been facilitated by making a regular size of room that is fitted with services for intermediate and intensive care such as gas and IT. The overall building plan is open ended to allow for new additions in the future.

St Olave's University Hospital, Trondheim

Architect:	FRISK Arkitekten and Medplan
Client:	Central Norway Regional Health Authority
Date:	Phase 1 completion 2006
Area:	186,000 m²

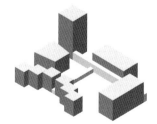

The University hospital includes St Olave's Hospital and the faculty of medicine. The hospital provides the main services for central Norway and a local hospital for the county.

The hospital is organised around several clinical centres aimed at improving resource utilisation and shortening lengths of stay, as a form of patient-centred care along the lines of the American Planetree model. This involves services being organised to come to the patient as far as possible; providing useful information resources that support shared decision-making; giving greater emphasis to the identity of the individual; and including carers and relatives as much

5.17
St Olave's proposed
aerial view

5.18
Street access to St Olave's

as possible. Changes in the organisational structures and operations are being developed alongside the design process, and one department has already adopted Planetree principles in the existing hospital.

The development involves extensive staff participation and, for the first time in Norway, considerable patient participation also. About 140 patient organisations have joined together to take part in the consultation at most levels. One outcome of this involvement has been to plan for single-patient rooms throughout the hospital. The wards are grouped in 'segetuns', like beads on a necklace, in groups of six to twelve, with support and workstations located in between to enable flexible management. Each group has one isolation room and most beds are visible from the workstation, which is open to encourage contact between patients, visitors and staff.

An international competition was held for the hospital and was won by FRISK Arkitekten with Ernst and Young; Medplan has since become involved in the development. Hospital ownership has been transferred from the private to the public sector.

The new hospital is being built in phases and will gradually replace the existing structure. The site is close to the Technical University and centre of Trondheim where the historic city is built on a fifteenth-century urban block structure with wide streets to prevent fires spreading among the wooden buildings. This is reflected in the masterplan for the hospital and was a key concept in the winning competition design.

The new hospital is divided into clinical centres that are based on diseases rather than specialties (that is, neuro, women and children, mobility, abdominal, environmental, cardiothoracic, psychiatric, emergency). These will be located in buildings that correspond in size to the urban blocks and thus integrate the hospital into the urban grain. The centres will be linked with glazed bridges and underground passages. The hospital is planned as a series of pavilions that has regard to human scale and a sense of normality over institutionalism. The entrance is given more emphasis, with an open public space that connects the hospital to its surroundings.

One advantage of the block system is the ability to adapt to changes in organisation and the building programme. However, there are some concerns about the staffing implications of such separate centres. While each block is designed for its particular function, there are some overarching planning strategies: technical and supply functions are in the basement, outpatients on ground level, diagnostic and treatment on the second, technical on the third, and the fourth is for inpatient wards. The overall grid size has also acted as a constraint into which the different pavilions have to fit and this has led to certain inefficiencies in the overall planning.

The design takes full advantage of the site and aims to maximise sunlight and views. Orientation is made easier by the scale of the centres, and the internal planning gives clues to help wayfinding.

5.19
Examination room and ward

France

Georges Pompidou Hospital, Paris

Architect:	A Zublena
Client:	Assistance Publique – Hopitaux de Paris (APHP)
Date:	1997
Area:	31,600 m^2
Cost:	€40m

The Georges Pompidou Hospital was opened in 1999 and is one of 51 or so hospitals run by the Assistance-Publique-Hospitaux de Paris (APHP), the Paris health authority. The development was the result of the rationalisation of four hospitals onto one site. The project involved significant challenges – both organisational and physical – in bringing together clinical and support staff from four separate hospitals into one environment. The design supports the integration of the organisation by, for example, providing a shared floor for medical equipment and rationalising services such as sterilising into one unit.

The hospital provides four main services: emergency, cardiology, oncology and transplants. The care is arranged around each organ or body part such as heart and blood vessels, lungs, kidneys, etc. These services are organised horizontally and each floor contains preventative treatment, diagnosis, monitoring, surgical treatment and rehabilitation. There are vertical connections around the same specialities such as cancer and organ transplants to maximise the use of equipment, skills and research. Each service has out- and inpatient services in one place,

5.20
Atrium to right and atrium to left, Georges Pompidou Hospital

5.21
Atrium from right, Georges Pompidou Hospital

and patients are met at the main reception and accompanied to the appropriate destination where their details are checked at a dedicated reception. This has significantly reduced the need for signage.

The majority (90%) of the patient bedrooms are single rooms with en suite bathrooms, and some provide overnight accommodation for carers. Each room has automatic taps, electronically controlled blinds, and air conditioning that can be operated from the bed. The provision of a single IT digital network that can transport, store and process data for the hospital administration and patient records has been installed.

The hospital, in south-west Paris on the banks of the Seine, is located on the site of the former Citroën factories and is close to two train stations and a public park. In scale and form the building responds to this distinguished urban site, taking account of the surrounding streets and buildings. A hospital mall runs the full length of the site, joining together two parts of the neighbourhood. This provides a significant public space along the spine of the building as well as connecting the various functions of the hospital. The metal bridges connecting upper floors, top lighting into the space, and the shop units, benches and plants all help to create a sense of scale, normality and comfort in such a large public building. The mall widens into a grand atrium between two ward blocks to create a public entrance to the hospital that is easily identified from inside and out.

The Bretonneau Hospital

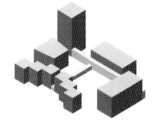

Architect:	Valode and Pistre Architects
Client:	Assistance Publique – Hopitaux de Paris (APHP)
Date:	2001
Area:	17,500 m²

The original hospital was built in the nineteenth century for medicine, surgery, infectious diseases and outpatients. These services were transferred to another site in 1988, enabling the redevelopment of this building as a nursing home for older people. The new addition consists of two parallel sets of pavilions, six in all, of two and three storeys, each of which accommodates around 15 residents.

The site is triangular in shape with the entrance to the hospital through the original buildings at the apex leading to a suite of rooms elegantly renovated to provide assessment for daily activities. The new pavilions are built to a rigorous grid that respects the scale of the original hospital. The buildings are built up to the boundaries of the site with the street outside and they are of a height and scale consistent with the surrounding residential buildings.

The inside of the site is formed around quiet gardens that give natural light and ventilation to the rooms and enable patients and visitors to enjoy the protected and secure outside spaces. Terraces and patios provide a subtle transition of space between inside and outside.

The nursing home entrance is separate and leads directly into the new buildings. The entrance opens onto an internal mall that has typically French-style hairdressers, cafeteria and shops to give a sense of normality as well as

5.22
Café bar in the nursing home
5.23
Kitchen in the nursing home

5.24
Gardens, Bretonneau Hospital

convenience. The mall is easily accessible from each of the pavilions and serves as a place for social interaction for all residents, staff and visitors.

The rooms in each of the pavilions are designed to be intimate, private and domestic in scale. Each pavilion has a central social space with a kitchen and a dining room that offers a place to gather for meals and other occasions. This makes a sensitive transition between public and private spaces where people can mingle and chat.

The new pavilions are built to complement the original hospital exterior in terms of form and scale and they unhesitatingly use modern materials and large windows to advantage. Horizontal bands of coursed brickwork, cladding and concrete help to reduce the scale and complement the original hospital built with brick coursing and stone quoins. The design has cleverly harmonised old and new.

Sweden

Bollnas Hospital

Architect:	Carlstad Architects
Client:	Local county council
Date:	1995
Area:	12,850 m^2

Bollnas was one of five hospitals serving a local population of 41,000 north of Stockholm. It provided local hospital services and consisted of three main buildings: a psychiatric unit built in the 1960s with 600 beds; a nursing home built in the 1970s with 130 places; and a general hospital. A major restructuring of hospital services undertaken in the mid-1990s resulted in a planned reduction of the existing hospital from some 1,200 beds to about 120 and the joining together of two hospitals to rationalise general hospital services.

5.25
Bollnas entrance

The psychiatric services were dispersed into small units and the acute services moved to another hospital. The nursing home for older people was reduced to eight to ten beds and otherwise people were offered rehabilitation in their own homes. The older buildings from the 1920s were considered unsuitable for modern surgical and medical care except for the wards (by Putsep), which were upgraded. The design for a more efficient and compact building was developed. Services offered at Bollnas include medical, surgical, gynaecology, rehabilitation and emergency with technical and support services. Outpatients services for ENT and eye are also provided.

The main entrance to the hospital is distinguished by the architectural style, which reflects some of the language of the local vernacular buildings. It is highly decorated and draws

5.26
Main hospital street and main hospital library

attention to the entrance, making it visible and distinctive for patients and visitors. The main hospital street is a double-height space with mezzanine balcony. It give a welcoming feeling and is flooded with light at both levels; its curved seats invite passers-by to stop and enjoy the view. A book library open to everyone is included in the street, and high-backed seats, like settles, make cosy places to stop and read. Artwork and landscaping bring a quality of intimacy and sensitivity to the interior, which is calm, colourful and comforting.

Several innovations were developed in the planning and design of the hospital. For example, the maternity service was planned on the LDRP (labour, delivery, recovery, post-partum) model of single rooms for patients, who remain in one room throughout their stay. It was among the first hospitals in Sweden to adopt this plan. The rooms were fitted with beds to enable partners to stay, en suite bathrooms and a place to sit beside the bed. The design sought to provide an intimate and domestic interior that was positive and supportive with the minimum level of clinical intervention unless required.

5.27
Maternity LDRP room

The offices for staff were designed in one location rather than being scattered throughout the hospital. This involved a combination of dedicated offices and general spaces. Some desks were available for solitary work in glass cubicles, others in larger shared rooms, and general facilities for printing, mail, etc. were arranged in a shared space for everyone. A small place for beverages was also included to give some social space for staff in this area. While this is not a new idea in office design, it was, and is still, a relatively new departure for health.

Norrtalje Hospital

Architect:	ETV Architects
Client:	Local county council
Date:	1996
Area:	14,000 m²

Norrtalje Hospital is a general hospital linked to four other general hospitals and two academic hospitals near to Stockholm. It was built on the site of an existing hospital of 40 beds that is over 100 years old. The existing buildings are retained largely for administrative uses.

Services in the new building are for surgery, medicine, radiotherapy, psychiatry and rehabilitation, and also include some specialist services for maternity, gynaecology and ENT. The 96 beds are arranged in three wards for medical, surgical and rehabilitation patients. The population fluctuates over the year with three times more patients in the summer than in the winter. The beds are arranged in groups of eight with three single rooms, one three-bedded room and one double. Staff work in teams with two or three nurses allocated to eight patients. The arrangement of beds was arrived at from findings of a research project that sought to identify the optimum size and arrangement of beds to give privacy and allow observation.

A unique feature of the ward design in Norrtalje is the day space that is provided in the middle of the wards. A living and dining area fitted with full domestic appliances serves as a peaceful place to sit, wait or entertain. It overlooks an outside garden landscaped with plants and paving to entice patients and visitors out in suitable weather. The staff bases were designed to be open and not enclosed in offices with glass screens, which was the more common arrangement in Sweden.

5.28
Norrtalje
hospital
entrance

A significant concept for the designers was the development of a design that was sustainable, and due attention has been given to the specification of ecologically sound materials that are respectful of limited resources and also acknowledge the need for recycling in years to come.

The colours and paints have been selected for calmness, and care has been taken to create, with integrated artwork, an interior that is sensitive, social and uplifting.

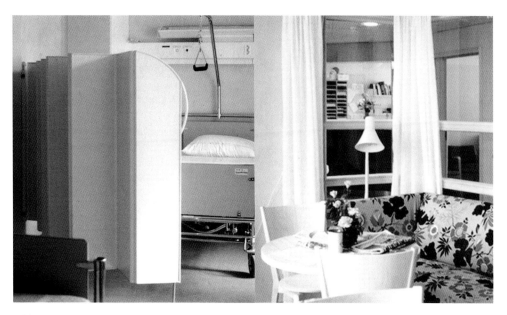

5.29
Norrtalje ward and staff space

Germany

Marzahn Hospital, Berlin

Architect:	Schmucker and Schmucker
	Architects
Client:	Berlin regional government
Date:	1997

As part of a programme of upgrading facilities in the former East Berlin, this hospital was developed as a trauma hospital for a catchment population of about 7 million people. As well as the new trauma services, the hospital offers general care and rehabilitation. It is the first model in Germany to combine trauma with general services.

The hospital is built on the site of the former psychiatric hospital of Wilhem Griesinger that was designed by Blankenstien in the 1890s. This has a typical pavilion-style layout of low-rise brick buildings in extensive parkland. The new hospital, which opened in 1997, is separate from the existing structures. Whereas the site was once an isolated place on the outskirts of the city, it is now connected by public transport and surrounded by residential areas. However, the hospital buildings are located deep into the site and are sheltered from the surrounding neighbourhood by the parkland and landscaped gardens. One of the key planning constraints was for low-rise development with no buildings higher than the tree line.

5.30
Marzahn Hospital

The main entrance to the hospital is denoted by a covered glass roof and leads onto a mall with flower and newspaper shops and a café. This creates a pleasant welcoming space and one that is used by patients, some of whom may have extended lengths of stay because of their severe injuries.

The hospital includes some specialist services particularly for burns and head injuries. An air ambulance service flies in patients three or four times a week and the hospital has a reputation for treating particularly severe cases.

The aim for the hospital to be as paper-free and film-free as possible has been achieved to a great extent. A totally digital radiology system that is fully filmless is in operation. There are 24 high-quality workstations and other lower-quality workstations throughout the hospital. Clinical images are sent to the diagnostic workstations in radiology and to viewing stations in various clinical departments. Group discussions can be arranged around large screens to display images from all modalities.

The rehabilitation department is fitted with a full-size Mercedes car that patients can use to practise mobility, especially wheelchair transfer in and out of the vehicle. A hydrotherapy pool and other pieces of exercise equipment are based in a well-lit building away from the main entrance.

Belgium

De Bijtjes Hospital

Architect:	FDA Architects
Client:	Royale H'pital De Bijtjes
Date:	1996
Area:	15,245 m²

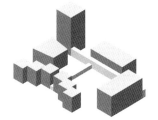

This is a special hospital for rehabilitation services which provides a wide range of therapies including physio, OT, speech, psychological and social. Many of the patients are treated for severe injuries and some are still comatose during their stay. About 60% of patients return to their homes and others move to special housing that gives them appropriate physical and social support.

The hospital is located in a beautiful renovated country house and estate with significant new additions. Great care has been taken in the design to provide for the needs of this severely immobilised group: the detailed design at the bedside provides mirrors angled to enable

5.31
Park, De Bijtjes Hospital

5.32
Exterior walkway, De Bijtjes Hospital

wheelchair users to see themselves; the circulation inside and outside the building provides for wheelchair users and other people with impairments.

One of the most uplifting spaces in the hospital is a central piazza. Designed like a town square, it is a place where all users – patients, visitors and staff – can gather in a more normal environment to sit and chat. Many patients are here for extended periods and often need time to adjust to a new lifestyle after traumatic accidents and extensive injuries. The hospital, both inside and through the extensive grounds, provides places for contemplation and connectivity.

Conclusion

While there may appear to be many differences among the health systems in Europe, there are many similarities and principles that are shared: systems that aim to provide equity for all, based on social insurance or taxation, and largely free at the point of use.

In terms of the building infrastructure, there is increasing convergence between the different systems for financing and procurement. For design, there are three overarching issues that are driving innovation and change: the relationship of the hospital to the city, the creation of a humanising environment for care, and advances and progress leading to greater technical sophistication and sustainability.

The examples of individual schemes illustrate the key design trends and provide a body of experience and lessons that can be shared to advantage in the UK, across Europe and potentially worldwide. What emerges from the European examples is a confident and inventive approach to design that is increasingly making links with ideas common to mainstream architectural practice.

However, there are some issues that are not addressed here: for example, the relationship of the hospital to primary and intermediate care. As services are relocated to more local and community settings, what will this mean for the hospital of the future? Will it become smaller, more specialised, and a place of last resort? What buildings will be required in the community and how different will these be from the current provision?

It is well understood that clinical models of care are constantly developing, and that buildings need to reflect these different changes and to be flexible enough to accommodate emerging ones. It is not possible to predict these changes in a precise way, but we know that change is likely and possibly inevitable. So how do we develop design principles that can accommodate such uncertainties?

Much has been aired recently about the achievements of the French system, which appears to provide hospitals of higher design quality, with better patient outcomes for lower construction costs compared with the UK.[7] But detailed studies of costs, construction and procurement methods are revealing some of the difficulties of comparing European systems, where different methods of measurement are proving incompatible.[8] However, all can agree that the capital cost of buildings is small relative to the overall cost of maintaining the buildings and running the services over their lifetime. We need to make a stronger argument for the business case for investing in design and service improvements together for the longer-term benefits of the patients, the staff and the hospital organisation.

As the issue of patient safety grows in importance alongside the recognition that system changes are required to help improve hospital performance, the contribution of the design of the environment is being investigated. Much attention has been paid to the design of single rooms and provision of hand-washing facilities to help reduce healthcare-acquired infections (HCAI). It is now recognised that this issue is multi-factorial, requiring consideration of clinical decisions about care, value-based decisions about patient services, operational considerations of effective and efficient management, and financial considerations about affordability of capital costs and revenue consequences. What is becoming better understood is that single rooms offer many advantages for patient privacy and dignity, for flexibility of bed management in relation to gender separation and managing fluctuating demands, and for reducing the movement of patients, which is strongly linked with clinical errors. Already many European countries are developing policies to recommend an increase in the percentage of single rooms to a minimum of 50% and preferably more, and to lower occupancy rates to around 83%, in order to gain improvements in health outcomes.

The winning entry in the recent Netherlands Board of Hospital Facilities competition for the 'Future Competitive and Healing Hospital' describes the concept for the scheme as:

a core hospital concentrating on specialist care, all other functions are outsourced. This lean core hospital fits in practically every city. A hotel with an outdoor connection is an essential part of the concept. It offers extensibility and flexibility to the hospital, to high quality service and low care nursing facilities. The hotel also attracts patients' relatives, tourists and businessmen.

The patient is offered an effective healing environment in the direct vicinity of markets, shops, restaurants and city life. Shops and facilities on street level can be entered from both the hospital and the city. The hospital itself focuses on diagnostics and treatment. A variety of gardens and terraces allow light to penetrate deep into the volume. Semi-transparent, white interior walls reflect and filter the light and different patterns on the walls create privacy and transparency at the same time.

Similarly, the winning entry for a competition for a new hospital and research institute for the Karolinska in Stockholm, a prestigious research and teaching institution, sets out a vision for a structure that creates a strong link between research and hospital, and the hospital building and a green academic pathway represent this symbolic collaboration.

The main entrance is located at the new square 'Karolinaplatsen', bringing together commercial and social activities with the hospital and creating a social arena between the medical university and the city. This will be the setting for the magnificent 'Aula Karolina' and the square will continue into the main lobby where different public activities will be offered in a pavilion-like environment. In November every year the limousines from the Nobel Prize ceremonies will decorate the nearby streets – the square is a part of everyday life but also a platform for ceremonies and festivities.

Clearly both these projects are bringing progressive thinking about the organisation of care, strengthening of links between research and medical practice, and the design concepts that are familiar to mainstream urban design and architectural discourse. Perhaps they will, in a small way, help to define the values and aspirations for future hospital designs in Europe where there is likely to be significant convergence of strategic concepts alongside considerable local cultural variation. While these endeavours are extremely encouraging, turning such aspirations into reality will take a little longer!

Developing a new language

One of the factors inhibiting the dialogue about hospital design is the absence of a shared language to help visualise and articulate the kind of design that will express the concepts and principles for the future. We need to develop words and images that capture the mood and intention in a new way. In this endeavour we need the combined efforts of practitioners, academics and journalists to develop, practise and publish the emerging concepts. While this is beginning to happen, it has yet to become common in the highly specialised world of hospital planning and design.

Whereas we used to describe the appearance of the hospital as 'utilitarian', we currently use terms such as 'corporate' or 'like an office block' as a way of bringing hospitals in line with more commercial building types. But if we want to develop a greater integration with public services and systems, perhaps we need to define and illustrate what we mean by making buildings with 'civic presence' that contribute to the neighbourhood in a social and physical manner.

Hospital streets were once evaluated for their ability to deliver people and goods (often known as 'traffic') efficiently; now we describe them as being like a concourse in an airport or a shopping mall; and in future we may see them as offering vital communication networks that foster informal exchange and support good communication and teamwork.

Waiting spaces were assessed for their sufficiency to serve a process; now they are expected to be comfortable like a hotel; in future, with booking arrangements and schedules that are supported by IT, we can perhaps expect to reduce waiting times and make these into multi-functional and social spaces where patients can spend their time more purposefully, for example to work in a business centre, move around the building until paged, or sit with friends in a café between appointments.

Finally, we designed private spaces to be clinically functional; we now want that combined with a sense of domesticity, like a home; in future, we may aspire to make places that are sensitive, stimulating and controllable.

The following table helps to illustrate these ideas:

Space	Old	Current	Future
Hospital	Utilitarian	Corporate, like an office	A civic building
Hospital street	Efficient	Concourse, like an airport	A communication network
Waiting spaces	Sufficient	Comfortable, like a hotel	Multi-functional and social
Private spaces, clinical rooms	Clinically functional	A sense of domesticity	Sensitive, stimulating and controllable

Finally, then, what can we learn from looking at policy and practice in Europe? There is a rich and diverse experience with much common ground. Local cultural variations and regulations will determine the precise interpretation for each country. But there is much to be gained, and many lessons to be learned from the projects, past and present.

Notes and references

1. Assistance-Publique-Hospitaux de Paris (APHP), *Hospital Heritage: A Journey Through Europe* (Paris, 2001).
2. Cor Wagenaar (ed.) *The Architecture of Hospitals.* (Rotterdam: Nai Publishers, 2005).
3. *European Healthcare Infrastructure* (Study commissioned by the Netherlands Board for Hospital Facilities and presented to the EU Health Property Network meeting in October 2002).
4. EU Observatory on Healthcare Systems, *Healthcare Systems in Eight Countries: Trends and Challenges* (London: London School of Economics, 2002).
5. NHS Estates, HBN 4: *In-patient Accommodation: Options for Choice Volume 2: European Case Studies* (London: The Stationery Office, 1998).
6. EU Health Property Network, research studies in progress on costs, procurement and design. Interim reports presented to the 7th Member Meeting in Edinburgh, November 2004.
7. Building Design Partnership, *Learning from French Hospital Design* (BDP, 2004).
8. Various information packs from individual hospital projects.

CHAPTER SIX

Changing hospital design in the USA

DOUGLAS OLSON

with assistance from LARRY BONGORT

Healthcare facilities in the United States are faced with mounting pressure for increasingly shorter cycles of renewal in order to keep pace with the forces of change within the healthcare marketplace. The origins of this pressure are diverse and collectively have a significant impact on the determination of the physical environment. This chapter identifies the key forces or drivers that set the context for change including demographics, financing, 'consumerism', technology, sustainability and regulations. It then examines trends that respond to those drivers. In some instances these trends anticipate a deeper integration between functional need and the physical environment. The chapter concludes with examples of positive innovation in hospital design, which suggest future directions for hospital development.

Context for change

Demographics

Growing population

The future may not be certain but demographic trends are fairly predictable. One sure thing is that the population is growing. In 2000, the US population comprised approximately 282 million people and it is expected to reach nearly 336 million by 2020 – an increase of almost 19%.[1] This increase in population, along with political and economic factors, will generate significant impacts for healthcare services.

Cultural diversity

Rapid increases in immigration and birth rate differentials among ethnic groups in the US have resulted in a population much more diverse than it was 20 years ago. Healthcare providers are adapting to more heterogeneous thinking and cultural attitudes within the population they serve. One example of this response is the growing recognition of the family as part of the patient's care team and the provision of hospital space to accommodate family members as they become a more integral part of the inpatient care setting.

Ageing population

By 2010, 13% of the US population will be 65 years of age or older. By 2030, 19.6% of the population – an estimated 71.5 million people – will have moved beyond 65, twice as many

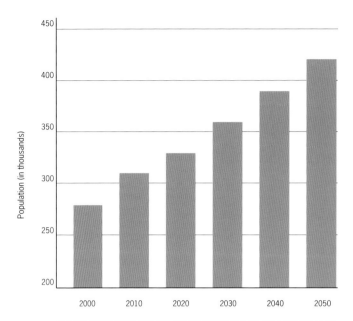

Source: U.S. Census Bureau, 2004, "U.S. Interim Projections by Age, Sex, Race and Hispanic Origin"

6.1
Growing population – projected
population of the US, 2000–50

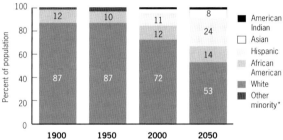

*American Indians, Asians, and Hispanics combined. These three groups
combined made up less than 3 percent of the population in 1900 and 1950.
Note: Hispanics are excluded from American Indian, Asian, African American,
and White categories. Hispanics may be of any race.

6.2
Cultural diversity – US population
by race and ethnicity, 1900–2050

people as today.[2] 'Seniors', once stereotyped as elderly grandparents, are now leading more
active lives.[3] In 2002 the US Bureau of Labor Statistics estimated that 4.3 million Americans over
the age of 65 continued to work – a record number.[4] In addition, the burgeoning fields of medical
technology and pharmaceuticals are contributing factors in prolonging life and transforming
many terminal diseases into manageable chronic conditions. There is a growing recognition
of the need for new models of care and suitable facilities to provide dignified and appropriate
services for an increasingly older population.[5]

Retiring 'baby boomers'
The baby boomer generation – those born after the Second World War and prior to 1960 – are
nearing retirement age. Many of them have realised that they will probably outlive their

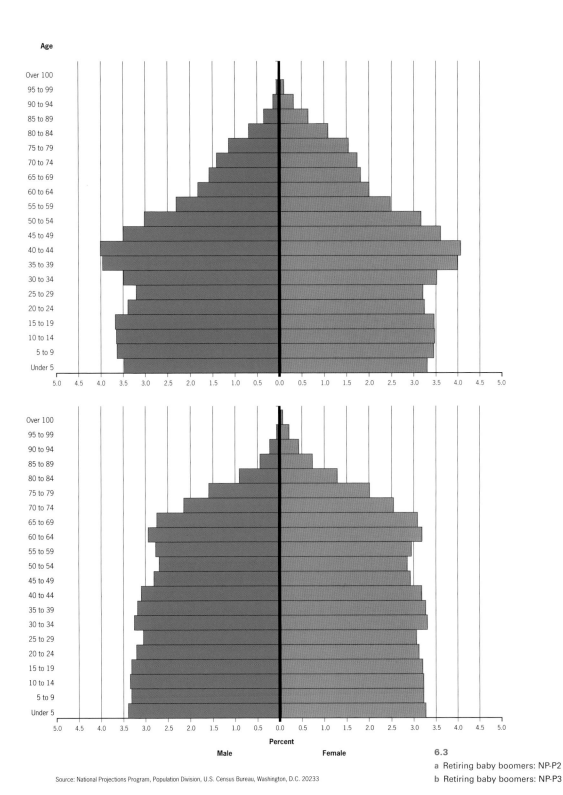

Source: National Projections Program, Population Division, U.S. Census Bureau, Washington, D.C. 20233

6.3
a Retiring baby boomers: NP-P2
b Retiring baby boomers: NP-P3

pensions, especially after having seen their retirement investments shrink as a result of volatile market trends. At the same time there are proportionately fewer young people entering the workforce. Currently, there are about 40 people at working age for every person aged 85 or older. By 2040 the proportion will be less than 14:1.[6]

The population pyramid (Figure 6.3) shows population distribution by age. A distinct bulge can be seen in the 30 to 50 year age range with relatively small percentages of the population in the 75 to 100 year age ranges. When we look ahead 25 years, the baby boomer 'bulge' will move into the 70 to 85 year range, and by 2050 many of the boomers will still be hanging in there, vastly expanding the ranks of those 80 to 105 years old.[7] People in these advanced age brackets use healthcare services at a much greater rate than those who are younger. The average healthcare expenditures for people aged 85 and older are almost three times the average for those in the 65 to 69 age bracket.[8] This demographic shift and its subsequent economic impact will be a major factor shaping the future of healthcare services.

Shrinking healthcare workforce

The demographics of an ageing population also apply to the healthcare workforce. The average age of an American registered nurse (RN) currently stands at 43.3 years. In 2004, a survey by the Bernard Hodes Group (staffing and recruitment consultants) recorded the greatest shortage ever of RNs in the US, with 13.9% of nursing positions unfilled and a staggering annual turnover rate of 15.5%.[9] Moreover, nurses are increasingly relied upon for their specialised expertise, leaving the routine, but no less important, tasks of daily care-giving to less trained staff and family members. Burnout and job dissatisfaction are widespread. Given such statistics, it is not surprising that many are choosing to retire, move on to more supportive facilities or move into different professions altogether.[10] There are similar shortages in other healthcare fields. Clinical laboratory technicians[11] and pharmacists[12] are also in short supply.

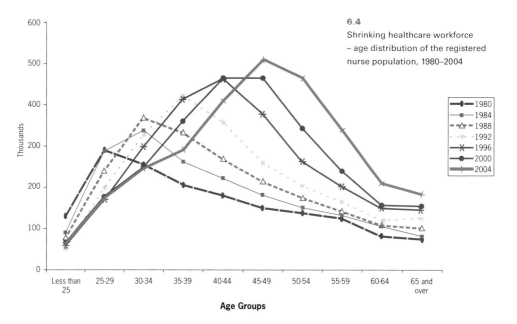

6.4
Shrinking healthcare workforce – age distribution of the registered nurse population, 1980–2004

Source: "Bureau of Health Professionals/U.S. Dept. of Health and Human Services"
Accessed: 28 August 2006

At the same time, fewer young people are training for careers in the healthcare field. For example, there has been a steady decline over the past 20 years in numbers of nursing school graduates as well as those taking the national licensure examination for nursing, a trend that has only begun to reverse itself in the last two years.[13] These trends, when combined, have created acute shortages of skilled staff whose numbers are not expected to keep pace with needs for the foreseeable future.

Concurrent with the national nursing shortage is a growing recognition of the need to accommodate an older workforce. Well-designed environments in which staff enjoy working and that make efficient use of staff time will be key to staff retention. Physical implications of design and planning include:

- reduction or elimination of intra-departmental travel;
- reduction of travel distances between patient rooms;
- facilitation of patient lifting and transfers;
- reduction of patient transfers;
- separate staff dining and rest areas;
- specification of flooring products for foot comfort;
- ergonomically designed equipment and planning;
- acoustical comfort in the work environment.

In rare cases medical providers are creating respite centres where staff can 'get away from it all'. The Beth Israel Medical Center in New York City recently dedicated the Beatrice Renfield Center for Nursing Excellence in support of the nursing staff. Envisioned as a place for peer support and personal development, the facility was designed by Guenther 5 Architects as a dedicated centre for education, research and moments of personal or group reflection (Figure 6.5).

Lifestyle and societal factors

Many health outcomes resulting from lifestyle choices and social conditions are having an influence on healthcare planning and design. Alcoholism, drug addiction and smoking, which are linked to the top three causes of death – heart disease, cancer and stroke – are expected to effect change in the coming years.

One condition having an immediate impact on healthcare design and planning is obesity. An increasingly sedentary lifestyle, poor dietary choices, and a growing reliance on fast food, coupled with a food industry intent on selling high-margin, highly processed products, have combined to expand the US waistline. While adult obesity has approximately doubled over the last 30 years, the prevalence of obesity in children has quadrupled in that same time period.[14] Demands for improved accommodation for this population are being addressed, with real impacts for the design of healthcare environments. Bariatric chairs and equipment, with modified dimensions and load design, can now be found in most healthcare equipment catalogues. Larger patient rooms and bathrooms with built-in lift and transfer equipment are becoming prevalent as healthcare providers seek to accommodate larger patients while avoiding workplace injuries for their staff.

6.5
Staff respite area at Beth Israel Medical Center in New York City

Healthcare financing

Current financing system

The current American healthcare financing system took shape approximately 40 years ago and, outside of military benefits, comprises Medicare, Medicaid and private insurance. Medicare provides medical benefits to those aged 65 and older. Medicaid extends benefits to those under the age of 65 based upon financial need. Private insurance provides a range of benefit coverage to consumers, primarily through their employers. Those not falling into any of these three categories remain uninsured.

Impact of the uninsured

In 2002, the number of US citizens without healthcare coverage was 43.6 million, roughly 15% of all residents.[15] It is predicted that by 2010 this number will increase to 60 million.[16] This does not account for an estimated 11 million 'undocumented immigrants' mixed into the society. For the uninsured or under-insured, the lack of access to primary care leaves few alternatives for medical treatment except at emergency departments of hospitals across the country.

In 1986 the Medicare Act was amended by the Emergency Treatment and Active Labor Act (EMTALA). This federal law requires hospitals participating in Medicare programmes to provide emergency screening and to stabilise emergency conditions found in any patient presenting at the emergency department regardless of the patient's ability to pay, thus creating an unfunded mandate to provide charity care. EMTALA relies on the ability of hospitals to cross-subsidise uncompensated care for the uninsured and thereby provide a safety net for the uninsured population.[17] Ultimately, it is the careful blending of the more profitable medical services that subsidises this unfunded care. This places increased pressure on each facility to maximise the efficiencies required to maintain the financial bottom line.

Private insurance – managed care

Managed care developed in the late 1970s and the early 1980s, primarily in reaction to spiralling healthcare costs. Managed care plans (also termed health maintenance organisations or HMOs) emerged by the mid-1990s as the dominant model for employer-sponsored medical coverage. While these were effective in stabilising healthcare's share of GDP, dissatisfaction arose with managed care. Although costs were contained, few improvements were seen in health status or patient outcomes.[18] Patient choice was being curtailed as coverage disputes and inappropriate denials of coverage were widely reported. Through various payment and financial incentive schemes, physicians were being encouraged to stint on care and achieve productivity goals. The managed-care system came to be seen as 'more mean than lean', naturally engendering a backlash.

Managed care has not proved entirely successful in the US as consumers will not accept limits on provider choice. Managed care leaders with a fully integrated system of quality health plans, facilities and provider employment, such as Kaiser Permanente, are among the few exceptions. However, even they continue to explore other care delivery models. The cultural aspects of US healthcare consumers, the operational nature of healthcare providers and the government's healthcare policies are simply not in alignment for managed care to be successful in this country at this time. The changes required from all to attain managed care in some form are not unrelated to the inability to provide universal care for everyone in the US.

Patients' Bill of Rights

Americans' concerns with the abusive excesses of managed care soon moved into the political arena. The idea of a Patients' Bill of Rights took shape in proposed federal legislation and Patient Protection Acts. Both Houses of Congress repeatedly passed regulations to govern managed care, only to have them fail at the conference stage when faced by intensive lobbying by the managed healthcare industry.[19] It is important to note that these legislative attempts focused on the rights of those who already had insurance. They did not consider the uninsured.

The idea of a right to healthcare has not developed in the US. Instead, calls for universal healthcare are stated in terms of governmental obligation or the elimination of the waste inherent in the current system, which is top-heavy with administration costs. The concept of 'solidarity' is strong in Canada and western Europe, but seldom part of American political thought.[20]

Nonetheless, there is renewed discussion of universal healthcare. Corporate America is waking up to the impact of healthcare costs on companies, workers and customers.[21] Studies have shown that the money wasted each year in healthcare bureaucracy should be enough to provide medical coverage for all of the 43 million Americans currently uninsured.[22]

State-based healthcare reform

There is growing interest in simplifying the entire healthcare system, with 'single-payer' systems being discussed. With gridlock in Washington, where insurance companies and drug manufacturers hold a great deal of political influence, many are looking for meaningful reform to begin at the state level. The healthcare system is economically challenged in many localities to provide care to those who cannot afford to pay. While several states are considering universal health plans, the costs of such programmes are likely to be transferred to taxpayers, employers, insurers and individuals who can pay, compounding the tension between cost and value. This growing tension will have profound impacts for an industry that consumes 15% of the gross domestic product (projected to reach 17.7% by 2012)[23] and for consumers with set views founded on generations of expectations. It is likely that the system will struggle in years to come before there is enough support for meaningful reform.

Consumerism

As part of healthcare financing reform, health insurers continue to shift greater responsibility to the patient in an effort to balance cost pressures. These consumer-driven health plans are intended to involve consumers in the decision-making process, whereby the costs for healthcare benefits are reduced without limiting the quality or availability of care. Central to this consumer-driven strategy is being able to shift from a deeply rooted perception of health coverage as a 'benefit to be expended at will' to the view that it is an 'asset to be carefully managed'. Strategies have included increased co-payments and cost-sharing as well as the concept of creating transferable patient health accounts, which the consumer can move from one employer to another.

As patients grow more accountable for their own health choices, consumer expectations of healthcare delivery are changing. Expectations for faster and higher levels of service and improved ambience and amenities are on the rise. Concurrently, interest in and the use of alternative medicines, non-traditional procedures and therapies, etc. continue to shape consumer decisions. As consumers play a more active role in health decisions, direct marketing of prescription-based pharmaceuticals and medical technologies has become commonplace.

Regardless of the health delivery strategy, choice remains a much-protected aspect of the US healthcare system. Healthcare consumers have demanded and received greater choice in who provides their care and where they receive it. As a result, consumers are better informed than they were in the past, primarily through internet access, about illness, procedures, products, physicians and facilities.

Responding to consumer interests, various healthcare rating systems have been introduced, which influence both the consumer's judgement criteria and the healthcare provider's decisions on ways to remain competitive. These include Health Grades, the *US News* list of the top 100 hospitals and the Leapfrog Group's quality initiatives. Healthcare providers are becoming focused on quality and measurable outcomes because such information is increasingly being made available to the public. The goal of improving patient satisfaction and positive outcomes also fosters investment in facilities and technology.

Free market conditions

In the past, both public and private medical providers were required to engage in a process called Certificate of Need (CON) to demonstrate the need for expansion and construction of new facilities. Most states have dropped the CON process and now operate in a free market environment where competition for patients is a major factor influencing the decision of operators (where to build, what to build, etc.). This has spurred healthcare providers of both for-profit and non-profit organisations into the development of brand image and relationship marketing to influence consumer choice. This is particularly the case in the higher-income-producing services such as cancer and cardiology.

The consumer market will increasingly demand that environments support the efficient delivery of core services while creating a positive experience for patients and for staff, thus improving outcomes. As healthcare facilities continually work to ensure higher levels of services, improved infection control and tightened security, the expectations of the consumer will focus on physical comfort, positive distractions and quality acoustics, all of which promote peace and tranquillity during convalescence. The role of design is of increasing value in defining and ensuring a positive patient experience.

Technology

Long-established models of care are rapidly evolving to encompass new options afforded by smaller, faster, more information-rich systems. Advances in medical technology are also allowing for significant improvements in patient diagnosis, treatment and care. Technology trends can be seen in biotechnology, clinical technology and information systems.

Biotechnology

Biotechnology includes genomics or genetic manipulation, which will allow for customised prescriptions based upon the unique gene structure of the individual, prolonging health and life. Genomics will also allow for lifelong health profiling anticipating, detecting and treating illness in earlier stages, transitioning terminal diseases to a more chronic status. Chemo and radiation therapy may be replaced with genetic treatments. Gene therapy, which modifies the blood to resist certain cancers, is already being tested.

Clinical technology

Clinical technology reaches into areas such as non-invasive imaging, minimally invasive surgery and robotics. The operating theatre is an excellent example of technology's impact on planning and design. Combined therapies are becoming common, such as the use of ultrasound, fluoroscopy or X-ray during surgical procedures. This allows for real-time observation of tumours, or complex injuries hidden by major organs or bone, thereby allowing for more successful and less intrusive procedures. Minimally invasive procedures will soon become normal practice. Cardiac procedures are changing rapidly through the use of implantable devices, injectable monitors, and overall miniaturisation of surgical devices.

Ohio State University Hospital's state-of-the-art orthopaedic surgery suite is an example of a facility where advanced use of technology has led the design. Two operating theatres have been designed based on the model of an aviator's cockpit, where controls are meticulously built around the ergonomic and logical needs of the surgeon. Elements of the design include voice-activated instrumentation, ergonomic furniture, ceiling-mounted booms and consoles, and the latest surgical tools, all incorporated into technologically advanced suites used for arthroscopic and other video-assisted surgical procedures. In addition to carrying out surgical instrument commands, the voice-activated system allows the surgeon to dictate operative reports for the hospital's billing department, instantly calling up radiographs and other images, and teleconference live on the computer screens. Utilisation has exceeded expectations as a result of shorter procedures and faster cleaning and sterilisation between operations.

Information systems

Healthcare information systems include electronic medical records (EMR), wireless technology (including hand-held devices for bedside charting) and point of care systems. Advances in general communication systems have great potential, especially for EMR. One current drawback is that investment is substantial and the industry is in the early stages of growth, meaning great risk of change and obsolescence. Only 13% of hospitals in America have instituted EMR. Access to electronic information and portable medical records are still in the planning stages at most institutions.

The advanced capability necessary for the growth of such technologies is a result of more complex IT systems and infrastructure. While computing capacity is occurring in ever smaller spaces, there is a corresponding increase in spatial needs for specialised equipment, 'smart' walls, floors and ceilings, and the technicians to support them.

As the myriad of medical offerings made available by technology expands, so too does the expectation for their use. These advances, combined with increasing staffing shortages, are forcing the most out of technology, stimulating smaller, more integrated systems. Given the average five to seven years taken to build a major medical centre, many decisions regarding technology may already be out of date within a few years of use, an unsettling concern for most hospital administrators.

Sustainability

Sustainability is slowly gaining importance in US healthcare as a result of an increasingly educated and active marketplace. Federal and state-wide support through accreditation and energy rebates, documented reductions in operating costs and increased energy savings, as well as growing evidence of improved patient outcomes, have allowed sustainability to become globally understood as an imperative for the future with widening acceptance in the consumer marketplace. Institutions are seeking to incorporate such principles to demonstrate corporate responsibility and attract patients as well as care-givers.

From an operational standpoint, the mandate for a medical facility to sponsor sustainable principles is grounded in simple facts. Hospitals are the fourth highest consumer of energy of all building types, accounting for 10–15% of all commercial consumption in the US, totalling more than $3 billion per year. The healthcare industry also contributes 5 million tons of solid waste annually to the nation's landfill. Hospitals must function at high performance levels 24 hours per day, seven days per week. Clinical demands may require contrasting heating and cooling of adjacent functional spaces throughout the year. Finishes and materials must perform to very high expectations in terms of both safety and maintenance.[24]

If taking into account the sheer volume of flooring, casework, lighting, wall protection, cleaning products, etc. that a hospital building consumes, the selection of interior materials can make a considerable contribution to meeting sustainable goals. Budgets are gradually allowing for not only capital costs but also life cycle costs and impact to environmental quality, including air and light.

Environmental stewardship is not a new idea. The general principles of traditional planning and design form the foundation of sustainability. Campus planning is logically an extension of the urban infrastructure having impacts far beyond property lines. Campus planning can participate in local urban redevelopment initiatives and allow for integration of public transit, protection of open spaces and strategic land banking for future development. Building orientation can exploit the varying qualities of the site for positive ends, including situating the main building entrance according to natural light and seasonal prevailing winds. Building envelopes and roof forms can be managed for efficient drainage and solar control. Dispensation of brief elements can include the strategic unbundling of functions into reused or appropriately designed buildings.

With an ageing nursing population, building design, systems and interior products are increasingly designed and specified with consideration for physical comfort, back care, ergonomics, acoustical comfort and an injury-free work environment. The key is to initiate sustainability as a priority early in the design process. Switching midway or reconciling upon completion can prove difficult and costly.

A recent example of national recognition for a sustainable hospital is Boulder Community Hospital in Colorado. This is the first certified hospital in the Leadership in Energy and Environmental Design (LEED) initiative. Members of the US Green Building Council representing all segments of the building industry have developed and oversee a rigorous set of standards emphasising state-of-the-art strategies for sustainable site development, water savings, energy efficiency, materials selection and indoor environmental quality.

Boulder Community Hospital's newly constructed Foothills Campus recently received v2 Silver rating, awarded for environmental leadership in the building industry. The certification marks the first time a hospital facility has been recognised with this designation. Some sustainable design elements incorporated into the new Foothills Campus include a resource-conserving energy centre, cost-saving motion-activated lights, recycling stations and rooms, waterless urinals and extensive water-conserving landscape techniques. In addition, the architects minimised the hospital's footprint to avoid disturbing more land than necessary. Further information is contained in the case study at the end of this chapter.

The regulatory environment

As with the design of any building type, the level of regulatory involvement is directly proportional to the complexity of function, the density of environment and, with healthcare, the medical capacity of the occupants. Below are listed some of the regulatory topics influencing healthcare design in the US.

The Health Insurance Portability and Privacy Act (HIPAA)

HIPAA is a new federal law providing privacy standards to protect patients' medical records and other health information provided to a health insurer's doctors, hospitals and other healthcare providers. These new standards provide patients with access to their medical records and more control over how their personal health information is used and disclosed.

HIPAA includes provisions designed to encourage electronic transactions and also requires new safeguards to protect the security and confidentiality of health information. In effect from April 2003, HIPAA guarantees privacy standards to patients that have an impact on the design of healthcare facilities as well as care delivery. For example, under the privacy rule, patients can request that their doctors, health insurance providers and other covered entities take reasonable steps to ensure that their communications with the patient remain confidential. This has translated into physical changes to patient and examination rooms, nursing units and workstations, and admission areas where audible and visual mitigation of individually identifiable health information of the patient is necessary.

Hospital as an essential service at the time of an emergency or natural disaster – terrorism and major disasters

Even prior to September 11, the Washington Hospital Center in Washington DC began looking at a prototypical emergency department design, called ER One, that could be responsive in any emergency situation. The goal of ER One was to establish operational procedures and design strategies to enable an emergency department to be ready for any major catastrophe and to be highly scalable, given the unpredictability of such an event.

The hospital assembled nine task forces, including architects, to examine ways to deal with disasters affecting from 20 to 20,000 people at any time. Understanding how planning for emergency situations impacted on the design of the department in terms of function, aesthetics and protection was considered critical. The main issues studied were strategic location, scalability, traffic management, immune building and blast mitigation.

The planning was based upon a flexible configuration of treatment areas and robust scalability to move response team size up and down quickly within a given template. This included open space immediately outside the emergency department to provide an expanded treatment area for patient stations and mobile units and provisions for docking stations. Traffic management focused on solutions for easing potential crowding in the ambulance bay.

Immune building design included the portal concept. Portals allow future technologies to attach to the department while mitigating contamination or potential security breaches. The ventilation systems were examined for compartmentalisation and control by computerised systems that could shut down sectors if they became contaminated, thereby avoiding transmission throughout the building system. Blast mitigation looked at overall building structure reinforcement, energy-absorbing wall technologies, and laminated glazing to reduce sharding.[25]

Seismic disaster

More localised initiatives include California's Senate Bill 1953, passed after the devastating 1994 Northridge Earthquake. SB1953 has overturned all 'grandfather clauses'[26] for seismic code conformity, forcing a rethinking of accepted code and design standards. The Senate Bill mandated upgrades at most acute care institutions, creating large pressures to replace outdated, non-conforming buildings instead of refurbishing them.

National Institutes of Health
There are new federal guidelines published by the National Institutes of Health and others that affect the mechanical systems and infection control aspects of healthcare facilities. These have recently been upgraded.

Drug price regulation
With prescription drug spending making up a significant part of the growth in healthcare costs, there will be greater pressure for some control of drug costs. However, drug manufacturers have significant political influence and will resist any pricing controls. Access to prescription medications is regulated by the FDA in the US. The length of time taken to obtain approvals can have a direct affect on patient care, quality of care and even length of stay. There are ongoing efforts to expedite the implementation of various drugs. The cost of some medications (for example, the HIV/AIDS drug regimens) often precludes many individuals in the US, and indeed around the world, from making use of them.

Characteristics of change

Adaptability

The evolution in structure of the current US healthcare market shows no real indication of slowing down in the near future. As healthcare delivery systems undergo rapid change, requiring substantial investment of resources, the importance of an adaptable design becomes essential to the strategic success of an institution.

Long-term adaptability
Healthcare is unique in its inward approach to design. Institutions are recognising the downside of the natural tendency to think in the short term, backing into growth and change and exhausting increasingly valuable real estate and future alternatives through small incremental additions. Ten-, thirty- or even fifty-year plans are becoming more commonplace in establishing masterplans for healthcare campuses. The value of a long-term plan lies in its service as a roadmap for near-term needs. It is increasingly common for comprehensive masterplan studies to include full evaluations of likely service upgrades, possible additions, functional transformations and removal of yet-to-be built work.

Shorter building lifespans
With medically related refurbishment and replacement activity currently driving the majority of the healthcare construction marketplace, the concept of a fixed 50-year hospital physical plant shows every indication of having exceeded its useful life. Innovations in technology, operational transformations, economic competition and governmental regulations are all driving continual shifts in how hospitals function. Even the most flexible buildings, considered hallmarks of adaptable design by today's standards, may not be able to sustain the momentum of change anticipated in the decades to follow. The ability to adapt and change is fundamental to the long-term life of a facility.

Adaptable building infrastructure

Current investments in new construction anticipate greater flexibility in the reuse of space. Elements of flexibility include a more rigorous structural system with dimensions capable of accommodating a variety of services, greater floor loading, reduced vibration, greater floor-to-floor heights, and increased mechanical and electrical capacity. Contemporary design calls for as much free-span space as possible. Hard utilities, such as elevators, utility shafts and stairwells, are commonly moved to the perimeter or sited within shared zones of the building, thereby allowing for increased interior flexibility.

The perimeter placement of utilities also improves access for repairs and upgrades, keeping occupied space in operation as long as possible and allowing systems to evolve separately from the building itself. Certain functional priorities may dictate some internal allocations but these principles are of great benefit in organising early planning choices.

Modular planning

In planning, there is a greater push for more repetitive room types, such as patient rooms or interventional rooms, providing more flexibility to accommodate a wider range of clinical applications. Planning modularity allows expansion potential for functions without the need to construct separate footprints or to execute refurbishments causing major disruption. This is done through clusters of 'soft space' such as offices or other easily relocated areas being sited adjacent to treatment areas to allow expansion with minimal refurbishment. Increasingly, similar spaces throughout a facility are being designed in a consistent manner.

Mobile and modular cabinetry is becoming a standard. While initial costs may surpass those of built-in furnishings, there are measurable savings with reduced construction times, improved operating costs, and greater adaptability to changes in functional use over time.

Functional adaptability

The need for functional adaptability may occur on a daily or seasonal basis. Although there is certainly the need for specialised rooms dedicated to specific functions, many spaces can be adapted to multiple functions that occur in the course of a day rather than being reserved for specific purposes or for use only at certain times. For example, surgery recovery areas change constantly during a typical day. In the morning hours patient preparation areas may be full while recovery areas are virtually empty. By designing the recovery areas in such a way that the

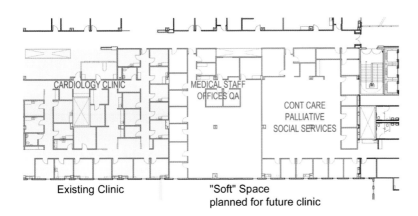

Existing Clinic

"Soft" Space
planned for future clinic

6.6
Modular planning

preparation and recovery areas are co-joined and each bay is essentially the same, the ebb and flow of patients during the day can be easily accommodated.

Adaptable design allows a building to live longer as a modern facility rather than be merely tolerated as it is 'force fit' with burgeoning technological and functional demands. High adaptability is required to ensure flexibility to changing demands based on patient type, clinical practice models, staffing patterns, communication technologies or the redistribution of diagnostic and treatment services.

Patient-centred care

Patient-centred care is generally defined as healthcare that establishes a partnership among practitioners, patients and their families to ensure that a patient's needs and preferences are respected and that education and support is in place to enable the patient to make decisions and participate in their own care. The discussion here of patient-centred care focuses on the design of the patient room.

Family care

Patient-centred care has seen the return of the family as an integral part of care-giving. Studies in the US have shown that the involvement of family and 'care partners' actually reduces length of stay. Making the family a part of the care-giving team and providing space, services and care for them as providers will become increasingly necessary and desirable.

In response to the incorporation of the family as part of the care model, nursing units are now being developed with space for a daybed in the patient room or enlarged waiting areas with increased amenities. Furniture manufacturers are responding with seating that can convert to a twin bed for family overnight stays.

Single-bed rooms

Hospitals are moving away from nursing units that have a mix of private and semi-private patient rooms to units that are exclusively single bed. The higher cost per bed is justified by a measurable reduction in nosocomial infections, reduced lengths of stay and increased patient and family satisfaction. The larger unit size is offset by changes in work patterns, enhanced electronic staff-to-staff and patient-to-staff communication systems, and distributed supplies and equipment to reduce staff travel and allow the faster and more efficient delivery of care.

The single room also allows more types of care to be provided at the bedside without the need to move a patient to a separate procedure room. This supports patient-centred focus by moving care to the patient rather than moving the patient to the point of care. Also, single bed units can operate at almost 100% occupancy, whereas units with predominantly two-bed rooms generally achieve only 80% occupancy.

Care moves to the patient

As patient acuity levels rise, the complexity, risk and cost of moving a patient also increase. Some facilities are finding that bringing care to the patient can be more cost-effective. This includes strategies such as the acuity-adaptable patient room with cross-trained nursing staff, where the patient remains in one location as his or her needs change from intensive care, to step-down, to general acute care. This can eliminate transfers from one nursing unit to another in the course of a patient's stay. For the patient it eliminates the physical and psychological stress that a move entails. The consistency of staffing enhances patient care and reduces stress for the patient.

Patient transfers can also be a significant contributor to patient dissatisfaction as records are sometimes lost or personal needs and concerns overlooked. Family members may arrive at a patient room only to find that their loved one is now being cared for in a different unit. The advent of portable diagnostic imaging equipment allows images to be taken in the patient room rather than patient being moved to a separate imaging department. With an increase in acuity-adaptable rooms and cross-trained staff and the advent of portable X-ray devices, the need for patient transfers can be minimised or eliminated.

Reducing patient transfers also reduces staff injuries. Nursing staff experience a very high rate of work-related injuries, many incurred while lifting and transferring patients. To protect staff, many facilities have instituted 'no-lift' work rules. This means that patients must be lifted using a mechanical device rather than directly by staff. Whether with a portable lift device or with a built-in lift system, the process of assisting a patient becomes much more complicated and time-consuming – a further reason to avoid patient transfer.

As technology supports greater portability of equipment, technology will move increasingly to the patient, thereby raising the potential for patient-centred care.

Pervasive computing

Computer systems are fast becoming the most critical element of the hospital infrastructure. The following functions rely on computer systems and will ultimately feed real-time information into the data network:

- communication systems;
- medical records;
- physician order entry;
- clinical decision support systems;
- pharmacy systems;
- imaging systems;
- patient monitoring;
- biomedical equipment;
- security systems;
- building control systems.

With the increasing use of and reliance on digital systems, almost every space in the hospital needs to be planned to accommodate computers.

In the patient room, bedside stand-alone computer systems were first introduced in the mid-1980s.[27] Today, bedside computers are being introduced that integrate charting, medication control, patient education and entertainment. For example, one bedside computer system replaces the bedside table with a flat touch-screen monitor mounted on an articulated arm with an integrated cabinet below housing patient medications and personal items. The back of the screen has a biometric scanner that reads fingerprints, by which nursing staff can access the charting and medication features. The patient can use the touch screen to access cable or in-house programming and education resources. Every office and workstation requires computer access, whether for the chief of staff, the housekeeping supervisor or the unit clerk in a nursing unit. In examination, treatment, procedure and consultation rooms, computers are used to access patient records, digital images and laboratory results, to place orders for tests and prescriptions, and to provide images to support patient education.

Facilities are integrating staff identification badges with access control. These 'one-card' systems utilise swipe or proximity cards that allow access to staff parking, the staff entrance, locker areas and work areas. Staff can use them to clock in and out, and bill cafeteria charges to their own account. They can allow and track access to supply rooms and medication rooms. Lost cards or the cards of former employees can be immediately and inexpensively removed from the access system.

Computer systems are being used to track equipment and supplies by infrared emitters or radio-frequency identification tags, allowing increased control and access. Similar systems, integrated with communication and charting, are being used to track staff, allowing for staff-to-staff communication and the tracking of staff response to patient calls.

Diagnostic imaging, clinical laboratories, pharmacies and material management departments have been transformed by digital systems. As imaging systems move from analogue to digital, film file rooms are eliminated, patient throughput is increased, images can be made available almost anywhere and massive amounts of digital information need to be stored and managed.

Laboratories are increasingly automated, allowing tests to be faster and more accurate while requiring smaller samples to work from. Medication can be ordered by the physician, verified by the pharmacist, and picked and delivered robotically to the point of care. From here it can be positively matched to the patient, recorded and billed, all through the computer system, drastically reducing medication errors, while tightly controlling medications and efficiently billing for them. Supply inventories can be tracked, allowing for reductions in inventory, automated reordering and just-in-time restocking.

These omnipresent computers take up space, even where flat screens are used. They also require an extensive cabling network and sizeable support spaces. This means that individual rooms must be sized to accept the computers and that the building gross needs to allow for data and communication rooms.

Increasingly acute hospital

Rising acuity levels

Several of the drivers mentioned in the first part of this chapter have converged with the effect of significantly raising the acuity level of hospital inpatients. Faced by the cost-containment pressures of managed care, hospitals seek to provide care in the least expensive setting possible. Providers are encouraged to move patients to lower levels of care and discharge them as quickly as possible. Patients are moved more rapidly from critical care to an acute care unit, and from there to an intermediate care facility or to their home.

Improved imaging and minimally invasive surgical procedures contribute to faster recovery. Surgical cases that would have required significant critical care stays can now be managed in the acute care unit or even on an outpatient basis. Remote monitoring technology, on-line patient–provider communication tools and home health nursing visits provide care to patients recovering at home while avoiding the costs of an inpatient stay. The results of these changes are remarkable. Hospitals admissions in the US fell from 38.9 million in 1980 to 35.6 million in 2001, with the average length of stay dropping from 9.9 days to 6.7 days.[28]

Migration to ambulatory services

A significant factor in the increase in hospital acuity levels is the rise of ambulatory services. With changes in technology, techniques and treatment protocols, care that formerly had been provided on an inpatient basis has migrated to ambulatory care settings. Outpatient surgeries in non-federal hospitals made up only 16.3% of all surgeries in 1980 but by 2001 accounted for 63% of all surgeries.[29] Thus, as overall bed days and lengths of stay declined, the inpatients being cared for were those who could not be cared for as outpatients or in less acute settings and the acuity level of inpatients rose. Hospitals have discovered that by providing excellent care to their increasingly acute patients they not only achieved better outcomes but concurrently were able to reduce costs.[30]

Preventive medicine and wellness

Maintaining a healthy lifestyle can prove beneficial to one's health as well as the wallet and at the same time keep people out of the hospital and healthcare system as long as possible. With the advent of the internet information age, rising healthcare premiums for employees and increasing medical errors, patients have taken their health and well-being more and more into their own hands. Health insurance systems and employers have shifted more cost burdens to the consumer mainly out of financial necessity. So with the click of a mouse or by participating in a lecture, people are becoming more educated about their symptoms and prognosis, their options and how one prevents hereditary illnesses such as heart disease.

Patients are starting to realise and appreciate the cost of their care and are finding ways to prevent the onset of illnesses before it is too late – when it becomes more expensive to treat. Fitness centres, education programs or wellness centres, which may consist of both, prove increasingly successful in promoting wellness, health and preventative care.

In 2004, Kaiser Permanente launched their 'Thrive' campaign to encourage members and non-members to lead a more healthy lifestyle. As part of this campaign, an award-winning online 'Healthy Lifestyles' educational programme was introduced to instil behaviour change around critical health issues such as weight loss, physical fitness, stress reduction and smoking cessation.[31] Other positive collaborations between healthcare institutions and local business have proven successful. For example, Kaiser Permanente has teamed up with local grocery stores to promote nutritional awareness and encourage healthy food choices. They have also introduced 'farmers' markets' at many of their hospital campuses where local farmers are invited to gather and sell their fresh produce for the convenience of patients and staff.

Complementary and holistic medicine

Until recently in the US, treatments and therapies such acupuncture, massage, homeopathic medicine, naturopathic medicine, meditation, herbal remedies and energy therapies have not been considered as viable avenues for treatment and healing. Today more and more people are tapping into these 'eastern' and 'holistic' approaches as a way to complement, and sometimes replace, their 'western' medical care. It is important to team up with one's doctor to get the most out of both schools of medicine. Depending on the doctor's openness to and awareness of available and effective complementary medicine, patients may seek treatment on their own.

Cancer patients will often use alternative treatments to help them cope with the side effects of cancer treatments and to comfort themselves and ease the worries of cancer-related stress. These treatments have the added value of allowing patients to feel they are actively involved beyond the clinical treatment of their illness.

Specialisation of care

A further contributor to the increasing acuity of general hospital inpatients has been the rise of the specialty or 'boutique' hospital. Typically small in size, specialty hospitals have developed in the areas of cardiac care, orthopaedic care, surgery and women's services. Because of their focused missions, these hospitals can provide high-quality specialty services more efficiently than general hospitals, achieve excellent outcomes and offer their patients levels of comfort and convenience not ordinarily found in general hospitals.

However, critics of these for-profit medical centres contend that they focus only on the most profitable procedures and serve only those patients that have the fewest complicating conditions. Since reimbursements are lump sums based on the patient diagnosis rather than the actual expenses incurred, the specialty hospital enjoys reduced costs and maximum profits while leaving general hospitals with the sicker, higher-cost patient population.[32]

The boutique hospital avoids the financial burdens of an emergency room and Emergency Treatment and Active Labor Act mandated care that full-service hospitals face. There have been recent efforts in various state legislatures to ban the construction of any hospital that does not include a full-service emergency department, effectively deterring the creation of boutique hospitals.

Integration of technology

As new technologies improve and become more widely available, the sophisticated levels of care currently provided at quaternary[33] or tertiary facilities will begin to be readily available in the community hospital, reducing the need for patients to travel to distant facilities to receive the best in care. Advances in information technology as clinical and administrative information merge are allowing community hospitals to quickly and efficiently access the most recent sub-specialty diagnostic and treatment information. Telemedicine and robotics will allow them to receive remote assistance ranging from real-time consultations with specialists for live procedures, effectively making the sub-specialty depth of the referral hospital available at the local level.

The consequence of the characteristics of change identified here is that hospitals are increasingly focusing on their core acute services of emergency services, critical care, acute care and complex diagnosis and treatment. This is happening as ambulatory care migrates into less expensive buildings either on campus in dedicated structures with close functional adjacencies or in off-campus locations integrated into the community. The same kinds of technology that are beginning to support a symbiotic relationship between community hospitals and referral medical centres are also allowing the community hospitals to unbundle their ambulatory services, reaching more effectively into the community. Yet, as technology advances, healthcare will remain a hands-on process where human skill and knowledge is its most essential element.

Makers of change – Case studies

If asked to imagine a hospital setting, most would quickly conjure up images drawn from personal experience. For many, the impression of receiving healthcare is of having been the subject of a clinical process. Traditionally, and to this day, the healthcare environment has been built to support the process of treating disease. Healthcare regulations, building guidelines, operational models and health insurance have all contributed to the institutionalisation of 'the process'. The patient has had little choice but to tolerate rather than participate in or exercise control over their own treatment or the environment of their care. Yet healthcare is shedding the 'disease' model in favour of a 'patient-centred' model and is slowly moving towards a finely integrated set of priorities that strives to provide care in collaboration with patients and their family and friends.

Hospital design encompasses a breadth of knowledge and engages a host of contributors unparalleled in the building industry. The building type is unique in its complexity of functional demands and insistence on inwardly focused priorities. A high percentage of the development and delivery process is primarily asked to respond to, rather than inform, strategic development decisions.

As healthcare delivery systems undergo rapid change, demanding substantial investments of resources, critical design is seen as a vital component for the long-term success of any institution. Because of a hospital's innate complexity, the act of generating and maintaining a clear and rigorous concept or resolving a localised matter with a simple, gracious gesture can become complicated in its own right. The design process has as much potential as those willing to lead such an effort are able to give it.

The following facilities represent clients and their design teams who advocated a break from established assumptions. While striving to meet a host of requirements and constraints, each has offered clear directions for future environments of healthcare. Every facility is intentionally different, expressing a diversity of needs and conditions including site, brief and budget, and predisposition of medical staff, as well as the training and vision of the architect.

High Desert Medical Center, Los Angeles, California

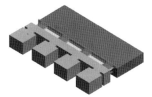

Architect:	Anshen + Allen Architects
Joint venture architects:	Stone Marraccini Patterson (now Smith Group International)
	Langdon Wilson
	Villanueva/Arnoni Architects
Client:	County of Los Angeles, Department of Health Services
Date:	Unbuilt
Description:	New hospital-based comprehensive medical centre – 200 beds
Area:	454,436 ft^2
Cost:	US$143m

While ultimately unbuilt, this scheme demonstrates the potential for thoughtful architectural integration of unbundled and decanted acute and ambulatory care functions. The scheme reaches beyond a well-ordered and patient/staff-friendly environment to offer spatial purpose and value.

Situated on a broad expanse of desert highland north-east of Los Angeles, the High Desert Medical Center brings inpatient, outpatient and health education services to a young, expanding community. Interconnected but separate structures in an unbundled arrangement house the various services of the medical centre, allowing flexibility and expandability. The north–south axis of the gardens defines the character of the medical centre and helps organise and unite its various components. The design makes use of the landscape, both natural and cultivated, to create an environment that encourages healing and rehabilitation.

The organisation of these elements achieves effective functional relationships, logical expandability, and discrete public access to individual service components. The key to the latter

6.7
a Model of High Desert Medical Center
b Impression of High Desert Medical Center

is a site plan that organises access and parking in ways that make wayfinding intuitive and therefore inevitable. The spaces around and between the buildings are as elegant and serene as the buildings themselves.

The nursing pods are positioned at the centre of the campus framed by the diagnostic and treatment centre to the west and outpatient services to the east. Carefully positioned as a backdrop to the main entrance, the towers are enveloped in a rich palette of landscape and hardscape, giving scale and privacy to the patient care environment while providing a successful wayfinding strategy. By this simple yet controversial move, the towers serve as anchoring elements and come to represent icons of care presented to arriving patients, families and visitors.

The diagnostic and treatment component has carefully collected vertical circulation and mechanical and electrical services into a shared spine leaving the primary floor plate as a clinical block unencumbered and open for future change. Exit stair towers have been pulled free of the primary block in support of the same end. Circulation for outpatient, emergent and materials services are all clearly designated off the major entry access road and accessible from individual site access points. The scheme is considerate of future growth for all aspects of care with a clear and understandable pattern for expansion without being interpreted as unfinished.

Northwestern Memorial Hospital, Chicago, Illinois

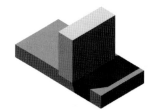

Architect:	Ellerbe Becket/Hellmuth, Obata & Kassabaum, Inc. (HOK) Chicago, Illinois
Joint venture architects:	VOA Associates, Inc., Chicago, Illinois
Client:	Northwestern Memorial Hospital
Date:	1999
Description:	Replacement hospital and new medical office building – 492 beds
Area:	2,100,000 ft^2
Cost:	US$380m

The patient experience is the guiding principle for many design decisions for this major medical centre. This philosophy is best reflected in the patient room where home comfort and technological care have been carefully balanced. The significance of a patient-centred approach becomes clear when it is considered that the resultant features were found virtually nowhere in the US healthcare system at this time.

In the late 1980s, the healthcare industry was faced with significant challenges, including changes in reimbursement and managed care, excess bed capacity and ageing facilities. During this time of great flux, Northwestern Memorial, in 1990, began to plan for what would become the nation's largest hospital building project of the decade. Along with the joint venture design team of Ellerbe Becket/HOK and VO, Northwestern Memorial created a new vision for healthcare practice and architecture. Drawing upon the medical centre's long-standing mission of 'Patients First', the team sought to strategically incorporate this philosophy into the planning and design of its new facility. At the time of its opening in 1999, the 492-bed, 17-storey Feinberg Inpatient Pavilion and twin 22-storey Galter Outpatient Pavilion were considered one of the nation's and perhaps the world's most progressive, patient-focused medical centres.

Because of its dense urban setting, space was limited and a 'bundled' approach to planning and organisation was implemented. The bundled approach stacks inpatient nursing units together on top of a diagnostic and treatment block. Northwestern Memorial went one step further and co-located inpatient services from the Feinberg Inpatient Pavilion, such as surgery, imaging and lab, with corresponding ambulatory services and linked them to the Galter Outpatient Pavilion. The outpatient pavilion has stacked clinical services and physician offices over the diagnostic and treatment block. This arrangement allows patients to see their primary physician in the ambulatory setting, undergo tests and consult with a specialist without having to leave the building. This approach, which recognised the increased trend towards ambulatory services, was unrivalled at the time.

The architecture creates a setting that communicates that patient, family and staff are all of key importance. The planning and design reflects the medical centre's culture and understands patient flow as part of the patient experience. Given the scale and complexity of the facility, dedicated circulation and a clear path of travel for the patient and visitor drove the major conceptual arrangements. The patient experience begins at the main entrance and continues throughout the site. Direct access to the main building entrances from the parking structure is clearly marked and as short as possible. Primary public circulation where elevators and waiting

areas are connected is placed along one edge of each of the buildings. This is separate from staff circulation, thus sponsoring a concept of 'front of house' separation from a 'back of house'.

Functional integration served as a high design priority. Since diagnostic and treatment facilities serve both inpatient and ambulatory needs, each floor contains a particular medical specialty. For example, all cardiology functions, such as nuclear imaging, stress testing, electronic monitoring, catheterisation and the cardiac intensive care unit are located on one floor. The consolidation of staffing for these specialties is an added benefit and creates greater efficiencies.

Ultimately, the patient experience is centred on the patient room where the inpatient spends most of his or her time. Each patient room is private and is a balance of home comfort and technological care with provisions for the family. Incorporated within each patient room is a window seat/day bed that seats three people and can convert to a single bed for family overnight stays. The window sill is set as low as possible, maximising patient views and natural light into the room. Cabinetry for personal belongings and mementos frames the window so that the patient can easily view and enjoy.

Family-centred care and the ability to respond to the needs of culturally diverse patients have been recognised as critical aids to healing and patient comfort. Since the new facility opened, these design concepts have become industry standards for many new hospitals in the US and around the world.

6.8
Northwestern Memorial Hospital Galter:
a Exterior
b Interior

Arrowhead Regional Medical Center, Colton, California

Architect:	Bobrow/Thomas and Associates
Associate architect:	Perkins & Will, Chicago, Illinois
Client:	Arrowhead Regional Medical Center
Date:	1998
Description:	Hospital-based medical centre in a park; acute hospital – 373 beds
Area:	927,000 ft^2 (five buildings)
Cost:	US$276m

With fully digital and paperless operations, private and universal patient rooms, and distinct zones for inpatient, outpatient, diagnostic and testing areas in discrete buildings along a landscaped circulation spine, this scheme manifests many current design trends, all conceived nearly a decade ago.

The design process itself was exemplary. Activities such as benchmarking of comparable healthcare centres, establishing hierarchical prioritisation for decision-making, and clear and continuous client/design team collaboration all contributed to early and strong design concepts and rigorous refinement.

Opened in 1999, this 927,000 ft^2 replacement hospital was one of the largest new healthcare facilities constructed in the US. Designed as a flagship hospital for county facilities, the planning concepts emphasise flexibility, operational efficiency and patient convenience. A unique feature is its innovative seismic safeguards – a base isolation system capable of maintaining operations following a magnitude 8.3 earthquake.

Design concepts include fully digital and paperless operations, private and universal patient rooms, and a 'medical centre in a park' concept that creates distinct zones for inpatient, outpatient, diagnostic and testing areas. With a campus of distinct buildings along a landscaped pedestrian circulation spine, or a park, the structures are placed within a series of individually landscaped parking courts connected by outdoor pathways and seating areas.

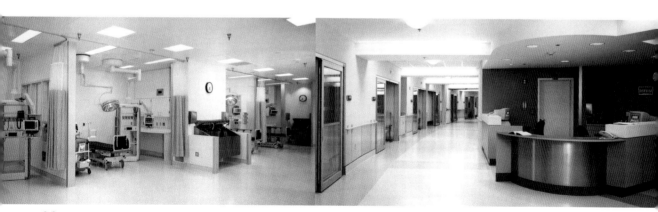

6.9
Arrowhead Regional Medical Center – interior: a examination cubicles; b desk

6.10
Arrowhead Regional Medical Centre – exterior

A plethora of elements were considered and integrated in the final design of the 373-bed medical centre including a variety of outpatient clinics, medical/surgical and specialised nursing, telemetry, maternal and child health nursing and inpatient psychiatric care. The programme also includes a full range of ancillary and patient services to support all campus facilities.

Aside from the design and planning, a unique and in many ways innovative move was the selection of the design team and the design process itself. It is rare and immensely valuable to be able to draw upon the experience of other architects in their approach to their craft. The following are selected excerpts from an interview conducted by McGraw-Hill one year before completion of the project, which best represent the thinking of the architects at the time. The discussion is with the design principals, Michael Bobrow, Julia Thomas and Robert Cull from the architect of record Bobrow/Thomas and Associates, Los Angeles, and their associates, Jean Mah and Jocelyn Lum Frederick from Chicago-based Perkins & Will.

Why do you think your firm was chosen to design the project?

Julia Thomas: Our proposal was very straightforward. We did a lot of research on the hospital – its market share, the types of services in place, etc. In putting together a presentation, we decided to focus on their role as a hospital that includes a teaching function as well as a large primary care function. We approached the project with three basic concepts that the County desired:

- the project needed to be designed from the inside out to ensure it was highly functional;
- it should be state-of-the-art, not cutting edge; and
- it needed to be flexible to accommodate changes in future use.

We viewed the project as one that had many interesting components that had to be approached with a flexible plan and programme because of the lengths of time it would take to build the project.

In addition to the hospital's programming needs, what factors significantly dictated the design?

Jocelyn Lum Frederick: The design plan was established early in the research period when we travelled to approximately a half-dozen other comparable healthcare centres around the country. We then put together a hierarchy of issues – building systems, site use, circulations, lifecycle costs, etc. – and compiled a coherent menu that everybody could agree to. Once the issues were agreed upon and prioritised, it was not difficult for us to develop a variety of solutions.

How are the buildings organised?

Michael Bobrow: This site organisation separates elements by medical function with distinct facilities for nursing, diagnostic and treatment zones serving inpatients and clinic. The distinct quality of the individual buildings, articulated as simple shapes based on platonic forms, allows the organisation of services to be clear, despite the very large size of the 72-acre campus. The entries are placed in such a way that it is possible to go into the hospital and not have to become involved with other areas of the hospital.

6.11
Arrowhead Regional Medical Center – front entrance

What design components were implemented to provide for flexibility in the future use of the Center?

Jean Mah: We have addressed continually changing healthcare by designing flexibility in the centre through maximum horizontal expansion potential on virtually every floor of the building. Just as the circulation corridors are arranged around the east–west spine, the mechanical systems are organised to achieve large open spaces with no shafts to maximise flexibility for change in the future.

Public buildings are scrutinised in terms of 'architectural enhancements'. How did you address this issue in your design?

Jocelyn Lum Frederick: The issue of enhancement needs to be looked at from the perspective of the life-cycle costs of the building. The County needed the centre to be competitive, and to resist wear and tear both inside and out. The building's use was a major issue for them so if we spent a little more on materials that resulted in less maintenance and replacement, the County considered that a long-term saving and accepted our recommendations.

The development of the interior finish palette followed the same strict durability requirements as the building systems. A simple colour scheme, which includes deep, rich tones, is rendered in a variety of textures through a wide range of materials, all of which underwent thorough life-cycle and damage testing before selection.

Although the curved frontage of the nursing tower is quite dramatic, what purpose did it serve in the functionality of the hospital?

Michael Bobrow: Each floor of the nursing tower is designed as three triangular 24-bed nursing units positioned to achieve a continuum of patient beds. Our concept of clustering beds around a central support unit increased the efficiency of the operation of the nursing units. We adapted triangular nursing units to pull all the units closer in to the central support unit, thus dictating a curved outer wall. Glass walls are utilised on the interior corridor to allow the nursing staff to view the patients in each room without having to enter the rooms. This configuration provides flexibility to reallocate beds as occupancy rates change. Also, since the tower is 350 feet long, by slightly curving the corridor the sense of it being long and never-ending is eliminated.

What was the role of the County and the hospital in the design?

Jean Mah: The County did their homework and travelled across the country to look at other facilities. Early in the design process, a hospital steering committee, including doctors, nurses and other senior management, held a series of meetings with the users to discuss the design affecting each of their departments. These meetings allowed us to get input from the users in a very directed and focused way. By the end of each session, we had closure on issues which moved the design through quickly. They also had the foresight to anticipate problems and provided budget contingencies to cover those items. Timely decisions prevented the design schedule from getting into a bind during the final design stages.

Michael Bobrow: Also, early in the design stage, the hospital painted the 350-foot nursing tower on a parking lot and erected 'walls'. Every hospital employee was given a chance to walk through and feel the distances from the nursing station to the room, the sizes of the rooms, etc. Even furniture was put into the mocked-up rooms.

Community Hospital of the Monterey Peninsula, Monterey, California

Original hospital

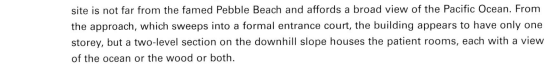

Architect:	Edward Durell Stone Architects
Client:	Community Hospital of the Monterey Peninsula
Date:	1962 and 1965
Description:	New hospital-based acute care – 142 beds
Area:	Phase 1 (1962): 82,618 ft^2
	Phase 2 (1965): 125,000 ft^2
Cost:	Phase 1 (1962): US$2.2m
	Phase 2 (1963): US$4.5m

Hospital expansion

Architect:	Hellmuth, Obata & Kassabaum, Inc. (HOK)
Client:	Community Hospital of the Monterey Peninsula
Date:	2004
Description:	Hospital-based acute care – 140 beds
Area:	New: 195,600 ft^2
Refurbishment:	338,000 ft^2
Cost:	US$150m

Given that this project was built in 1962, it might be thought unusual to include it within the category of 'Makers of change'. However, with regard to a successful marriage of planning and design, this scheme remains highly innovative and exemplary of what might be accomplished in the future.

Located between the towns of Monterey and Carmel, 125 miles south of San Francisco, the low white building was designed by noted architect Edward Durell Stone. The hospital nestles on a 22-acre knoll of wooded pine and wind-twisted cypress for which the area is famous. The site is not far from the famed Pebble Beach and affords a broad view of the Pacific Ocean. From the approach, which sweeps into a formal entrance court, the building appears to have only one storey, but a two-level section on the downhill slope houses the patient rooms, each with a view of the ocean or the wood or both.

6.12
Monterey Peninsula
Monterey Inpatient
Hospital

One of the stated goals for the architect was to provide a 'healthy emotional atmosphere for the patient' and to 'build a hospital that doesn't look like a hospital', avoiding an institutional look and feel. To this end the architect introduced some fundamental elements, innovative both at the time and by today's standards.

Relation to landscape

The hospital has a siting and relation to the landscape that most hospitals, or any other buildings, can rarely attempt. This is due, in part, to the spectacular setting in a Monterey pine forest and the advantage of a down-slope site. The building lies low and integrates beautifully, contrasting poetically with the forest in both form and palette. The approach is picturesque and site circulation is sympathetic to landscape.

Central courtyard

The core identity for the hospital is a series of three open courts beginning at the main entrance drop-off and ending with a rear plaza facing out onto the wooded hillside and framed by the patient wings. The second of three courtyards is a central domed area. Initially considered 'non-functional' and to be usurping valuable space at the heart of the building, the space sets the tone and atmosphere for the entire facility and almost immediately became a major amenity, drawing patients, visitors and staff to enjoy its café-garden and gracious exposure to sun, sky and water. The nursing wings are arranged around the central court. Flanking the central court are two large inner garden lobbies with skylit bubble-domes over stairways that negotiate the lower level patient units. These two-storey spaces exhibit the work of the local Carmel artist community.

Clarity of circulation

The building is clearly organised around a central public space. Natural light is used extensively. The nursing wings are open and visible so there is no confusion about where to go. Corridors are wide and almost always end with a view to the forest. The main circulation spine utilises floor to ceiling glass, again with views to the forest. Waiting areas are open and glassy, many with the feeling of being in a forest pavilion. Stairs are skylit from above, making them comfortable and inviting. There is a presence of natural light in almost every space and path in the building.

Single-patient rooms

The hospital was built with all private patient rooms, which in the words of Thomas Tonkin, the hospital administrator at the time, give the patient '… dignity, status and position as a human being'. Such considerations are strikingly consistent with

6.13
Monterey Peninsula Monterey Inpatient Hospital:
a Waiting area
b Pool
c Ward

6.14
Community Hospital of the Monterey Peninsula – stairway

patient-centred care. All patient rooms are uniquely arranged in clusters of four around a porch or balcony. Each main-storey bedroom opens to a skylit balcony and each lower-storey bedroom opens to a patio. The sawtooth arrangement of the clusters allows for more compact plans, shortening the corridor length – a key goal of the design brief.

While this was not the first hospital to be built using the single-patient room model, the concept was all but unheard of in the early 1960s when semi-private patient rooms and four-bed critical care wards were the norm. Prior to making the controversial decision, the hospital conducted an 18-month trial mock-up in the old hospital. The staff and patients gave their almost unanimous support for the idea, and detailed cost studies reflected no loss in income. When the hospital building was opened occupancy rates held between 94% and 99% with no measurable strain on nursing or other support staff. Nursing hours per patient dropped by 8%, from 5.1 to 4.7 hours per day. Average length of stay of the patient also dropped more than 10% from 6.6 to 5.9 days. Patient satisfaction increased from 83% at the previous facility to 96% at the new.

Expandable concept
The single-bed concept has been adhered to through several expansions and is continuing with a new major expansion scheduled for completion in 2004. The building additions and refurbishments are planned to support a new emergency department as well as an additional 140 hospital beds. The current addition maintains the scale and character of the original design.

Community Hospital of the Monterey Peninsula – Ryan Ranch Outpatient Campus, Monterey, California

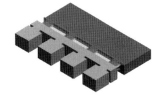

Architect:	Chong Partners Architecture
Client:	Community Hospital of the Monterey Peninsula
Date:	2004
Description:	New ambulatory care in stand-alone campus
Area:	125,000 ft² (including single level of structured parking)
Cost:	US$88.5m

Client goal

This project establishes a new outpatient campus to expand and support clinical programmes associated with the Community Hospital of the Monterey Peninsula (CHOMP). The current expansion and refurbishment of the existing hospital are made possible, in part, by this new outpatient campus. In order to meet the future demands of a growing and ageing population, advancements in medical technologies, and competitive markets, CHOMP elected to develop a new campus primarily focused on outpatient medical care and the support and consolidation of administration functions.

The first phase of the campus consists of 125,000 ft² of built space. This includes a medical office building for 35 doctors, an imaging centre, a sleep centre, a home care centre, a diagnostic laboratory, rehabilitation services and an education centre.

Design intent

The site is located within the Ryan Ranch Business Park Development, a 309-acre office park in the rolling coastal hills five miles east of central Monterey and six miles from the hospital. The sandy topography of the 21-acre site falls gently to the south over 40 feet in elevation and is covered in coastal live oak trees. Primary views are to the south and south-west towards the hills east of downtown Monterey and the coast.

The masterplan calls for seven campus buildings each designed to integrate with the landscape and topography. The site concept includes the Monterey Peninsula, which is to say that the design strategy refers to the site in terms of a larger context including the land form of the hillsides and rolling sand dunes, and the native landscape.

Each of the two initial buildings is constructed over one level of underground parking. This is done to conserve the site for future development, as well as for ease of access for patients. The buildings are designed to harmonise with their natural setting while continuing a statement of quality consistent with the hospital's reputation in the community.

The buildings 'dig into' the site with textured structural concrete retaining walls that help define the public areas between buildings. These walls also mark points of entry and circulation. The low-slung broken rooflines, or 'roofscape', are designed to harmonise with the rolling topography of the site and as a continuation of the landscape. The roofscape is an integral part of the overall aesthetic and spatial strategy for the campus.

The building and campus programme areas are captured by the roofscape. The interior functions are made as transparent and accessible to the outdoors as possible by the framing of

6.15
Ryan Ranch Outpatient Campus, Monterey
(and overleaf)
a North and East elevations; b South and west elevations

ANCILLARY BUILDING

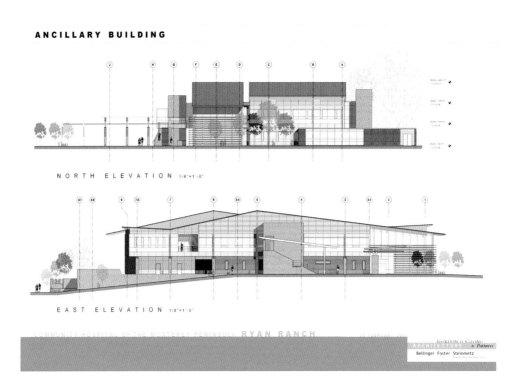

NORTH ELEVATION 1/8"=1'-0"

EAST ELEVATION 1/8"=1'-0"

ANCILLARY BUILDING

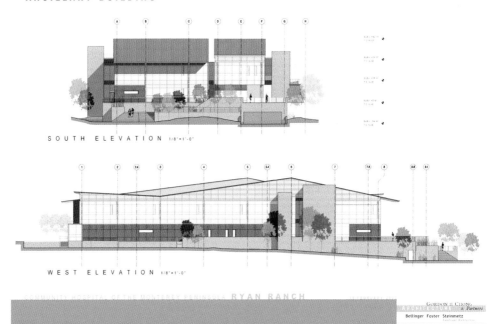

SOUTH ELEVATION 1/8"=1'-0"

WEST ELEVATION 1/8"=1'-0"

views out and drawing in of daylight. Glass curtain wall, western red cedar and weathered steel form the skin of the buildings and provide a material connection to the site's rugged nature. Circulation between buildings engages visitors with the natural landscape. Interior circulation and waiting spaces flow between the inside and outside through material use and visual connection.

The patient pathways from arrival point to waiting areas are easily followed and offer abundant natural light and views. Waiting areas are adjacent to exterior windows. Internal departmental circulation allows for easy access to treatment areas. Departments are planned so that common areas, such as copy rooms and break rooms, can be shared. Site expansion is planned, so the infrastructure will support new buildings without compromising planning and design concepts.

Boulder Community Foothills Hospital, Boulder, Colorado

Architect:	OZ Architecture/Boulder Associates	
Client:	Boulder Community Foothills Hospital	
Date:	2003	
Description:	New hospital-based acute care	
Area:	154,000 ft^2	
Cost:	US$46m	

Boulder Community Foothills Hospital is a new women's and children's centre located on a 49-acre site in Boulder, Colorado. The 154,000 ft^2, 60-bed hospital, complemented by a 67,000 ft^2 outpatient services building, provides comprehensive obstetrics, gynaecological and paediatrics services, and features private neonatal intensive care family suites. Other services include imaging, surgery, laboratory and emergency care.

The facility is the first LEED^{TM} Certified hospital in the US. LEED stands for Leadership in Energy and Environmental Design. Members of the US Green Building Council representing all segments of the building industry have developed and oversee a rigorous set of standards emphasising state-of-the-art strategies for sustainable site development, water savings, energy efficiency, materials selection and indoor environmental quality.

Masterplanned for 400,000 ft^2, the campus will eventually occupy 17 acres of the site. The remaining 32 acres have been dedicated to the City as permanent open space. The architects minimised the hospital's footprint to avoid disturbing more land than necessary. Boulder Community Hospital's newly constructed Foothills Campus recently received a LEED Silver rating, awarded for environmental leadership in the building industry. The certification marks the first time a hospital facility has been recognised with this designation. A list of sustainable actions is provided.

Site
- Erosion and sedimentation control used during construction.
- Alternative transportation:
  - public transportation access;
  - bicycle storage and changing rooms;
  - Boulder Creek bicycle path serves hospital;
  - parking capacity reduced to encourage alternative transportation.

6.16
Boulder
Community
Foothills
Hospital exterior
and corridor

- Reduced site disturbance:
    - minimised building footprint;
    - 31 acres of property left untouched, some of which includes a wetland and a wildlife corridor;
    - prairie dog colony left mostly undisturbed.
- Storm water management treatment on site.
- Landscape and exterior design to reduce heat island effect:
    - use of a white roof.

- Light pollution reduction of exterior lighting.
- Hospital-owned cars provided for necessary workday travel for employees who cycle or bus to work.

Water efficiency
- Water efficient landscaping:
  - used extensive 'xeriscaping' or landscaping with slow-growing, drought-tolerant plants on the site.
- Waterless urinals.

Energy and atmosphere
- Building commissioning included in design work as well as after construction.
- Optimised energy performance:
  - annual energy savings calculated at more than 27.6% above code mandate;
  - annual energy savings for the energy centre over a distributed system calculated at more than 21%;
  - use of motion-activated lights.
- Use of wind energy, from a local wind farm, for some energy requirements.

Materials and resources
- Storage and collection of recyclables incorporated into the building brief.
- Construction waste management:
  - more than 64% of waste diverted from landfill.
- Recycled content added to many materials, including concrete (fly ash), steel and reinforcing bar, metal studs, exterior and interior sound insulation, thermal insulation, carpet, acoustical ceiling tile, casework, wall guards, task chairs and roller shades.
- Local/regional materials – up to 52% of the materials were locally manufactured, of which 59% were locally harvested, including concrete, gravel, brick, gypsum board and sandstone.
- Rapidly renewable materials used, including linoleum flooring and cork/linoleum tack boards.

Indoor environmental quality
- Minimum Indoor Air Quality (IAQ) performance.
- Construction IAQ management plan during construction and before occupancy:
  - unfinished ductwork capped until work completed;
  - tracks vacuumed before drywall installed;
  - flushed out building for two weeks prior to occupancy.
- Environmental tobacco smoke control:
  - no smoking allowed on campus during construction.
- Carbon dioxide monitoring.
- Increased ventilation effectiveness of system.
- Low-emitting materials (low VOCs), including adhesives, sealants, paints and coatings, carpet, composite wood products for casework and cornice boards, fire-treated wood blocking and wood doors.
- Indoor chemical and pollutant source control.
- Thermal comfort – installed permanent monitoring system.

In addition to USGBC LEED v2 Silver rating, the hospital is also protecting and preserving the community by:

- Meeting or exceeding all environmental laws and regulations.
- Supporting and encouraging recycling (and reuse in some cases) of many materials used in the hospital, some of which include alcohol, batteries, light bulbs, X-ray materials, old linens, computers, envelopes, wheelchairs and crutches, computer parts, printer cartridges and medical equipment.
- Reducing waste by using real silverware and dishes, using cloth nappies instead of disposable, composting landscaping debris and issuing bus passes to employees.

Kaiser Permanente Template Hospital, Modesto, Antioch, Irvine, and Vacaville CA

Architect:	Chong Partners Architecture, Inc., San Francisco, CA & SmithGroup Inc., San Francisco, CA
Client:	Kaiser Foundation Hospitals
Description:	Acute care
Date:	2007–09
Area:	340,000–430,000 GSF (includes shell)
Cost:	US$140m–160m (excludes sitework)

Chong Partners Architecture in joint venture with SmithGroup was selected to lead the development of Kaiser Permanente's Template Hospital Project, an innovative new programme elevating hospital design standards for the HMO. In response to Kaiser Permanente's current and anticipated membership growth, the template project sets guidelines and standards for the development of up to 13 new California Kaiser Permanente hospitals over the next decade.

Kaiser Permanente is currently experiencing the most monumental building programme in the organisation's history. In addition to their response for growth, Kaiser Permanente has been committed to leveraging best practices in their operations through standardisation. Since the launch of 'Templates 2000', an internal template and standards programme from equipment procurement to room layout and sizing, Kaiser Permanente has documented and implemented ways of doing things that help them provide better services and be 'good stewards of members' money'. These building blocks have gone through many iterations culminating in what is now known as the Template Hospital – a standardised hospital that can be built on multiple greenfield sites.

The Template Hospital contains essential services as required by state code such as Emergency, Imaging, Inpatient Pharmacy and Lab, Surgical Services, Inpatient Nursing, Dietary Services, some Administrative Space, Central Sterile Supply, Material Management and Loading Dock. Labor and Delivery and Postpartum services are also included as a business strategy rather than an essential service.

Conceptually, the hospital is attached to an adjacent Hospital Support Building which could also be a Medical Office Building and/or Ambulatory Surgery Center, where the non-essential and outpatient services are located. Departments that contain inpatient and outpatient services are matched up to one another to form one cohesive department between the two 'buildings'. For example, the inpatient imaging required by code to be conducted in the hospital can be placed directly adjacent to modalities that can be located in an outpatient imaging setting. From a patient and public perspective it appears as one department and one building structure but from a code and cost standpoint it is two separate buildings.

The hospital is organised with a central spine, with the main entry at one end and a secondary entry, as the Emergency walk-in entrance, at the other end. One side of the spine houses the diagnostic and treatment 'block' including Emergency, Imaging, Surgery and Labor and Delivery. Nursing units, cafeteria, pharmacy and lab are located on the other side.

The triangular nursing unit design allows maximum exterior perimeter for patient rooms with a condensed central core for essential support and nursing functions. A central meeting space promotes private and group staffing collaboration. Decentralized nursing allows more direct visual communication with patient rooms as well as reducing travel distances. Each patient room is designed as a 'Universal Room' where single-bed rooms are promoted for patient-centred care. Nursing units easily stack for infrastructure and operational reasons.

Opportunities for expansion are built-in by adding triangular nursing units and lengthening the D&T block linearly along the spine. Expansion, adaptability and the marriage of inpatient and outpatient facilities built into Kaiser Permanente's 'Hospital of the Future' provided them with the flexibility and standardisation that they set out to accomplish.

6.17
Kaiser Permanente Template Hospital Sand Canyon: exterior rendering, aerial view and patient room

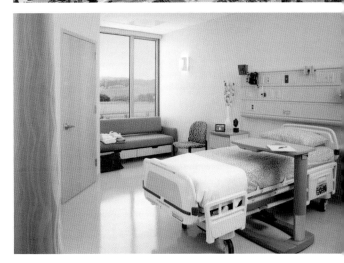

219

Memorial Sloan-Kettering Cancer Center Surgery Suite, New York, New York

Architect:	Executive Architect (Core & Shell): Granary Associates; Surgery Architect (Lead Medical Planning): KMD; Associate Architect (Interiors): Perkins Eastman Architects
Client:	Memorial Sloan-Kettering Cancer Center
Description:	Acute care – Cancer Center
Date:	2006
Area:	70,000 GSF (20,000 GSF New, 50,000 GSF Alter)
Cost:	US$35m

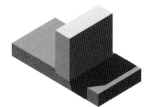

Memorial Sloan-Kettering Cancer Center (MSKCC) has opened a new 70,000 ft^2 surgical centre that was uniquely designed to take advantage of the latest medical technology. Their introduction of technological integration such as radiation therapy, MRI or CT imaging in surgery for specialized cancer care has kept them at the forefront and cutting edge of medicine.

This new 21-operating-room suite opened in May 2006. It occupies one floor in a four-storey extension that was built on top of an existing structure, suspended – as if from a bridge – and supported by four enormous columns driven through the existing hospital building (six floors plus two basement levels) to bedrock. The Surgical Center is located on the sixth floor of Memorial Hospital and incorporates the new infill construction as well as four older MSKCC buildings that ranged in date from the 1930s to the 1970s.

Their operating rooms range in size from 600 to 800 ft^2; the four 800 ft^2 rooms are specially designed to accommodate orthopaedic and neurosurgeries and three of these are specifically designed to accommodate MRI technology with structural reinforcement, roof hatches and provision for special shielding. These three operating rooms were identified for this unique function owing to their location within the new infill construction, where the additional structure could be accommodated. All 21 operating rooms are equipped for minimally invasive surgery and feature full digital integration for room control and intercommunication.

Two lead-lined intra-operative radiation rooms are designed to deliver targeted radiotherapy during surgery. This reduces the number of times a patient needs to endure a procedure and allows surgeons to investigate, locate and eradicate tumours on the spot without transport or follow-up.

An unusual arrangement was used for the 21 operating rooms: they are in small clusters ranging from three ORs to six ORs. This arrangement was

6.18
a (facing page) Integration operating room
b (above left) Control desk
c (above right) Integration and wall of knowledge

selected to foster a sub-specialty model for each of the small clusters. For instance, one cluster is focused on orthopaedic surgery; another is focused on hepato-biliary procedures. The small clusters, rather than a single large core, which had been the model in the previous surgical suite, are proving to successfully foster the desired team focus developing at MSKCC as part of their work in process engineering.

Pre-op and Recovery, located in a single suite adjacent to surgery, is organised in such a way that 20 Post-Anesthesia Care Unit (PACU) bays are located at one end closest to the surgical suite, 17 Pre-Surgery bays at the other end and 15 'Swing' bays in between which can be used in the mornings for pre-surgical patients and later in the day to care for post-surgical patients. Two separate paediatric rooms are located in the Pre-Surgical Center (PSC) as well as three isolation rooms for infection control in the PACU/PSC. A unique cluster design was employed for the PSC, PACU and Swing beds, which was a radical departure from the open ward concept typical of most prep and recovery facilities. The beds are clustered into groups of three or four beds with a small nurse-charting position in each cluster. Initial feedback has shown that families are more comfortable, patients are recovering faster with the family present and the staff is less distracted and capable of focusing on their assigned patients.

Notes and references

1.   US Census Bureau, *US Interim Projections by Age, Sex, Race, and Hispanic Origin.* Internet release date 18 March, 2004 (accessed 20 April 2004). http://www.census.gov/ipc/www/usinterimproj/
2.   Ibid.
3.   Rick Adler, 'Stereotypes won't work with seniors anymore', *Advertising Age,* 11 November 1996: 32.
4.   US Department of Labor, Bureau of Labor Statistics (accessed 20 April 2004). http://www.bls.gov/#content
5.   George P. Moschis, 'Live stages of the mature market', *American Demographics,* September 1996: 44–47.
6.   US Census Bureau, *US Interim Projections.*
7.   Ibid.

8.   Federal Interagency Forum on Aging-Related Statistics, *Older Americans 2000: Key Indicators of Well-Being* (accessed 20 April 2004). http://www.agingstats.gov/chartbook2000/tables-healthcare.html#Indicator%2025

9.   Bernard Hodes Group, *Health Care Metrics Survey – National Sample 3, November 2003* (accessed 20 April 2004). http://www.hodes.com/hcrecruiting/

10. Ibid.

11. Department of Health and Human Services (USA), *The Pharmacist Workforce: A Study of the Supply and Demand for Pharmacists,* Health Resources and Services Administration Bureau of Health Professions, December 2000. ftp://ftp.hrsa.gov/bhpr/nationalcenter/pharmacy/pharmstudy.pdf

12. Ira D. Godwin, 'Can we afford competency in light of personnel shortages?', *American Society for Clinical Pathology Member News,* March 2001 (accessed 20 April 2004). https://www.ascp.org/general/afford.asp

13. National Council of State Boards of Nursing, *NCLEX Examination Pass Rates* (accessed: 20 April 2004). http://www.ncsbn.org/regulation/epls.asp

14. American Obesity Association Fact Sheets (accessed 21 April 2004). http://www.obesity.org/

15. US Census Bureau, *Health Insurance Coverage in the United States: 2002* (September 2003), 60–223 (accessed 23 April 2004). http://www.census.gov/prod/2003pubs/p60-223.pdf

16. Terese Hudson Thrall and Dagmara Scalise, *America's Uninsured Hospitals & Health Networks* (November 2002). http://www.findarticles.com/p/articles/mi_hb3156/is_200211/ai_n7857889

17. Clark C. Havighurst, 'American Health Care and the Law', in M. Gregg Bloche (ed.), *The Privatization of Health Care Reform: Legal and Regulatory Perspectives* (New York: Oxford University Press, 2003), 16–17.

18. M. Gregg Bloche, 'One Step Ahead of the Law: Market Pressures and the Evolution of Managed Care', in Bloche (ed.), *The Privatization of Health Care Reform*, 22–48.

19. Ibid.

20. Daniel Callahan, *What Price Better Health Care? Hazards of the Research Imperative* (Berkeley, CA: University of California Press, 2003), 62–3.

21. David Lazarus, 'Health care, the flashpoint', *San Francisco Chronicle,* 8 February 2004: I1,I6.

22. David Lazarus, 'What premiums pay for', *San Francisco Chronicle,* 16 January 2004: B1,B6.

23. Robert Pear, 'Health spending rises to record 15% of economy', *New York Times*, 9 January 2004, late edition: A16.

24. Jens Mammen and Paul Strohm, 'Healthcare sizes up sustainability', *Healthcare Design Magazine* 3 (2).

25. Craig Feied, Michael Pietrzak and Ralph Hawkins, 'ER One Project', in *Proceedings from the PDC 2002: Essential Partners in Patient Care* (International Conference and Exhibition on Health Facility Planning, Design and Construction, AIA Academy of Architecture for Health and the AAH American Society for Healthcare Engineering, Orlando, FL., 24–27 March, 2002).

26. 'Grandfather clauses': buildings designed under a previous Building Code cannot be forced to upgrade upon enactment of new codes. The building's compliance is 'grandfathered' along with the superseded code.

27. Stephen Verderber and David J. Fine, *Healthcare Architecture in an Era of Radical Transformation* (New Haven, CT: Yale University Press, 2000).

28. National Center for Health Statistics, *Health, United States, 2003* (Hyattsville, MD, 2003), 285. http://www.cdc.gov/nchs/data/hus/hus03.pdf.

29. Ibid.

30. Society of Critical Care Medicine, *Better Care is Less Expensive: The New Model for Hospital ICUs* (E-Factsheet). http://www.sccm.org/public_affairs/advocacy_resources/documents/eFACTSHEET-ICUModel.pdf

31. Kaiser Permanente. 'Kaiser Permanente's 'Healthy Lifestyles' Wins Innovations in Healthcare (SM) Award' June 2006. http://ckp.kp.org/newsroom/national/archive/nat_060620_healthylifestyles_award.html (accessed: 20 August 2006).

32. US General Accounting Office, *Specialty Hospitals: Geographic Location, Services Provided, and Financial Performance,* GAO-04–167, October 2003. http://www.gao.gov/new.items/d04167.pdf

33. Quaternary hospitals: a tertiary care hospital provides a full range of services across the continuum of care, including some of the most highly specialised services – that is, specialised services with the exception of organ transplantation, which is considered 'quaternary'. Tertiary and quaternary medical centres are generally affiliated with schools of medicine, participate in undergraduate and graduate medical education, and serve as regional referral centres.

CHAPTER SEVEN

Changing hospital design in Australia

LAWRENCE NIELD

Lawrence Nield worked with the well-known British architectural firm of YRM before going on to design not only hospitals but also sports stadia and airports in Australia. In the first of his two contributions to this book he surveys the development of hospital design in Australia. He points out that when, in the 1970s, the Whitlam government opened an era of major investment in social infrastructure, the first results were an importation of hospital building forms developed in the UK, but without any development of indigenous processes of brief and standard-setting. These were to follow, and Australia has developed a hospital design culture that is similar to those of Europe and North America. In the last 20 years Australian hospital stock has largely been rebuilt. However, Nield observes that the hospital typologies are almost identical to western ones, despite differences in climate and culture. The changes in technology, patient pathways and models of care should see new typologies emerge, guided by what he calls the 'primacy of design' rather than the lowest-cost culture, which is threatening to dominate.

A landmark report in 1974

To review changing design in recent Australian hospitals it is necessary to go back to the early 1970s when government funding of hospitals dramatically changed. In 1972 the Whitlam Labor government was elected and introduced major Australian government funding for hospitals.

Australia has three levels of government: local government serving populations of up to about a quarter of a million, the eight states and territory governments, and the central Australian government (which collects the taxes). Prior to 1972 the states and a private insurance system were the main funders of hospitals. The Whitlam government introduced major initiatives in relation to health and hospitals, including a universal health insurance system called Medicare, which was initially funded by a 2% tax on people's incomes. The system provided universal healthcare at all levels for the Australian population. People wanting private beds and choice of doctor usually took out private insurance, which paid most of the difference in cost.

As well as introducing a new universal healthcare system, the Whitlam government commissioned a report on hospitals in Australia. This significant report was the result of study and research by a committee chaired by Dr Sidney Sax.[1] The committee surveyed all hospital assets in Australia including nursing homes and mental health institutions. It considered all aspects of hospitals in Australia – utilisation, physical state, age, distribution and key demographic indicators. The report proposed a new philosophy for delivering health, a plan for improving hospital services and new benchmarks for assessment of need and sizing of hospitals. It also made recommendations on capital funding – apportioning funds to each state on a per capita basis. It further recommended major central government involvement in all areas of health and proposed new regional administrations, the restructuring of finance, new licensing and controls for private hospitals and the introduction of computers into hospitals as a capital cost item. It recommended a bed ratio of 4.5 acute beds per 1,000 of population, age-weighted, excluding referral hospitals.

1978 Westmead Hospital in Sydney's west

The first major project developing from this report was Westmead Hospital in Sydney's west. For nearly 200 years hospitals had clustered around the original colonial city centres and adjacent to the major universities. Population, of course, had spread away from the original city centres and by the 1970s Sydney was a city of 3.5 million with more than half of its population living west of Parramatta (which is 20 km west of the centre of Sydney) with very inadequate hospital services. A hospital at Westmead, a suburb adjoining Parramatta, had been suggested for some years, particularly by the University of Sydney, but there had been dispute and prevarication.

The Whitlam government's initiatives brought focus and reality to the proposal at Westmead and planning started in 1973, led by the English architectural practice Llewelyn-Davies Weeks Forestier-Walker & Borr (Llewelyn-Davies Weeks) in association with the Government Architect of the NSW Public Works Department. For many years the NSW Public Works Department, a descendent of the Colonial Architect's Office, had been involved in major hospitals in New South Wales. (Generally their hospitals prior to 1970 were not thoughtful in terms of functional order or architectural response.)

7.1
The Children's Hospital, Westmead

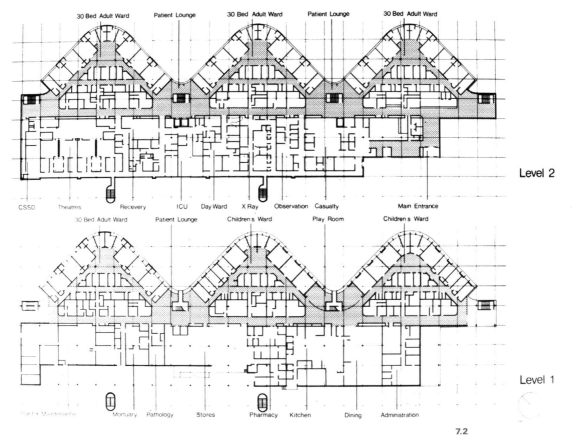

7.2
Mount Druitt Hospital, Sydney

Llewelyn-Davies Weeks introduced quite radical thinking at Westmead, about both individual hospital units and overall planning strategies, particularly growth and change. This new operational order brought with it a new hospital typology: six-storey inpatient buildings between three-storey service blocks serviced by major movement 'streets' with plenty of capability for future growth and change.[2] The strategies developed at the Nuffield Provincial Hospitals Trust and first tested at High Wycombe and Greenock in Glasgow and then later in Northwick Park were also used in full measure at Westmead, which was a major referral hospital, and teaching hospital of the University of Sydney and had initially 925 beds.[3]

In terms of building tectonics, as in England, the hospital used a universal structural grid, often 7.2 m x 7.2 m, and huge quantities of steel-framed plasterboard walling (in non-wet areas). It brought British planning to Australia and in so doing brought a new level of awareness of the interaction between functions, future growth and change, and building fabric.

The strategies employed at Westmead were continued at the Flinders Medical Centre in southern Adelaide, also planned by Llewelyn-Davies Weeks and employing English practices. This hospital again emphasised the whole hospital strategy of 'indeterminacy'. Weeks theorised that hospital buildings were susceptible to both planned and unplanned growth and change. He described medical practice and technology as changing unpredictably and therefore having an unpredictable effect on the building framing their activities. He called this 'indeterminacy'.

Westmead brought UK practices to Australia but not UK standards. In Australia there was nothing like the Health Building Notes published by the then British Department of Health and Social Security. Interest increased in these standards while the large project at Westmead was being completed. In the Western Metropolitan Health Region standards were initially set up in a series of planning and building notes. These set the 'vital statistics' – number of beds in nursing units, number of operating theatres, space standards, etc.

The first hospital to employ these standards was the 200-bed district hospital at Mount Druitt, about 5 km to the west of the Westmead project. Generally hospitals of this size had been developed as five- or six-storey slab blocks. Mount Druitt was a two-storey hospital employing the new benchmarks and using a computer planning program developed by the Australian government scientific organisation (the CSIRO) to maximise the locational efficiency of departments.[4] In fact this program showed that for small to medium-sized hospitals, two to three storeys was more efficient than higher hospitals. HRH The Duke of Edinburgh remarked at the opening of Mount Druitt Hospital that this was very different from hospitals in Britain.[5]

Nevertheless, benchmarking and the development of advisory standards and notes continued. In the 1980s in New South Wales, the Hospital Planning and Environment Centre (HOSPLAN)[6] continued to develop the hospital planning units originally initiated in planning in the Mount Druitt Hospital. These developed benchmarks for space and operations in hospital departments. By the end of the 1980s these guides were complete for most departments of specialist care centres. Benchmarks still needed to be developed for super-specialty teaching centres and for smaller country hospitals. This provided a useful database in New South Wales, which was generally adopted by other states.

These pioneering hospitals of the middle and late 1970s set the planning formula and the range of hospital fabric for the next 30 years.

The rise of the hospital procurement industry

New hospitals in the 1970s and early 1980s reflected new concerns and interests in hospitals by the Australian government and by state governments. The resultant increase in funding produced a new procurement industry and further standards, hurdles and benchmarks. A 'kit of parts' for hospitals had been established by Westmead and Mount Druitt. In rolling out new hospitals all over Australia, governments moved away from their traditional method of procurement (using public works departments) to new capital works departments in state departments of health.

Health departments had seldom done this before and were clearly anxious about the complexity and risks of sponsoring very large buildings. They turned to project managers – small project managers rather than large construction companies.

By using project managers, state departments of health could have relatively small capital works offices and could draw on the knowledge and experience of industry. Project managers soon began to specialise in health and employed health planners – usually nurse planners. Quite often they were also involved in the selection of architects, more so than under the sponsorship of public works departments. 'First-time' cost became the central criterion of design rather than operational order, appropriate occupancy and movement or operational costs. Hospital building is complicated and intricate – a fertile area for 'value-management' exercises by project managers. By the 1990s the role of the project management companies in hospital procurement had brought a narrow focus on capital cost at the expense of operational order, productivity and sustainability.

Hospitals cost too much to run – capital and operating costs

In the early 1990s, the state governments of Australia realised that there was a link between hospital spatial arrangement (configuration of departments and rooms) and operating cost. The planning and three-dimensional arrangement of a building affected staffing levels. New hospitals had to be not only better in terms of care and location but also cheaper to run, which meant using staff more effectively. This proved difficult to achieve.

New hospitals, even those the same size as older ones, usually had more complex medical services and more complex building services. Medical equipment, air conditioning and lifts often come with expensive maintenance contracts. Staffing in new hospitals is often at a higher level than in older hospitals. However, by sharing spaces, 'swinging' beds between wards (providing more efficient bed utilisation) and the efficient location of critical departments, staff and cost savings could be made. Staff travel (with or without patients) takes up to 15% of salary costs.[7] Travel is 'wasted' time. By the efficient spatial arrangement of key departments travel time can be minimised. All hospital projects now have to give defensible forecasts of their future operating costs.

The biggest efficiency gain was in reducing the length of stay. This was achieved by new medical procedural work such as minimally invasive surgery and the tendency for more and more medical disciplines to treat on a day-case basis. Changing work practices, so-called multi-skilling, made staff more efficient. Better relations with primary care organisations and GPs also reduced hospital stays. With resources being distributed only to areas of need, the overall number of hospitals was reduced while services were aggregated and provided from the remaining extended hospitals. For example, in Canberra, a city of 300,000 people, where before 1990 there were three major hospitals, the Royal Canberra Hospital was closed in the centre of Canberra and the two hospitals to the north and south of the city strengthened.

An extensive and wide-ranging hospital programme

In the 1980s state health services were generally administered through regions. Sydney, for example, had four regions. Initially, hospitals were not part of regional administration and had their own Boards, but by the 1990s more streamlined health authorities had been formed, which included all levels of care. There was a considerable difference between large metropolitan health authorities that might administer populations of over 1 million and country health authorities that might have fewer than 100,000 residents.

The 1990s saw many country hospitals close and the strengthening of services in major country centres. Smaller country towns had clinics with GPs, and sometimes visiting specialists, but no beds. Better transport allowed more convenient travel over long distances. Special health programmes for Aboriginal peoples were administered across Australia by the central Department of Health and by states' departments of health. The improving health profile of the majority of Australians was not shared by the Aboriginal population and governments realised that they needed to increase their funding to Aboriginal health services.[8] Specialist Aboriginal primary care buildings began to appear in both the outback and Aboriginal population centres in cities.

However, by the 1990s the state governments began to blame standards and Hospital Planning Notes for what they perceived as the high cost of hospitals, and in New South Wales HOSPLAN was abandoned and space standards no longer benchmarked. At the same time governments and project managers forced down the fees of design teams so there was little fee available or incentive to innovate and question the form of the hospital. Generally, the paradigm of hospital departments with local circulation (local streets) linked by primary (through hospital-corridor 'freeways') together with the use of the 'neutral and universal grid', made the hospital into an industrial and anonymous complex. Hospitals, with exceptions, became pathology factories with hierarchical staff organisation and the anonymous power of industrial medicine.

Though the architecture and feeling of many of the hospitals may be anonymous, there has been an extraordinary hospital programme in Australia over the last 20 years where virtually all major specialist centres have been redeveloped or relocated. Generally, hospitals have been located or relocated to meet demographic demand and most major cities now have specialist hospitals close to or at population centres. Many inner city hospitals that did not serve existing or growing populations have been closed. In addition, there has been growth in private health – a number of new private hospitals have been built despite only a minority of the population holding private insurance. In 2000 the number of Australians holding private insurance was below 30%. In the 1970s most inner-city hospitals (more than 25) were using facilities, according to the Sax Report, that were more than 50 years old. By 2000, fewer than six specialist care centres in Australia were using obsolescent facilities.

A distinct architectural language?

'The Australian Modern hospital holds a pivotal place both in the development of Australian Modernism and in the advancement of Australian health. They used a distinctly modern language, drawing upon the latest medical and architectural theories of the time. In doing so, they also introduced Modernism to the Australian public, seeding a fundamental shift in Australian architectural aesthetics,' Willis explains in 'Machines for Healing'.[9]

The Melbourne architect, Arthur Stevenson, reinvigorated hospital design in the 1930s after trips to Europe where he saw many pioneering buildings. He moved hospitals away from blocky brick designs to the elegance of floating balconies and the new tectonics of Alvar Aalto.

7.3
The Royal Melbourne Hospital

His influence continued right through to the 1960s. He won the RIBA Gold Medal in 1947 for the Royal Melbourne Hospital and his early hospitals. A new hospital form came in the 1970s, particularly with Westmead Hospital, with a series of distinct blocks with brise-soleil. Balconies did not reappear. The need for sunlight and air – those characteristics of modernism – was no longer thought important.

'What ideas, though, can plausibly drive hospital design? What kind of idea could even get a look-in, in so highly programmed a building type? What, for that matter, might architecture's main idea-material – space, light, beauty, even – really contribute to the sick or dying?' E.M. Farelly observes.[10]

In the 1970s and 1980s different architectural languages began developing in Brisbane, Sydney and Melbourne. In Brisbane a lightweight verandahed and shaded language grew from the sub-tropical Queenslander house to become the 'south-east Queensland style'. In Sydney, influenced by Glen Murcutt, there was an interest in precise metal buildings, often using 'common' corrugated iron. In Melbourne there was less interest in everyday materials and more interest in style. Melbourne, though a more staid city than Sydney, embraced postmodernism, initiated in houses and small public buildings by Peter Corrigan. The RMIT University particularly encouraged postmodernism in university buildings. Personal ideas expressed by architects developed into a language and imagery ranging from parody to cosmology. These regional languages began to influence hospitals. The variations in language can be seen at St Vincent's in Sydney (Figure 7.10) and Sunshine Hospital in Melbourne (Figure 7.6).

In the 1980s, in hospitals such as Westmead, Mount Druitt and the Alfred, traditional procurement provided a reasonable cost base. However, with the rise of project managers, both architects' fees and the cost per square metre of hospitals were reduced, and every part of the fee structure and the building fabric was worked over to reduce cost. This impacted on the sustainability, serviceability and architectural language of Australian hospitals.

Hospitals were no longer seen as a symbol of a modern and healthy society as they were in Britain in the 1950s and in Australia in the 1970s and 1980s. Hospitals were seen in a sense as a charity, as in the early nineteenth century when the destitute attended hospitals and the wealthy were treated at home. In the 1990s many public hospitals gave out signals and associations of charity, while the wealthy attended private hospitals. This propensity for government and project managers to underfund public hospitals meant that it was hard to rethink the forms, materials and order of the hospital, though there was room to some degree to experiment on the exteriors. This experimentation largely involved materials, expressions of the internal (neutral) grid or various brise-soleils.

During the 1970s and 1980s hospitals were usually designed by specialist hospital architects. There were probably only ten significant practices across Australia. For example, in Queensland, Conrad and Gargett designed almost all the big hospitals, while in Victoria, Stephenson and Turner continued their run from the 1940s and 1950s. In New South Wales, the Government Architect of the NSW Public Works Department designed most of the district hospitals, as did the Public Works Department in South Australia and Western Australia. The new funding initiatives in the late 1970s and 1980s began to change this group, though the so-called hospital architects remained a small and specialist part of the profession. This increased the skill level in hospital design, but it mitigated the effect of ideas and paradigms coming from other building types.

The exception to this was the use of teams of architects to do different parts of a major hospital project at the same time and in a coordinated way. Of course many hospitals are designed by different architects over time, but there seems to be merit, in a constrained cost environment, in gaining some changes of architectural expression by using different architects simultaneously. The approach of having a team of architectural practices was used on both the New Sydney Children's Hospital and the Prince of Wales Hospital, major projects of the 1990s.

Given these constraints of money and project managers, it is not surprising that hospitals show less invention and richness than, say, houses and university buildings. There was still an overwhelming feeling of anonymity. The pivotal place that Australian hospitals held in the development of modern architecture has almost disappeared. It is difficult to see fundamental changes in type and language in the huge hospital programme that has occurred from the 1980s. The introduction in 2003 of unthoughtful PFIs (Private Finance Initiatives) in Victoria and New South Wales may further reduce cost, innovation and exploration. The Royal Melbourne Hospital has successfully operated for 60 years and is only now reaching the end of its service life. It is hard to think that some of the low-cost hospitals now being produced will be able to emulate this.

What follows are descriptions of key Australian hospitals that are chosen both because of their planning initiatives and because they are not as anonymous as many of their contemporaries. These are the (better) exceptions, not the rule.

> Despite squeezing architecture's play-space to near-zero ... the hospital needs its healing ministrations more than ever.[11]

Australian typologies – Case studies

When considering the spatial arrangement of activities, architects take account of context, access, site, circulation and current technologies. Hospitals resolve themselves into organisational paradigms. Typologies both facilitate and limit the organisational arrangements. The investigation of typologies is not just a taxometric exercise but a critical part of designing complex buildings – an intrinsically architectural activity because of its holistic nature. Both care patterns and technologies influence typologies. For example, tuberculosis has been a major design factor in the rise of the 'slab with balconies', while the introduction of fluorescent tube lighting increased the depth of blocks. Typologies have provided a cohesive theme in hospitals in different (western) countries generally over 80 years and more, particularly since the Second World War. Sunand Prasad has identified the following typologies:

1. Linked pavilion or finger plan.
2. Low-rise multi-courtyard or checkerboard.
3. Monoblock.
4a. Podium and slab/tower (also 'bundled' or 'stacked' in US).
4b. Podium with two or more towers/blocks over.
5. Street.
6. Atrium/galleria.
7. Unbundled.
8. Campus.

In the following, a selected but typical cross-section of Australian hospitals is considered in relation to these typologies. It is a selection by the author and considers probably about 20% of the large hospitals built over the last 25 years. Interestingly, all these typologies are represented except one. There is a fairly even distribution between typologies with the exception of typology 2, the low-rise multi-courtyard, which is not represented. Typology 4a slabs are seldom seen since the 1940s and 1950s.

Linked pavilions

This form is used in smaller country hospitals and in other suburban hospitals where new facilities are being added.

Blacktown Hospital, Sydney

Architect:	McConnel Smith and Johnson
Date:	2002
Area:	32,000 m²
Cost:	AUD$65m (excl. loose furniture, commissioning costs and fees)
Procurement route:	Lump sum

This project involved the redevelopment of a metropolitan district hospital while maintaining full service delivery, and was completed in 2000 at a cost of approximately AUD$65 million.

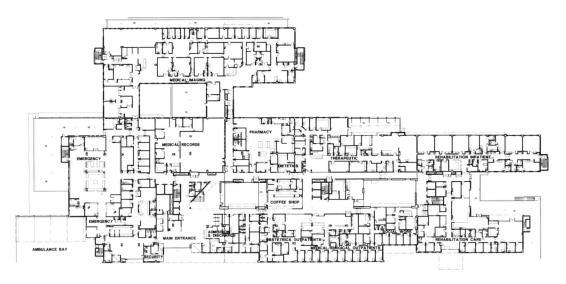

7.4
Blacktown Hospital, Sydney

The project principally comprised a new main building of approximately 32,000 m^2 with four usable storeys and accommodating 273 beds plus most of the hospital's other facilities. Other new and existing buildings accommodate about 100 beds.

The form of the new main building was strongly influenced by the size, shape and topography of the site able to be cleared on the edge of the campus. It is based on the fundamental principle of vertical zoning of functions to allow each the optimum building form and access routes.

The functions on the four levels of the building are: 1. general support; 2. restricted access 'hot floor'; 3. main entry and public access diagnostic and treatment; and 4. inpatient. The unusual configuration, with the main entry at the third level, results from the site topography and allows visitor access to the fourth level inpatient facilities by stair. To orientate people, a series of carefully scaled and modulated internal courtyards are integrated with the hospital's circulation.

The 'hot floor' includes birthing and newborn special care nursery, operating theatres/day surgery, intensive care/high-dependency, coronary care and cardiology 'step-down' units. The main entry level includes emergency, imaging, outpatient and therapies/rehabilitation units.

The general inpatient units are – as is strongly preferred by the users – of conventional single-corridor form, but the majority of units, all independently accessible, are arranged end-to-end in continuous 'strings' of three to allow adaptability of unit configuration.

Coffs Harbour Hospital, North Coast, New South Wales

Architect:	Woods Bagot
Date:	2002
Area:	27,000 m^2
Cost:	AUD$55m (excl. loose furniture, commissioning costs and fees)
Procurement route:	Managing contractor

Developed on a greenfield site, this AUD$80 million public hospital is a 202-bed facility and accommodates four operating theatres, day procedures and an endoscopic suite, together with ICU/CCU facilities. The development was designed around four distinct care centres, each with its own entrance and reception – critical care, family care, medical and therapeutic care, and mental and general well-being. A 'one-stop shop', the campus provides the whole gamut of health services on a single site.

This 27,000 m^2 development is configured in joined clusters providing considerable access to landscaped courtyards, views and natural light, and allowing for future adaptation and expansion. The resort-style setting, with its emphasis on access to external courtyards, takes advantage of the balmy Coffs Harbour climate and allows patients, including those in bed or undergoing treatment, to be treated outside.

The single-level buildings are oriented to take advantage of shade and cooling breezes to reduce air conditioning consumption, with rooms opening onto courtyards to provide natural light and outlook. Sensitive landscaping supports conservation of the surrounding rainforest ecosystem, and is low maintenance and planned to support lower energy use within buildings.

7.5
Coffs Harbour Hospital, New South Wales

Integrated into the design were many cultural needs that evolved from consultation with the community's Aboriginal elders. Courtyards and a tribal platform provide Aboriginal patients with private spaces for family/friends of the sick to give care in customary ways.

Sunshine Hospital, Melbourne

Architect:	Lyons
Date:	2002
Area:	6,000 m²
Cost:	AUD$15m (excl. loose furniture, commissioning costs and fees)
Procurement route:	Managing contractor

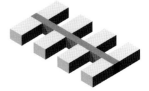

> Marry medicine and architecture and we have the modern hospital – the bastard child of politics and pragmatics, clad, if unlucky, in an aesthetic gesture, or, if lucky, in nothing at all.[12]

Sunshine Hospital is a district hospital in Melbourne's west that has been developed since the late 1970s. Recently a new ward building and hydrotherapy suite have been added. These additions overtly insist that they are architecture.[13] The buildings are faced with glazed brick arranged in pixelated patterns of grey, white, orange, yellow and blue. The hospital is turned into a billboard addressing the nearby ring road. A play is made between the window pattern and the pixelated wall pattern. A play on plan is also made, where the plan of the hydrotherapy building is a miniature plan of the ward block. As previously discussed, Melbourne has a preoccupation with the postmodern.

Though the architecture, wall play and configuration is undoubtedly interesting, inside the plan is a typical double-corridor nursing unit with four-bed and single-bed ward units that goes back to the Nuffield researches of the 1950s. The nurses' station is placed centrally. The architect, Corbett Lyon, is laudable in suggesting that the building 'interrogates the type'. In the normal sense of the word there is no interrogation or reconsideration of type in this building: it repeats a well-tried hospital ward type that is 50 years old. Their wall play is an appeal, a billboard to the community bringing Tom Wolfe and Las Vegas into the hospital. But as Tom Wolfe has explained, the vitality of Las Vegas comes from 'unconscious pretentiousness', not from pop designers. Andy Warhol would not have cut the mustard in Las Vegas.[14] But Lyon is right when he says 'the hospital is part hotel, part laboratory, part airport lounge, part business centre, part shopping centre and part hospital ward. Each of these types suggests a new way of conceptualising hospitals.' However, the type needs to be fundamentally reconsidered to make new hospitals with their new services' requirements work.

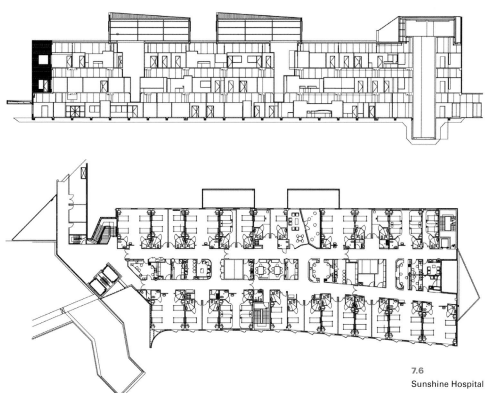

7.6
Sunshine Hospital

Podium and slab

Slab blocks alone have seldom been used since the Royal Melbourne which shows a direct influence of Aalto's Piamio Sanatorium in Finland. The 'slab' typology was used by designers from the 1930s to the 1960s.

The Royal Melbourne Hospital 1942–95

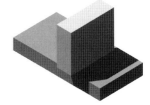

Architect:	Stephenson and Meldrum 1942;
	Daryl Jackson and Di Carlo Potts 1993
Date:	1942 and 1993
Area:	1942: 80,000 m^2
	1995: 50,000 m^2
Cost:	AUD$100m (excl. loose furniture,
	commissioning costs and fees)
Procurement route:	Lump sum

The Royal Melbourne is a specialist centre for major trauma and referral. Melbourne Health, its governing body, is responsible for care in Melbourne's north and west. The hospital has a distinguished history of medical research and shares its campus with the Walter and Eliza Hall Institute.

The Royal Melbourne was designed by Stephenson and Meldrum in 1942. It was a distinguished example of Arthur Stephenson's functionalist modernism, which started with the

Mercy Hospital in 1934 after a European trip where he inspected Bijvoet and Duiker's Zonnestraal Sanatorium (1928) and Alvar Aalto's Piamio Sanatorium (1932). The 1942 buildings have been extended by a new combined services building on the southern edge of the site as well as a new entrance and intensive care building. Further to the north, on Royal Parade, a private medical centre and private hospital have been introduced to the site next to a large underground car park. By demolishing a nurses' residence on the west of the site, a new site is being made for a women's hospital to adjoin the Stephenson and Meldrum 1942 main block. Because of its innovative planning in the 1930s and 1940s, the Royal Melbourne has lasted for 60 years with only these recent major additions

7.7
The Royal Melbourne Hospital

The podium and slab typology is common in Australia and was used on 30–40% of inner city hospitals before 1980. Even in recent hospitals, such as St Vincent's, this typology has been used – in this case determined by the site and existing buildings. Toowoomba Hospital puts a service 'podium' beside the existing ward 'slabs', allowing many inpatient, outpatient and clinical services to be located adjacent to each other on one floor.

The Alfred Hospital, Melbourne

Architect:	Stephenson and Turner
Date:	1990
Area:	5,000 m² Trauma Centre
Cost:	AUD$8m (excl. loose furniture, commissioning costs and fees)
Procurement route:	Managing contractor

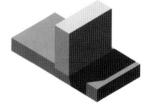

The Alfred Hospital is an anonymous major hospital whose major treatment and diagnostic facilities and slab ward blocks were built in the 1970s. Many of the 1970s facilities are now being redeveloped. It also houses a major research facility, the Baker Institute, and the Medical School of Monash University.

In 1990 Stephenson and Turner added a unique trauma centre serviced by both helicopters and ambulances. The hospital has a park opposite and a helicopter platform has been placed

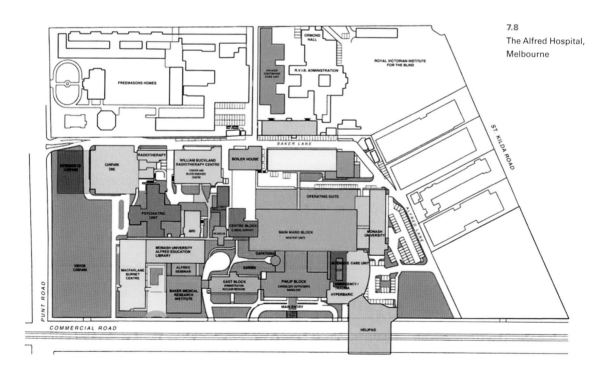

7.8
The Alfred Hospital, Melbourne

237

over a major road. This allows helicopter access from four major directions and safe approaches. Patients from the helicopter meet a stabilising team at the entrance and proceed immediately to the resuscitation bays, all on one level with radiology departments and CAT-scanning. Patients are able to receive the highest level of treatment within the 'golden hour'.

The Alfred was the first hospital with an integrated helicopter landing platform. The initiative, funded by the state road and traffic authority, led to reordering of facilities – creating what is now called a 'hot floor' – and the co-location of emergency, emergency beds, operating theatres, imaging, and intensive and cardiac care. Most specialist care centres adopted this zonal organisation (and helicopter landing pads) ten years later.

Toowoomba Base Hospital, Queensland

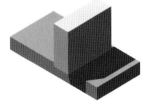

Architect:	Bligh Voller Nield
Date:	1997
Area:	20,000 m^2
Cost:	Stage 1: AUD\$43.5m;
	Stage 2: AUD\$5m (excl. loose furniture,
	commissioning costs and fees)
Procurement route:	Managing contractor

This redevelopment project comprised the construction of a new building to provide a new main entrance together with emergency, medical imaging, day procedures, operating suite, ICU/HDU and support departments. In addition, the project included the refurbishment of various departments in existing buildings and the construction of a new community health village on the hospital site. An 'institute' model of care was used to develop the planning strategy.

Each floor has contiguous inpatient, outpatient and clinical services. However, major treatment and diagnostic facilities such as operating theatres and radiology are still centralised. The patient, rather than the medical and nursing staff, has to do most of the travelling within the complex. On the other hand, at the primary level, there are conveniently organised services that will allow very convenient diagnosis and treatment in the health village.

7.9
Toowoomba Base Hospital,
Toowoomba, Queensland

238

St Vincent's Hospital, Sydney

Architect:	Lawrence Nield and Partners (Interior Design and Art Programme Andrea Nield)
Date:	2002
Area:	84,000 m²
Cost:	AUD$110m (excl. loose furniture, commissioning costs and fees)
Procurement route:	Lump sum

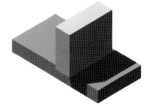

St Vincent's is situated in inner-city Darlinghurst, which has a 'difficult' population mix. There are many older people with complex conditions as well as young people and drug addicts. St Vincent's is a typical inner-city modern hospital that has halved its beds (to 310) while treating much greater numbers of patients. Three-day bed stays and huge increases in ambulatory care have meant that more than 60% of the activity of the hospital is on a day-only basis.

The redevelopment brings together a major public hospital and a private hospital, which now share their major treatment and diagnostic facilities as well as hotel facilities. There has been close consideration of shared space – for example, on the public ward floors there are large shared spaces between each ward. An extensive emergency department is on the ground floor, linked to radiology.

7.10
St Vincent's Hospital, Sydney:
(far left) patients, relatives and public in
the entrance garden, a parvis; (left) 'The
Gift' by Neil Roberts in main entrance

Escalators link to the ambulatory floor above, which has day surgery, cardiothoracic, oncology and associated clinics. Surgery, endoscopy, interventional radiology and the cath lab/EPS lab are located in a single zone. This was the first Sydney hospital to use 'planned' patient-centred zones.

As in the Children's Hospital (see below), there is an extensive art programme with a major glass piece called 'The Gift', by Neil Roberts, at the main entrance. This uses a cosmology of everyday drinking glasses. 'In so many circumstances – sickness, thirst, deprivation, crisis – an offering of water is the first expression of caring.' But it also gazes at the stars: 'The heavens express the infinite scale of the universe. To some they are a place of their God, to others simply an embodiment.' A garden outside the main entrance provides a place for interaction between patients and their families. Art and landscape provide engagement and mystery.

Monoblock

This typology in Australia seems to be a product of site constraints, air conditioning and fluorescent tube lighting.

Prince of Wales Hospital, Sydney

Architects:	Di Carlo Potts and Associates with Daryl Jackson, Robin Dyke: campus schematic design
	Bligh Voller Nield: 19-theatre operating suite fit-out; cardiac services fit-out; infectious disease unit
	Rice Daubney: paediatric 'hospital'
	McConnell Smith and Johnson: obstetric and gynaecology 'hospital'
	SJPH with Brown Brewer and Gregory, and Peter O'Neill and Partners: ambulatory care and services fit-out
	Di Carlo Potts and Associates: acute care services building
Date:	1995
Area:	6,000 m^2
Cost:	AUD$10m (excl. loose furniture, commissioning costs and fees)
Procurement route:	Lump sum

The Prince of Wales Hospital consolidated specialist care services in the eastern suburbs of Sydney and allowed the closure of the Prince Henry Hospital, a pre-war 'linked pavilions' hospital. As with the Children's Hospital Westmead, a team of architects worked simultaneously on various parts of the redevelopment.

The huge monoblock redevelopment includes:

- A new acute care services (ACS) building, which included the relocation of the Prince of Wales adult emergency department and the provision of a two-helicopter helipad and patient transfer facilities with direct access to the new intensive care department.

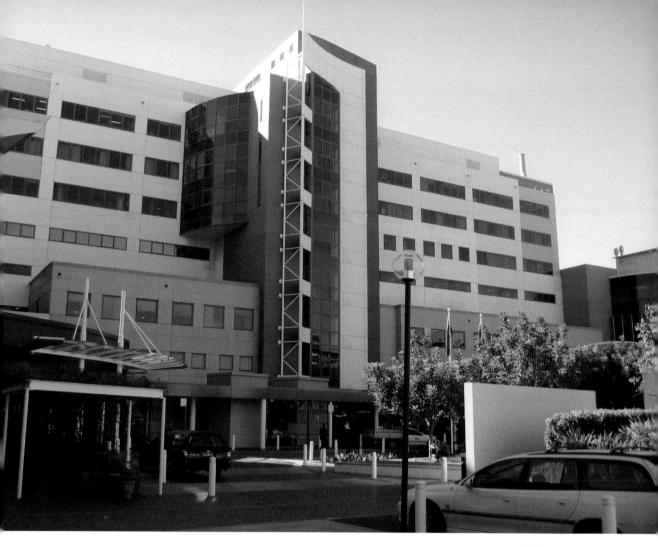

7.11
Prince of Wales Hospital,
Sydney

- Additions to the 243-bed children's hospital, including a new school, new main entry, haematology/oncology ward with day care facilities and a 21-bed intensive care unit.
- A new women's hospital features include extensive educational seminar and lecture theatre facilities, delivery suites and birthing centre, breast clinic and newborn intensive care unit.
- A new five-storey ambulatory care and services centre (ACSC), which incorporates a range of clinical and diagnostic services for both inpatients and outpatients for the major hospitals and houses the 19 co-located and integrated operating theatres. The centre also provides retail outlets and a landscaped forecourt for drop-offs and arrivals, and is the hub of the development. There is multi-level structured car parking directly under the majority of the new hospital buildings providing 1,600 parking spaces. Additional car parking spaces are planned, providing an overall total of 2,250 spaces.
- A three-storey 171-bed private hospital on top of the ACSC building.

The complex is remarkable for the full integration of ambulatory, medical, surgical, paediatrics, gynaecology, obstetrics and genetic services, and a 19-theatre operating theatre floor (at the time of building, the largest in Australia). It introduces both further zoning planning and a very high degree of centralised facilities. The use of six architects relieved the oppressiveness of the large monoblock.

241

Low-rise multi-courtyard

Despite Australia's benign climate in which you would expect courtyards to be an important amenity, there are few, if any, public acute hospitals using this special arrangement.

Street

Westmead Hospital is very much a diagram of 'freeways' and 'local roads'. The freeways and associated building services routes can expand endlessly. Mount Druitt Hospital is organised around a two-storey street, which can extend in two directions. Unlike Westmead, which has separate buildings connected to the 'freeways', Mount Druitt has continuous building on both sides with top-lighting to the street. The form of Westmead is one of low three-storey buildings flanking the five- and six-storey central ward blocks.

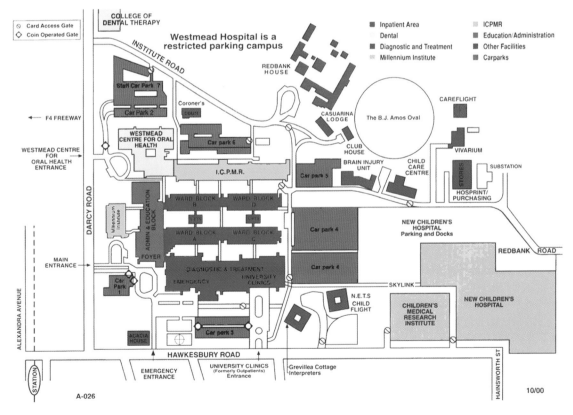

7.12
Westmead Hospital

Westmead Hospital, Sydney

Architect:	Llewelyn-Davies Weeks, Forestier-Walker and BOV with NSW Government Architect
Date:	1978
Area:	150,000 m^2
Cost:	AUD$150m (excl. loose furniture, commissioning costs and fees)
Procurement route:	Managing contractor

When Westmead was finished in 1980 it had 925 beds, a total that has subsequently been reduced by about 200 beds. This is an important example of John Weeks's principle of 'growth and change' and the 'endless street', which has been described earlier in this text.

Atrium/galleria

Atria and gallerias are a very useful primary circulation design tools in hospitals – particularly low-rise hospitals. They given orientation and 'comprehensibility' to visitors, patients and staff. They provide a significant room in a mix of rooms. In a children's hospital, this is particularly important.

The New Children's Hospital at Westmead, Sydney

Architect:	Government Architect PWD, Lawrence Nield and Partners, Woods Bagot, McConnel Smith and Johnson
Art programme:	Joanna Capon and Andrea Nield
Date:	1995
Area:	90,000 m^2
Cost:	AUD$300m (excl. loose furniture, commissioning costs and fees)
Procurement route:	Managing contractor

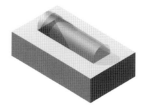

In 1995, 300 paediatric beds were added to the Westmead complex by closing the Royal Alexander Hospital for Children in inner Sydney. This very large series of buildings was given humanity and scale by using five architects. The main block of the new children's hospital, including the organising galleria, operating theatres and laboratories, was by Lawrence Nield and Partners; the outpatients building by McConnell Smith and Johnson; the services building by Woods Bagot; and the inpatient units by the NSW government architects.

The hospital had a very successful art programme. The principle underlying this programme was 'Does the work appeal to the parents, and relax them and therefore their children?'

7.13
The Children's Hospital, Westmead Hospital

This hospital is a major project of 'medical humanities'. There is nothing tame about the artwork in this large hospital, and children, parents and staff are enjoying it ten years after its completion.

Townsville Hospital, North Queensland

Architect:	Woods Bagot
Date:	2002
Area:	55,000 m²
Cost:	AUD$130m (excl. loose furniture, commissioning costs and fees)
Procurement route:	Managing contractor

The new Townsville Hospital provides 425 beds and offers a general acute level of medical support. It is a freestanding development replacing the original facility on the waterfront and follows the language of the Royal Melbourne Hospital with extensive balconies. The 'institute' model of care developed for the hospital clusters clinical services with inpatient and outpatient functions. This increases flexibility by bringing the clinical services into a direct relationship with the related bed spaces. The interconnection of the four key buildings creates a deep plan and gives a strong order by the clarity of the circulation patterns. The four-storey, naturally lit atrium running from east to west through the length of the main building anchors the horizontal and vertical circulation and gives an order to the overall pattern of circulation. The ambition to create a welcoming and enjoyable environment is sustained by emphasising the locations of the entry and main stairways by strongly pronounced, super-scaled blade walls and by the use of bright colour to punctuate the spaces.

7.14
Townsville Hospital,
Queensland

Unbundled

In Australia, the form of some hospitals seems to be determined by site and the need to maintain service delivery. The use of 'institute' models of care and the integration of outpatient and inpatient by discipline, together with the constraints of existing buildings, leads in the case of Princess Alexandra to a mixed (hybrid) typology. The beds are contained in a serpentine six-storey block with courtyards on the south side.

Mount Druitt Hospital, Sydney

Architect:	Lawrence Nield and Partners
	(now Bligh Voller Nield)
Date:	1980
Area:	17,070 m²
Cost:	AUD$14.4m (excl. loose furniture,
	commissioning costs and fees)
Procurement route:	Lump sum

Mount Druitt is a planned new town, 50 km from the centre of Sydney. The new hospital for the Western Metropolitan Region of the Health Commission of NSW contains 200 beds offering general medical, surgical and paediatric services, together with major accident and emergency facilities.

Computer studies of internal traffic in similar hospitals led to the spatial arrangement of activities. The programme used was called TOPAZ – Technique Of Placing Activities in Zones. This was developed by CSIRO (the Australian Government Research Organisation for urban planning). It relied on surveying return trips from origins to destinations by ten staff groups in an existing hospital then optimising these for the planned Mount Druitt Hospital. This simulation led the design team to the two-storey layout. The plan has two major user levels, with the two-level hospital street providing both the major circulation and the organising principle for future growth and change. On one side of the street are the nursing units and on the other the clinical and non-clinical services.

The wards have a triangular configuration, which provides good patient supervision and convenient intra-ward movement. The roof level contains engineering service spaces and allows maintenance and adjustment to be carried out without intrusion into clinical areas.

7.15
Mount Druitt Hospital

Princess Alexandra Hospital, Brisbane

Architect:	Cox MSJ
Date:	2002
Area:	90,000 m²
Cost:	AUD$200m (excl. loose furniture, commissioning costs and fees)
Procurement route:	Structure: lump sum contract; completion (fit-out): managing contractor with guaranteed maximum price

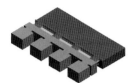

The project comprises the redevelopment of a metropolitan teaching hospital, including women's services. It includes a new main building, several other new buildings, and partial or complete upgrading/recycling of several existing buildings. The cost in 2002 was more than A$300 million.

The new main building is approximately 90,000 m² and has six usable storeys plus a basement car park. It accommodates 560 beds plus most of the hospital's other facilities. Other buildings accommodate about 200 beds.

The other new buildings accommodate research, pathology, mental health, ambulatory dialysis, central energy, etc. Retained buildings include the spinal injuries and geriatric assessment/rehabilitation units.

The form of the new main building was strongly influenced by the topography of the site able to be cleared in the centre of the campus, and is based on the following principles:

- Horizontal splitting into inpatient and support zones to allow each the optimum building forms and infrastructure, and to facilitate separation of disparate functions and access routes.
- A continuous inpatient zone accommodating 140 beds, only nominally divided into five completely flexible units.

The new main building is particularly notable for the 'institute' of associated inpatient and support facilities providing specialised co-located outpatient/inpatient consultation, diagnostic, treatment, allied health, teaching, research and administration facilities. Most ambulatory facilities are decentralised to these 'institutes'.

Other noteworthy features of the new main building include a 'hot floor' with 22 operating rooms and three cardiac catheter labs in an integrated facility for day-only and inpatient procedures, with adjacent critical care and coronary care inpatient units.

Changing models of care

From the beginning of the 1990s women's (including obstetric services) and children's health services were relocated with specialist care centres. This rationalisation of services is continuing. By 2004 there will probably be only one or two stand-alone sub-specialty hospitals.

7.16
Princess Alexandra

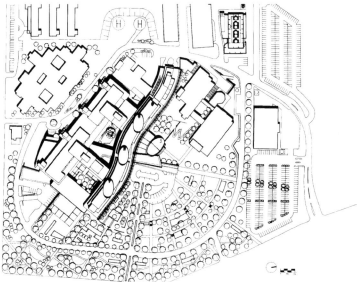

In Adelaide, the women's and children's hospitals were combined. In Sydney, the Princess Alexandra Children's Hospital was redeveloped with Westmead Hospital. The Prince of Wales Redevelopment Hospital brought all specialties and sub-specialties together. In Melbourne, the Royal Women's Hospital is presently being moved onto the Royal Melbourne site. Similarly, in Brisbane the Royal Brisbane Hospital and Princess Alexandra Hospital now bring together specialist care for women, children and general patients.

After 1995, the notion of a model of care became an important design requirement. The definition of 'model of care' is not precise and often has different meanings to various stakeholders in the planning process. However, the notion clearly concerns the organisation and delivery of medical and nursing services in the tertiary, secondary and primary care settings.

Changing medical practice has had a huge impact on the delivery of health services. Length of stay in hospital has decreased from 10 days in the 1980s to 3.5 days currently. This reduction seems to be due to changes in technology, minimally invasive surgical procedures, improved anaesthetic agents and government financial pressures. But there is still a focus on inpatient services and waiting lists.[15]

Ambulatory services are being increasingly developed, as less than a third of hospital services are now inpatient services. This move to specialist ambulatory care models is a fundamental shift and will further increase the efficiency and effectiveness of hospitals. Ambulatory service zones can provide a more efficient and flexible environment for medical practice and a less threatening environment for patients.[16]

Many hospitals in the 1980s and 1990s, such as Toowoomba and Princess Alexandra in Queensland, were developed on the so-called institute model, which locates disciplines geographically, including inpatient units. This model works well for the doctors but not for the patients who would be continually shuffled around the hospital. In this model it was very seldom that diagnosis and assessment of patients could be done in one day.

A patient-focused zonal model can give a better arrangement for both medical practice and patients. Increasingly in Australia, specialist care centres (referral hospitals) have critical care zones or hot floors, ambulatory zones, comprehensive cancer services, trauma and emergency services and 'centres for independence', all providing much more convenient arrangements for patients. These new treatment and diagnostic 'supermarkets' now largely 'occupy' existing hospitals – that is, traditional typologies. However, they will lead to new typologies

Changing hospitals

Australian hospitals generally seem to use the same typologies as those in other western countries. The effects of context, access, site, circulation, technology and model of care have affected typological outcomes. In terms of size, specialist care centres attached to ten universities have reduced from 1,000 beds to 600 acute beds or fewer, no doubt as a result of the reduction in bed-stay and increasing ambulatory care. This trend is continuing. The recent dialogue between 'institute' and 'zonal' care models will also perhaps change typologies, as will the ever increasing use of computer and information technology.

Australian hospital stock has largely been rebuilt over the last 20 years. Those described in this chapter are ones that exhibit both good design and effective spatial arrangement of activities.

Hospitals in the 1980s displayed optimism and confidence, but the increasingly misplaced emphasis on cheapness, project management and, in the state of Victoria, PFIs (private finance initiatives) controlled by the Treasury, has seen hospitals degenerate into an architecture of anxiety, often with visual cheapness and constraining typologies. Vitality has been lost. Designers must go on 'interrogating the type' to re-establish the primacy of design.

Notes and references

1. Hospital and Health Services Commission (Sidney Sax, Chairman), *A Report on Hospitals in Australia* (Canberra: AGPS, 1974).
2. R. Llewelyn-Davies, and H. M. C. Macaulay, *Hospital Planning and Administration* (Geneva: World Health Organisation, 1966).
3. A. Cox and P. Groves, *Hospitals and Health Care Facilities* (London: Butterworth, 1990), 54–65.
4. CSIRO Commonwealth Scientific and Industrial Research Organisation TOPAZ Programme.
5. Personal conversation with the author, October 1982.
6. New South Wales Hospital Planning Advisory Centre, *HOSPLAN Health Building Guidelines* (Sydney, 1973–).
7. South Australian Health Commission, *Royal Adelaide Cost Study* (1985).
8. ATSIC Aboriginal and Torres Strait Islander Commission, *Annual Report 1991–1992 Aboriginal Health Services* (Canberra: AGPS, Canberra, 1992).
9. Julie Willis, 'Machines for Healing', *Architecture Australia,* July/August 2002): 46.
10. Elizabeth Farrelly, 'Taming St Vincent's', *Architecture Australia*, July/August2002: 58.
11. Ibid.
12. Alan Bowen-James, 'An Examination of Hospital Buildings', *Architecture Bulletin*, May 1991: 4.
13. Trevor Mein, 'Sunshine', *Architecture Australia*, July/August 2002: 48–54.
14. T. Wolf, *The Kandy-Kolored Tangerine-Flake Streamline Baby* (New York: Farrer, Straus and Givoux, 1965).
15. Peter Brennan, *Melbourne Health: A Vision for a Healthy Future* (paper presented to Melbourne Health Board and Executive, 2003).
16. Ibid.

CHAPTER EIGHT

Postscript: Re-inventing the hospital

LAWRENCE NIELD

In the final chapter of this book Lawrence Nield speculates about a new paradigm for the design of hospitals. He compares twentieth-century advances in the design of airports and offices with the lack of equivalent advances in the design of hospitals. This brings us back to where this book began, noting the schism between architectural culture in general and the design of hospitals. Nield believes that the new paradigm, based on creating highly flexible and indeed movable buildings and open-plan spaces within a large-span building, will allow a break from the current highly specific and rigid paradigm based on a multiplicity of cellular spaces arranged on the basis of optimising clinical adjacencies. This new paradigm will not only offer far more effective environments for care, but will also re-engage more 'thinking architects' with hospital design. Though speculative, the vision is solidly grounded in Nield's experience of designing hospitals in the UK and Australia. And all its components already exist – from the robotic arms through which a surgeon in New York operates on a patient in Strasbourg, to the regulation of hospital environments and security through technology like that of flight information display systems in airports. Nield argues that only when free of the tyranny of planning grids, corridors and rooms can hospital environments be designed to better respond to the whole spectrum of patients' needs.

The architecture of 'people buildings'

Building a 2020 Vision: Future Health Care Environments considered the planning, location, design, delivery and construction of healthcare buildings.[1] It defined design quality as functionality, technical performance and 'impact' and sought a new vision for the range of healthcare buildings from primary care to specialist care. By implication, it said that design and architecture were lacking in healthcare building. It had suggestions about bringing healthcare design 'back into mainstream architecture'. It sought to stimulate a 'dialogue' between healthcare and architecture. This chapter aims to advance that dialogue, particularly in relation to hospitals and specialist care centres.

In relation to hospitals, it is useful to look at key factors in the architectural order of the best airports and offices. Contemporary airports process large numbers of people. The best contemporary offices have reinvented the concept of work. Many of the factors that have changed airports and offices are also present in hospitals. Of particular interest are the impact of computer and information technology, and non-hierarchical management and teamwork.

New modes of occupancy in airports and offices have made them both more productive and better places for all types of users. Airports, in particular, manage and process large numbers of people as they arrive and depart. Offices have changed as a result of the introduction of computer and information technology and the increasing realisation that much office work is team-oriented rather than hierarchical. Like hospitals, both airports and offices are 'people' buildings.

Hospitals are becoming more and more like airports. They need to enable a series of complex, related processes in one place and usually in one day. Almost two-thirds of modern hospital activity relates to patients visiting the hospital for the day and not staying the night. This ambulatory activity will increase. Even inpatients seldom stay longer than three or four days. Like airports, hospitals need optimum access for patients, visitors and staff.

Airports process people

Airport terminals process people and, like hospitals, use extensive wheeled traffic (luggage and trolleys). The better airport terminals, such as Hong Kong International Airport and Kansai in Japan, process large numbers of people, with easy wayfinding, and treat them decently in a variety of spaces ranging from large to small. Both the processing of the passengers and the management of spaces and gate lounges are controlled by sophisticated computer and information systems. The airport information and management system is the critical, but unseen, component of the management and planning of space.

The airport terminal information and management system is part of a network and suite of computer programs that inform the terminal's operations data bank. These include programs for

8.1
Kansai Airport Renzo Piano Building

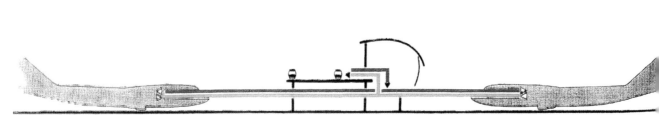

flight information display systems (FIDS), gate management, baggage reconciliation, wireless communication, common use equipment, security, booking and ticketing, finance, facilities management and local departure control. Furthermore, this suite of programs is linked to various external networks, such as airport operations and air traffic control. It is said that over a million discrete operations have to be carried out for a large modern airliner to take off. Successful terminals balance seamless internal operations, effective passenger wayfinding and information, together with retail and commercial activities.

FIDS is an active, integrated signage and information system. This system allows space to be programmed, for example gate lounges may be changed. It can also give information about plane delays, weather, etc. Linked to plasma screens which have audio-visual capabilities, FIDS can become more than just a navigation system.[2]

Airport departure and arrival halls are usually large-span structures. The Japanese architect and 1993 Pritzker prize-winner, Fumihiko Maki, identified large-span 'flexible' halls or hangar buildings as becoming increasingly important. They provide an envelope that can accommodate many different functions, events and architectural expressions (Figure 8.1).[3]

Offices discover work

Since the 1980s offices have changed quite radically to develop a new workplace with computer and information technology and to reflect teamworking. Despite exceptional offices – like the Larkin Building by Frank Lloyd Wright (1906) and the Johnson's Wax Building, also by Frank Lloyd Wright (1933), which began to investigate the workplace, staff leisure and opportunities for amenities at work – offices were highly influenced by Taylorism (Frederick Taylor's *The Principles of Scientific Management,* 1915), which organised offices into a hierarchical assembly process, similar to mass production in the manufacturing industry.[4]

Offices became further formularised with the introduction of the 'deep plan' facilitated by the invention of the fluorescent tube by General Electric in 1938.[5] Buildings such as 100 Park Avenue, New York, moved office workers well away from natural light coming in through the windows. Before the Second World War, office buildings such as the Empire State Building had large windows and relatively shallow floors because typing generally required natural light. The combination of air conditioning (which became common immediately before the war) and cheap, cool fluorescent lighting made big floor areas, in excess of 1,000 m^2 per floor, economical. These factors quickly developed the 'core and shell' office building and the ubiquitous 4 ft (1,200 mm) module of office buildings.[6] This paradigm is still quite common, particularly in speculative office building.

In 1963, in Germany, this formula began to be challenged. Burolandschaft (office landscape) considered plans determined by teams and workflow, including quiet zones, meeting facilities and cafés. The first office building planned on these principles was the Ninoflax Building, Nordhorn.[7] With its developed 'kit-of-parts' to make simple 'open-planned offices', it introduced a new and more pleasant way of working. However, with abbreviation and blurring of the concept, Burolandschaft became watered down and the office environment became less satisfactory. Speculative offices returned to the core and shell formula and introduced cubicles, work bays and work points within neutral structural grids and hermetically sealed building envelopes.

With the appearance of personal computers in the office, new influences were at work. This was appreciated by Frank Duffy and the work of DEGW in the late 1980s. More spacious layouts, flexible buildings with increased storey heights and more effective building services were proposed. Understanding that office staff worked in teams, even to the extent of placing key managers within their teams in open offices, changed office layout. Offices such as the Boots office in Nottingham, England, by DEGW showed new ways of designing and working.[8] This continued with the exploitation of networked systems and just-in-time management. New realisations and developments in sustainability introduced the office project as an agent of change – increasing productivity and improving the work environment while minimising environmental degradation.

Contemporary hospitals – how are you?

In comparison with airports and offices, contemporary hospitals are not well. They are often obsolescent when completed. Many hospitals designed only 25–30 years ago are now being replaced – for example, Charing Cross Hospital, London. Furthermore, they are often hostile, impersonal and monotonous environments. Much planning is done according to simple formulae and diagrams concentrating on the co-location of departments or zones and the cellularisation of activities. There is an inability to keep up with or 'frame' changing medical practice and models of care, for example the increasing procedural work for surgery, obstetrics, gynaecology and radiology. Because serious approaches to environmental sustainability cost more initially, sustainability is only token compared to the better offices and airports. Even at the everyday level of planning, hospitals have difficult wayfinding systems. In large specialist care complexes, finding your way is often difficult and confusing. Lastly, throwing away one of the most expensive buildings in the community every 25 or 30 years is hardly sustainable – it does not save energy or reduce greenhouse gases.

These disorders result not only from problems associated with changing models of care, access, equity and social inclusion, inappropriate networking and location, but also from current design strategies. The strategies affecting the form and life of hospitals are the over-particularisation of user requirements in briefing, the lack of full integration of computer and information technology and, most significantly, the continuance of an outdated paradigm. In short, the wrong sort of building is a major contributor to the poor health of hospital facilities.

One of the great paradoxes of architecture is that it has to deal with both the everyday and the long term. It has to meet the operational and ergonomic requirements of everyday activity while accepting change in that activity over time. Furthermore, it has to bring the framework of everyday activities into an overall integrated organisation. Successful architecture has to succeed both at the everyday level and at the higher level of organisational integration. We should think of architecture not, in the definition of Pevsner, as 'buildings designed with a view to aesthetic appeal', but as places for life events and activities.[9] It is not helpful to say 'hospitals are about functions first and we can fix the aesthetics afterwards'. This takes a narrow view of functions and an unsatisfactory view of aesthetics.

It is more useful to say 'operations' than 'functions'. Importantly, the operational order of a hospital has a number of levels. It is not simply the arrangement of rooms, corridors and equipment – this is a snapshot of what is a dynamic problem. Hospitals, and particularly specialist centres, are many series of changing events, changing workplace conditions and appropriate forms and frames for treatment, diagnosis and care. A hospital's 'functional brief' needs to consider overall operations and movement.

As a result of inadequate briefing and inherent conservatism (the use and reuse of the 'lying-in' paradigm), hospitals and particularly specialist centres are in very poor health.

Hospital symptoms

The poor health of hospitals is characterised by the following symptoms:

- **Difficult wayfinding**
  This may seem a minor ailment but it usually reveals systematic planning problems.
- **Walls get in the way**
  The ubiquitous double-loaded corridor with cellularised facilities does not respond to workflow and changing events. Furthermore, wall dependency means the facility is hard to change over time. Over-particularisation of hospitals often reflects one snapshot of user requirements. Particularisation of hospitals often reflects static requirements rather than more general dynamic requirements. Hospitals have become demand-driven rather than seeking a balance between supply and demand. They are seen as a fixed setting, not a 'movement economy'.
- **Growth, change and the 'neutral and universal grid'**
  Since the research of the Nuffield Trust in the 1950s there has been very widespread use of the 'neutral and universal grid'. This is a structural grid that can house the key facilities of a hospital – four-bed wards, single-bed wards, operating theatres, etc. Within this grid plasterboard rooms are constructed, often with the walls laced with services. The aim of such construction is to allow future change. In hindsight, we can see that this change has not happened particularly gracefully, if at all. The inherent irony of plasterboard walls (and office partitions) is that they have to be destroyed to change the space. On the whole the 'neutral and universal grid', which varies from 6.9 m × 6.9 m to 7.8 m × 7.8 m, has constrained planning and thinking and has not been an agent for incremental change. Similarly, the development of hierarchies in circulation with through 'streets' and local 'streets' has very seldom led to structured extension or alteration. For example, in London, Northwick Park's great circulation armature is still waiting for new pieces 30 years after its completion. In contrast, large-span structures in airports have been able to sustain many refits, for example Dulles Airport in Washington DC.
- **Static rather than dynamic**
  The very close fit of rooms and circulations with the requirements of users often freezes a hospital around one activity. In fact, like offices and airports, hospitals are dealing with a series of events rather than with static functions. Most buildings, for example, sporting stadia and convention centres, have new facilities and equipment for different events. Similarly, in hospitals there are changing settings over the seasons and even over the working week. Furthermore, medical practice and technology is rapidly changing.
- **Inherent conservatism – the 'lying-in' paradigm**
  There have been important changes in hospitals since the Second World War, but in the last 30 years there have been relatively few changes despite changing technologies and radically reduced lengths of stay. It seems that when people set out to design a hospital they seek to improve the existing model or type, rather than question it. There used to be

similar conservatism in office buildings but changing work practices and computer and information technology have forced change.

- **Natural light**

    The planning of hospitals with their increasing size and complexity is easier on large floor plates with little natural light. The invention of the fluorescent tube and mechanical ventilation has allowed very deep floor plates in both offices and hospitals. However, Dr Roger Ulrich has shown that natural light and engagement with the outside world – landscape in particular – can help patients to recover more quickly, use fewer analgesics and have lower blood pressure.[10] Though obviously it is not possible to have natural light in some treatment and diagnostic facilities, it is important in waiting areas and nursing areas, even in intensive care and coronary care. The use of natural light can also conserve energy.

- **Sustainability**

    Hospitals, unlike other building types, have failed to implement new environmentally sustainable strategies and techniques. Ironically, in many cases they are the most unhealthy buildings in terms of material use, out-gassing, engagement with nature and production of CO_2.

- **Poor procurement policies**

    Present procurement policies mean that every part of the hospital is fitted-out down to the last thermometer holder. Many of these fit-outs were designed five years before they were implemented. In contrast, offices separate the base building and fit-out contracts. This allows design to be done much closer to implementation.

- **Impersonal institutionalism**

    > ... see, as they climb
    > To their appointed levels, how their eyes
    > Go to each other, guessing; on the way
    > Someone's wheeled past, in washed-to-rags ward clothes:
    > They see him, too. They're quiet. To realise
    > This new thing held in common makes them quiet,
    > For past these doors are rooms, and rooms past those,
    > And more rooms yet, each one further off
    > And harder to return from; and who knows
    > Which he will see, and when?
    >
    > Philip Larkin, 'The Building'[11]

For as long as planning relies on cellularisation, double-loaded corridors, and sequential waiting spaces, hospitals will be condemned to have '... rooms, and rooms past those, and more rooms yet'. As in airports, the use of computers, FIDS-type systems and a new organisational approach can develop a more pleasant and scaled environment. In airports, small-scale activities are often located in larger halls. Work and patient environments, rather than functional requirements and considerations, should be the basis of planning.

How did our large medical centres get this way? What is the illness underlying these symptoms?

An outdated paradigm

Hospitals developed in a similar way to office buildings over much of history. In the classical Greek cities hospitals and offices both used the stoa. At Kos and Epidaurus patients lay either in the colonnade or in the double hall behind. The Romans, as military casualties increased, converted barracks into hospitals. The Christians then took over the 'workhorse' building of the Romans, the basilica, and used it for churches, monasteries and convents. Convents and monasteries were often recycled as hospitals.

The first purpose-built hospital was the Ospedale Maggiore by Filarete (1456) in Milan. Men and women were separated in two cross-form wards. Canal sewage systems were below ground, and there was real ventilation and heating. This building was used for 450 years, until the 1950s. It is now the library of the University of Milan. About 150 years after the first hospital, the first office was built in Florence for the Medici family, the Uffizi by Giorgio Vasari. Our word 'office' comes from the Italian word 'uffici'.[12]

In the early eighteenth century the main hospital in Paris, the Hotel-Dieu (a converted monastery), was burnt down. A competition was instituted to build a new hospital further down the Seine, which produced extraordinary new plans. This competition considered both supervision and ventilation. It proposed 15 patients per ward, amended in the Third Report to the Academy of Science to 30 to 35 patients per ward (Figure 8.2).[13] However, the Revolution delayed implementation of these ideas and it was not until 1846 in the Hospital Larisboisiere that the

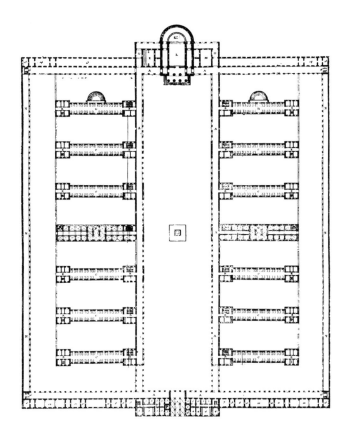

8.2
French pavilion hospital plan, This is the first time the term 'pavilion' is used. Each pavilion provided approximately 100 beds with 34 beds' per floor. Wide spacing is to avoid contagion. Third Report of the Hospital Commission to the Academy of Science 1788.

257

new 'pavilion hospital' appeared. Shortly after the completion of this hospital in Paris, Florence Nightingale (*Notes on Hospitals*, 1858, *Notes on Nursing*, 1859) developed the pavilion plan at the Herbert Hospital, Woolwich, setting a paradigm for hospitals for the next hundred years.[14]

The next significant paradigm was developed by Alvar Aalto at the Paimio Tuberculosis Sanatorium in Finland in 1932 (as a result of a competition held in 1928). This introduced the slab block with balconies for sun. This architectural type was widely copied around the world, for instance in the Mercy Hospital, Melbourne, in 1938 and the King George V Hospital for Women, Sydney, in 1942.[15]

The invention of the fluorescent tube and the increasing use of air conditioning, together with antibiotics, which reduced bed stay, produced deep-plan hospitals, particularly in the United States, at the same time as offices adopted deep-plan 'core and shell' typologies. In the 1950s research into hospitals began in England with the St Albans Hospital Study, the High Wycombe Hospital and the Nuffield experimental work at Greenock in Scotland. This produced a more rigorous understanding of hospitals. The use of the 'neutral and universal grid' began, which could conveniently house different-sized units.

In 1965 Le Corbusier showed an alternative to this in the extraordinary Ospedale Civile in Venice. This established the hospital on an urban grid but with ranges of different room sizes and clear wayfinding. Unlike his 'Ville Radieuse', it also worked well with the historic urban typology and grain of Venice. However, Le Corbusier's hospital plan had little influence on planning and typology – unlike his architectural language.[16]

Llewelyn-Davies and John Weeks developed the original Nuffield research into the strategy of 'indeterminacy', continuing the development of structural grids often 7.2 m × 7.2 m. By the 1980s offices were developing more spacious and flexible layouts with increased storey heights as a result of more effective building services and information technology. Computers began to be used in hospitals but initially for financial systems only, not as an integrated part of the design. During the 1990s workplace planning based on teams and non-hierarchical organisation greatly changed offices.

Over the last 20 years hospitals have adopted a conservative paradigm built around major circulation (freeways and strict zoning). In many ways they have similar characteristics to present-day urbanism. Instead of looking at hospitals as strategic foci where teams and equipment gather to 'address problems, isolate and resolve them', they are seen as rigid little cities of 'disciplines' and 'beds'.

Bill Hillier has argued in his description of cities and their origins that cities began as an urban grid with groups of continuous buildings in outward-facing, fairly regular clumps, among which is a defined, continuous system of space in the form of intersecting rings, with a greater or lesser degree of overall regularity.[17] The deformed grid gave towns a mechanism for generating contact.

In the nineteenth century, with the increasing size of towns and increased traffic, the traditional model of the city and the city itself became synonymous with moral depravity and political disorder. This gave rise to the value system of nineteenth-century urban planning encouraging dispersion and ruralisation. This paradigm has survived into the twenty-first century and has become embedded in institutional forms and structures. Streets lost their multi-purpose use and became traffic arteries only. Hillier suggests that these relics of an outdated paradigm threaten 'the natural functioning and sustainability of cities'.[18]

Much of this nineteenth-century thinking is still embedded in the 'lying-in' hospital: that is, regarding a hospital as a series of through-ways and departments rather than an overall movement economy. Through the pressure of technology, airports and offices have re-established some of the beneficial aspects of urbanism in their planning whereas hospitals have not.[19]

Hospital makers – ministries, users, management, boards, project managers, engineers and architects – have focused on the exact and economical responses to everyday activities. They have avoided, perhaps inadvertently, the importance of the strategic whole, of trying to understand and formulate the most appropriate architectural type. There are of course architectural types emerging in hospitals, particularly the mega hospital. For example, the use of deep plan with atria based on a repetitive grid, such as the McKinsey Health Sciences Centre in Edmonton, Alberta, which, as well as using deep plan with atria and nursing units in wings, has interstitial spaces for services. Similar forms can be seen in the Chelsea and Westminster Hospital in London and the Berlin-Neukölln Hospital. However, when 'interrogated', these types have not rethought the important opposition between the everyday and the strategic whole – they are still a development of the 'lying-in' hospital.

With new modes of occupancy in hospitals and new technologies, particularly the full integration of communication and information technology, both the form and face of hospitals will need to change to make them more productive and better places to be in for patients and staff. They need a new paradigm that supports their natural functioning and sustainability.

The 'neutral' grid

The widespread use of the fluorescent tube, which produced cheap light and little heat, permitted the deep plan. Natural light was ignored in many hospital areas. At the same time, antibiotics began to reduce bed stay and the balance between the area of nursing units and the area of treatment and diagnostic facilities began to change. In Florence Nightingale's Herbert Hospital, Woolwich, of 1859, about 90% of the area of the hospital was for nursing. By the 1940s, in hospitals such as the Massachusetts General Hospital, the beds were taking up between 40% and 50% of the area. Treatment and diagnostic areas were put in deep-plan blocks with the wards usually slabs above or beside them. But the tyranny of the fluorescent tube had brought in the 4 ft × 4 ft (1,200 mm × 1,200 mm) grid (Figure 8.3).

In the 1950s research began in hospital building in Europe and particularly in England with the Nuffield studies on early ambulation and their experimental buildings at St Albans, Greenock and High Wycombe. These were directed by Richard Llewelyn-Davies and John Weeks. In the 1960s Llewelyn-Davies and John Weeks developed this work into the planning principles that reflected 'indeterminacy'. Hospital buildings grow and change but a great part of this growth and change cannot be predetermined. Hospital planning in terms of circulation, building services and growth paths needed to have plenty of 'elbow room'. Hospital 'streets', the major circulation of the hospital, could expand in a number of directions. Ducts allowed for future building services (Figure 8.4).[20]

In the 1970s Richard Llewelyn-Davies and John Weeks began to put their theories into practice in Northwick Park in London and many other health sciences complexes around the world. In Britain the 'Nucleus' hospital and the 'Harness' and 'Best buy' were developed as ways of standardising and making hospitals more economic. However, by the 1970s hospitals had begun to adopt a conservative formula based in Europe and Australia on a 300 mm grid and a repetitive structural bay size of (usually) 7.2 m × 7.2 m. Planning then began with this neutral structural grid and rooms were filled in by 'connecting the dots'. Following Llewelyn-Davies, hospitals – where the site permitted – were six or seven storeys high rather than 20 storeys. Despite the oil crisis of 1973, there was little attempt at sustainability and energy minimisation.[21]

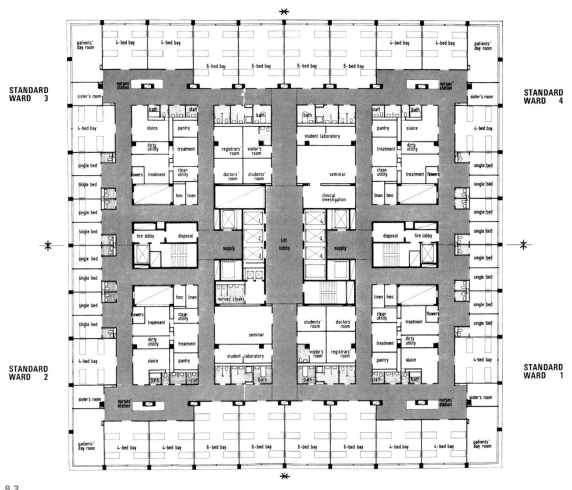

8.3
St Thomas' Hospital, London 1968, Yorke Rosenberg Mardell Architects

The forms and fabric of the 1970s have continued until today. The hospital is usually relatively low rise with division into treatment and diagnostic zones and with 'hot' areas such as emergency and operating theatres, nursing and 'hotel' areas, and non-clinical services. Sometimes the universal structural grid is applied across all these different uses; sometimes the three major uses have different grids and fabric. In the last five years this model has been improved by the introduction of atria or galleries. An atrium assists in wayfinding and makes a large complex more comprehensible for users, visitors and patients.

Nevertheless, though there has been some planning refinement in terms of making the spatial arrangement of activities of a hospital suit its model of care and there is now more understanding of the impact of physical layout on operational costs, the contemporary hospital is still a formula of universal grids, double-loaded corridors and multiple waiting areas. The columns of the 'neutral and universal grid' are structuring and controlling the working and environment of the hospital. More seriously, the planning and fabric of the present hospital does

8.4
Northwick Park – growth and change

not recognise it as an environment for teamworking. Hospitals are still organised around and promoting hierarchical working. They will not allow or encourage new work or medical practices. They are not agents of change. Columns and walls are getting in the way!

Developing a 'good enough' specialist care environment

The integration of computer and information technology is critical to improving healthcare buildings. Airport terminals are in one sense run by airport operations' data banks. Hospital computer and information systems need to be developed up to the level of those of airports. For example, a hospital operations data bank could include the following networked services:

- hospital information and management system
- patient services
- clinical services
- hotel services
- wayfinding and information display
- finance
- equipment
- logistics
- security
- facilities.

Many of these would be linked to external networks, for example to primary care centres and general practitioners. Some might even be linked to houses to provide for the home as a setting

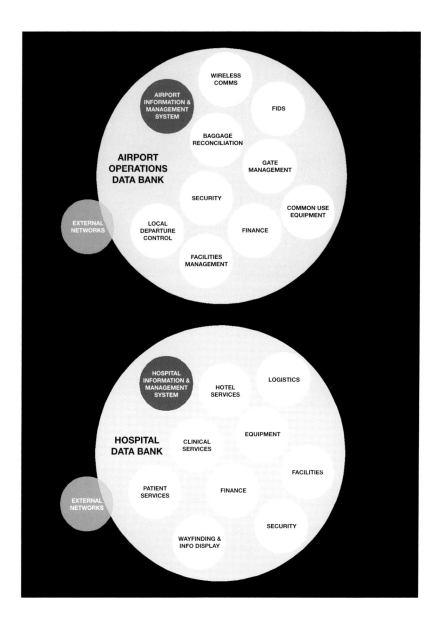

8.5
a Airport Information and
   Management System
b Hospital Information and
   Management System

for healthcare. As in airports, computer management has the ability to shorten or remove the endless waiting associated with specialist care and to allow programmed use of space (Figures 8.5a and 8.5b).

D. W. Winnicott, the famous English child psychoanalyst, said that mothers could not be, and need not be, perfect. They just needed to be 'good enough'.[22] Similarly, hospitals cannot be perfect, and the more attempts are made to make them perfect, the more problems over time will accrue. In planning for the future, a 'good enough' hospital should be proposed.

It is no longer reasonable to see a hospital as just meeting demographic needs in an effective location. Hospitals need to be pleasant and productive places in which to work. They need to

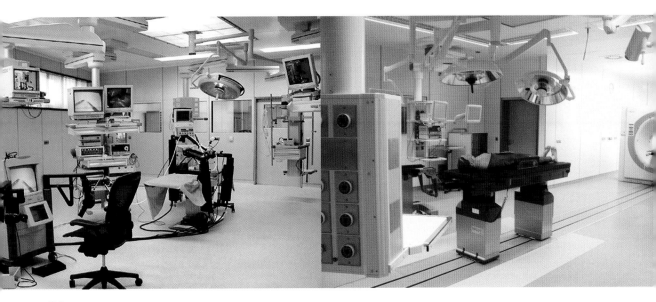

8.6

a Minimal invasive robotic theatre

b Increasing equipment in the operating theatre

accept changing practice more easily than the early 'hospital street' models of Llewelyn-Davies. By planning and designing new work and patient environments, a new architecture for specialist care centres can follow.

Hospitals are still in a transitional phase, moving away from the model of care largely based on long stays of patients in hospital for medical or surgical conditions. Over the last 20 years this model has been decreasing the length of overnight stays, while at the same time the number of patients not staying overnight has risen dramatically. Patients with complex conditions are being managed in clinical settings without the need for admission. Many disciplines have all but moved away from inpatient services (for example, dermatology, rheumatology, endocrinology, respiratory medicine, gastroenterology and ophthalmology). Almost every discipline has a large non-inpatient component.[23] By the year 2011 nearly three-quarters of all services will be provided in an ambulatory setting.[24] The ACAD at the Middlesex Hospital recognises this important trend.[25]

'Ambulatory services' has been a buzzword in health for more than ten years, but its impact has not been fully understood and neither has a suitable architectural response been given. Ambulatory service is not a new term for outpatient super-clinics and it cannot be equated to, or substituted for, primary care services. An ambulatory service now manages patients having complex investigations (angiography, angioplasty, liver biopsies, etc.) and patients having ongoing therapy for serious conditions (chemotherapy or renal dialysis). It is expected that a further and growing group of patients requiring the infusion of genetic and molecular material will join the ambulatory services as molecular biology is incorporated into clinical practice.

Ambulatory care, rather than blocks of inpatient accommodation, will become the centrepiece of the hospital. Hospitals over the last 20 years have moved from the departmental model (often expressed architecturally as a podium with a slab of beds above or beside it), through so-called institute models where all services are grouped geographically, to the grouping of services in a functional patient-oriented model. Rather than a medical model based on disciplines, we now see critical care zones or 'hot floors' where emergency, medical assessments and ICUs, theatres and diagnostics are located together. An ambulatory care zone is similar. This centrepiece of the hospital would include not only a full range of disciplines with a patient focus but also parking, child care, health information and education together with retail outlets and restaurants. This new space could be permeated with art and perhaps have an art gallery.

It seems that a new ambulatory service hall, perhaps with one or two levels of accommodation only, will be the centre of the new hospital. Rather than subdividing space with plasterboard walls, this would be a furniture system in a large-span space. It would be an assemblage of mobile walls, screens, glass walls which (at the flick of a switch) can become opaque, curtains and mobile changing areas. Services and much air conditioning would be under-floor and connected via power poles or 'umbilicals'. Email would provide silent and discreet communication. This furniture-based system could respond to events and could be rearranged at different times of the week or the year. A facilities manager would actively change the furniture system to meet changing events. I use the term 'aedicular architecture' for this, borrowed from Sir John Summerson.[26] He used the term to describe the smaller architectural components of Gothic architecture: *aedicule* is Latin for a small building (Figure 8.6).

I think in considering hospital futures there is little need to consider nursing units. This is because they are taking an ever diminishing part of the hospital and because there has already been considerable research into these units. Most patients will stay only two or three days. Only about a quarter of the services of a specialist care centre will be involved with patients 'lying in'.[27] Sufficient to say these should be in single-bed rooms. Single-bed rooms give many benefits but particularly with regard to infection control.

The real and the virtual – a new work environment

A good example of how work environments in specialist care centres are changing is the operating theatre. New surgical practice, such as minimally invasive surgery with laparoscopy and endoscopy, is requiring both new skills for surgeons and new environments.

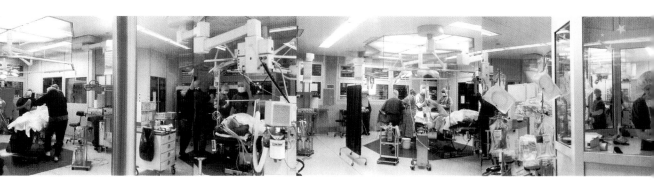

8.7
Wilhelm Schulthess Klink, Zurich – open-plan operating theatre

New specialist teaching centres are required for training in minimally invasive surgery, for example the European Surgical Institute in Hamburg and IRCAD in Strasbourg. Operating theatres are becoming studios where television screens are a fundamental part of the procedure. There is now a need for large communication modules in operating theatres, with cameras in theatre lights. This is extending into robotic surgery. Recently Professor Marasceau (of IRCAD) operated on a patient in Strasbourg robotically while he was in New York. These new techniques require not only new equipment but new rooms for editing and control of the images (Figures 8.6a and 8.6b). Operating theatres will require access to CAT-scanners and MRIs as well as the usual X-ray and image intensification facilities (Figure 8.6).[28]

These developments make the present cellularised operating theatre suite more and more inconvenient. There is no reason to maintain separate rooms; in fact there are considerable advantages in not having separate operating theatres. With laminar-flow air, a multi-table system can be kept sterile. The removal of walls also would eliminate many expensive doors (usually with automatic operation) and reduce the need for ancillary rooms for scrub-up, anaesthetic and change. An open-plan form would provide more space for imaging and robotic equipment. It would allow consultation between surgeons. One anaesthetist might look after four patients, with anaesthetic nurses monitoring at each table. Importantly, it would be easier to clean, as well as allowing capacity for 'events'. Of course, one or two theatres would need to remain as traditional rooms for particularly septic cases.

8.8
R. Vinoly Architect the Kimmel Center for the Performing Arts

There are already a few hospitals that work in this multi-table open-plan form. One of them is the Wilhelm Schulthess Klinik in Zurich, a largely orthopaedic hospital, which has four tables in one space doing quite complex operations such as total hip operations. Patient privacy is ensured by screens on wheels and drapes from the edge of the laminar-flow glass curtains (Figure 8.7).

Similar changes can be expected in the work environment for ambulatory services where patients are examined and treated. It is here that mobile walls, curtains and mobile changing areas could provide a furniture-based system. These areas would be supplied by under-floor servicing with umbilicals and could be stage-managed to meet changing clinics and changing frequencies during the year. It would be in these areas and in the emergency areas that a new environment could be built around teamworking rather than hierarchical working.

A new paradigm

The great expense of hospitals, together with their complexity and user requirements, mitigates against change. Should something that is untried be planned and built? But changes in medical practice, changing models of care, the increasing use of computers and information technology, and constraints on funding force us to question the existing paradigm. This applies to secondary level hospitals as well as tertiary specialist care centres, which are the most expensive element of the health system.

The existing paradigm is a development of the 'lying-in' hospital. Of course, in many contemporary facilities, such as the Medical Centre at the University of Aachen in Germany (1984) or the new hospital at Norwich in the UK, it is hard to perceive the original 'lying-in' hospital. But at their core these hospitals still rest on this old paradigm.

A new paradigm for hospitals is not simply a question of 'design quality' or 'function before form'. As in cities, particularly in English-speaking countries, where the community has continued to embrace the paradigm of 'ruralisation' to the exclusion of other paradigms for cities, so in hospitals we must work towards a new paradigm based on understanding both over-arching health strategies and individual work events. Therapeutic environments, the design of public, social and private spaces, and contribution to place and community are important but must be understood within a paradigm. It will be by the change of paradigm that thinking architects will once again become intrigued by the design of hospitals.

Research on the building types of offices, airports and hospitals indicates that the forces now existing in hospitals, particularly computer and information technology and new work practices, will promote a change of paradigm as they have in offices and airports. Furthermore, it is clear from both offices and airports that larger-span structures are central to the new paradigm. We cannot be restrained any longer by 'neutral and universal grids'.

A hospital, then, could be described as having a series of working environments. Within each environment there would be flexibility built around teamworking and changing events. All environments would be informed and to some degree managed by a hospital information and management system using large LCD or plasma screens, which would have both text and visual capabilities.

There would need to be full consideration of sustainability, particularly with regard to air, water and waste systems. There is strong evidence that patients recover more quickly when they can see or experience landscape. Therefore, along with the privacy and amenity strategies for patients, there should also be a landscape strategy. There are a number of studies in offices that also indicate the importance of engaging with the landscape.

Bringing all these considerations together suggests that the new specialist centre should be in a hall or series of halls; it should be a series of what might be called aedicular systems. Like airports, the primary spaces could become bigger, and not consist of repetitive low-ceilings, neutral grids and double-loaded corridors.

Louis Kahn said: 'Architecture comes from the making of a room ... The plan is a society of rooms ... The room is a place of the mind. In a small room one does not say what one would in a large room ... a room is not a room without natural light.'[29]

We might interpret this as meaning that a hospital is a society of environments within a large room or hall. By using a large hall, a large-span structure, we can provide natural light, and with aedicular architecture we can provide intimacy.

It is the ambulatory care zone, treatment and diagnostic, outpatient and emergency as well as operating theatres, intensive care and imaging (and their office and logistic support space) that are the key to rethinking the hospital work environment. As nursing units are taking a diminishing part of the hospital, probably reducing to 20% by area in the next ten years, it is the other ambulatory services and investigative services that will become the centre of the hospital. These can best be provided in a light-filled hall, a large-span structure over ever-changing aedicular architecture. This new hospital type would provide:

- a 'movement economy' where circulation spaces are multi-functional (like a city of streets – not motor roads);
- an operational order in planning for teamworking rather than hierarchical working;
- an operational order based on 'events' rather than 'rigid functions';
- patient amenity and privacy considerations that can be satisfied in a range of different settings;
- the introduction of computer and information technology as a stakeholder in the hospital;
- the rethinking of 'walls' in many hospital areas into 'vehicles', and as a consequence the relocation of services either under floors or into pedestal/power poles or umbilicals from the ceiling – the development of aedicular architecture;
- open-plan operating theatre for non-infectious cases;
- the use of natural ventilation and light and, where required, the use of more sophisticated air conditioning such as displacement systems and laminar flow;
- within a larger space, a smaller 'changing city' built on furniture-based systems – most of which would be on wheels.

Lastly, but not least, the new large-span hospital building will have to have a large footprint (approximately the size of a football field), with at least three levels. Wards with single-bed rooms would be at the periphery. It should not be compromised by unsuitable sites – such as crowded existing hospital sites.

An agreed new paradigm is the key to enabling the natural functioning and long-term sustainability of hospitals and specialist care centres. It is greatly needed.

Notes and references

1. Susan Francis and Rosemary Glanville, *Building a 2020 Vision: Future Health Care Environments*, Nuffield Trust and RIBA Future Studies (London: The Stationery Office, 2001).

2. Jess Barber, 'No longer an island', *Passenger Terminal World,* July 1998: 56–60. Bill Weissmueller, 'Resolution resolved', *Passenger Terminal World,* July 1999: 62–6.

3. Fumihiko Maki, *Wilkinson Memorial Address* (Sydney, 2000).

4. Frederick W. Taylor, *The Principles of Scientific Management* (New York: Harper, 1915).

5. http://www.gelighting.com/na/faq/basic_history.html

6. Ibid.

7. Thomas Arnold, 'From the Burolandschaft to the cityscape in the office', in R. Hascher, S. Jeska and B. Klauck, *Office Buildings: A Design Manual* (Basel: Birkhauser, 2002), 19.

8. Francis Duffy, *The New Office* (London: Conran Octopus, 1997).

9. Nikolaus Pevsner, *The Buildings of England* (Harmondsworth: Penguin, 1951–).

10. Roger S. Ulrich, 'Design for improving health outcomes: theory, research and practice', in A. Dilani (ed.) *Healthcare Buildings that Foster Wellness* (Stockholm: Royal Swedish Institute of Technology), 41–66. Roger S. Ulrich, 'Effects of gardens on health outcomes: theory and research', in C. Marcus and M. Barnes (eds), *Healing Gardens* (New York: John Wiley, 1999).

11. Philip Larkin, *High Windows* (London: Faber and Faber,1974).

12. Simone Jeska, 'From ancient times to the twentieth century', in Hascher *et al.*, *Office Buildings*, 15.

13. Plan of the Third Report of the Hospital Commission to the Academy of Sciences 1788, in J. D. Thompson and G. Goldin, *The Hospital: A Social and Architectural History* (New Haven, CT: Yale University Press, 1975), 140.

14. Plan of the Herbert Hospital, Woolwich England, 1859–1864, in Thompson and Goldin, *The Hospital*, 163.

15. Julie Willis, 'Machines for healing', *Architecture Australia,* July/August 2002: 46–7.

16. R. Dubbini and R. Sordina *H VEN LC Hopital de Venise Le Corbusier: Testimonianze* Venezia (IUAV AP Archivio Progetti,1999).

17. B. Hillier, *Space is the Machine: A Configurational Theory of Architecture* (Cambridge: Cambridge University Press,1996), 180.

18. Ibid., 181.

19. Peter Brennan, *Melbourne Health: A Vision for a Healthy Future* (paper presented to Melbourne Health Board and Executive, 2003).

20. A. Cox and P. Groves, *Hospitals and Health Care Facilities* (London: Butterworth, 1990), 54–5.

21. Rainer Hacher, 'Sustainable building concepts for office buildings', in Hascher *et al.*, *Office Buildings*, 47.

22. D. W. Winnicott, *Mother and Child: A Primer of First Relationships* (New York: Basic Books, 1957).

23. Brennan, *Melbourne Health*.

24. Ibid.

25. NHS Estates, *Diagnostic and Treatment Centres: ACAD Central Middlesex Hospital: An Evaluation* (London: The Stationery Office, 2001).

26. John Summerson, *Heavenly Mansions and Other Essays on Architecture* (New York: W. W. Norton,1963).

27. Brennan, *Melbourne Health*.

28. Observations by the author at IRCAD, Strasbourg, France, February 2002.

29. Heinz Ronner *et al.*, *Louis I. Kahn: Complete Works 1935–74* (Basel: Birkhauser, 1977).

Acknowledgements

This chapter was developed from a presentation given at the Nuffield Trust Conference on hospitals in London in February 2003. Special thanks must be given to Mr Bernie McKay, the former Commonwealth Director General of Health in the Australian Government, and Dr Peter Brennan, the former Medical Director and CEO of the Royal Melbourne Hospital, and Andrea Nield who have helped develop the ideas and approach in this chapter. Janine le Quesne and Skye Johnson typed the text and Rosa Cotrona and Maria Ferrara researched the bibliography and images. Jennifer Tweedie and Rosa Cortrona checked the text. Mistakes are mine alone.

Index

Picture credits

6.12–6.14 Carmel CA Architect: Edward Durell Stone. Photographer © Ezra Stoller; 6.15 Chong Partners Architecture ©Tim Griffith, exterior night shot © Sharon Risedorph; 6.16 OZ Architecture/ Boulder Associates, Boulder, Colorado; 6.17 Chong/ SmithGroup, aerial view © 111th Aerial Photography Squadron; 6.16 OZ Architecture/Boulder Associates, Boulder, Colorado; 6.17 Chong/SmithGroup, aerial view © 111th Aerial Photography Squadron; 6.18 Granary Associates Surgery Architect, KMD, Associate architect:Perkins Eastman Architects

Chapter 7

7.1 Llewellyn Davies Weeks in association with the NSW Public Works Department; 7.2 Lawrence Nield & Partners (now Bligh Voller Nield). Photographer Max Dupain; 7.3 Lawrence Nield & Partners (now Bligh Voller Nield). Photographer Max Dupain; 7.4 McConnel Smith & Johnson. Photographer Michael Nicholson; 7.5 Woods Bagot; 7.6 Lyons Architects. Photographer John Gollings; 7.7 Stephenson & Meldrum Jackson Di Carlo Potts; 7.8 Stevenson & Turner; 7.9 Bligh Voller Nield; 7.10 Bligh Voller Nield. Photographer Anthony Browell; 7.11 Di Carlo Potts & Associates with Daryl Jackson, Robin Dyke & Bligh Voller Nield; 7.12 Government Architect PWD, Lawrence Nield & Partners, Woods Bagot, McConnel Smith & Johnson; 7.13 Government Architect PWD, Lawrence Nield & Partners, Woods Bagot, McConnel Smith & Johnson; 7.14 Woods Bagot; 7.15 Lawrence Nield and Partners (now Bligh Voller Nield); 7.16 Cox MSJ

Chapter 8

8.1 Renzo Piano/Lawrence Nield of Bligh Voller Nield; 8.2 Lawrence Nield of Bligh Voller Nield; 8.3 Architect Yorke Rosenberg Mardell; 8.4 Architect Llewelyn Davies Yeang; 8.5 Lawrence Nield of Bligh Voller Nield; 8.6 IRCAD, Hôpital Civil, Strasbourg/ Marquet, Rastatt, Germany; 8.7 Schulthess Klinik, Zurich/Architects for Health; 8.8 © Rafael Vinoly Architects